MCGRAW-HILL

Microsoft Word *97*

Timothy J. O'Leary
Arizona State University

Linda I. O'Leary

**Irwin
McGraw-Hill**

Boston, Massachusetts   Burr Ridge, Illinois   Dubuque, Iowa
Madison, Wisconsin   New York, New York   San Francisco, California   St. Louis, Missouri

Irwin/McGraw-Hill

A Division of The McGraw·Hill Companies

Microsoft Word 97

This book is printed on acid-free paper.

domestic	3 4 5 6 7 8 9 0 BAN BAN 9 0 0 9
international	2 3 4 5 6 7 8 9 0 BAN BAN 9 0 0 9 8

ISBN 0-07-228253-3

The Sponsoring Editor was Rhonda Sands.
The Developmental Editor was Kristin Hepburn.
The Editorial Assistant was Kyle Thomes.
The Marketing Manager was James Rogers.
The Production Supervisor was Richard DeVitto.
The cover was designed by Lorna Lo.
Project management was by Elaine Brett, Fritz/Brett Associates.
Composition was by Pat Rogondino, Rogondino & Associates.
The typeface was ITC Clearface.
Banta Co. was the printer and binder.

Library of Congress Cataloging Card Number 97-72182

http://www.mhhe.com

Contents

Word Processing Overview

One of the most widely used software applications is a word processor. Putting your thoughts in writing, from the simplest note to the most complex book, is a time-consuming process. Even more time-consuming is the task of editing and retyping the document to make it better. With the introduction of word processing, errors should be nearly nonexistent—not because they are not made, but because they are easy to correct. Word processors let you throw away the correction fluid, scissors, paste, and erasers. Now, with a few keystrokes, you can easily correct errors, move paragraphs, and reprint your document.

Definition of Word Processing

Word processing software is a program that helps you create any type of written communication. A word processor can be used to manipulate text data to produce a letter, a report, a memo, or any other type of correspondence. Text data is any letter, number, or symbol that you can type on a keyboard. The grouping of the text data to form words, sentences, paragraphs, and pages of text results in the creation of a document. Through a word processor you can create, modify, store, retrieve, and print part or all of a document.

Advantages of Using a Word Processor

The speed of entering text data into the computer depends on the skill of the user. If you cannot type fast, a word processor will not improve your typing speed. However, a word processor will make it easier to correct and change your document. Consequently, your completed document will take less time to create.

Another time saver is word wrap. As you enter text you do not need to decide where to end each line, as you do on a typewriter. When a line is full, the program automatically wraps the text down to the next line.

A word processor excels in its ability to change, or edit, a document. Editing involves correcting spelling, grammar, and sentence-structure errors. As you enter characters using the keyboard, they are displayed on the screen and stored electronically in the computer's main memory. As you find errors, you can electronically delete or correct them. Once the document is the way you want it to appear, it can be permanently saved on a disk and printed on paper. Good-bye, correction fluid!

In addition to editing a document, you can easily revise or update it by inserting or deleting text. For example, a price list can easily be updated to reflect new prices. A document that details procedures can be revised by deleting old procedures and inserting new ones. This is especially helpful when a document is used repeatedly. Rather than recreating the whole document, you change only the parts that need to be revised.

Revision also includes the rearrangement of selected areas of text. For example, while writing a report you may decide to change the location of a single word or several paragraphs or pages of text. You can do it easily by "cutting" or removing selected text from one location, then "pasting" or placing the selected text in another location. The selection can also be duplicated or copied from one location to another.

Combining text in another file with text in your document is another advantage of word processors. An example of this is a group term paper where each section of the paper is written by a different person. Before printing the document, the text for all sections, which is stored in different files, is combined to create the complete paper. The opposite is also true: text that may not be appropriate in your document can easily be put in another file for later use.

Many word processors include additional support features to help you produce a perfect document. A spelling checker checks the spelling in a document by comparing each word to those in a dictionary stored in memory. If an error is found, the program suggests the correct spelling. A grammar checker electronically checks grammar, phrasing, capitalization, and other types of grammar errors. A thesaurus displays alternative words that have a meaning similar or opposite to the word you entered.

You can also easily control the appearance or format of the document. Formatting includes such operations as changing the line spacing and margin widths, adding page numbers, and displaying page headers and footers. You can also quickly change how your text is aligned with the left or right margin. For example, text can be centered between the margins, or justified—evenly aligned on both the left and right margins—as are these pages. Perhaps the most noticeable formatting feature is the ability to apply different fonts (type styles and sizes) and text appearance changes such as bold, italics, and color to all or selected portions of the document. Most word processing programs also have the ability to produce and display graphic lines and boxes. Graphic boxes can then be used to hold text or graphic images that you place into the document.

Word Processing Terminology

The following terms and definitions are generic in nature and are associated with most word processing programs.

Bold: Produces dark or heavy print.

Center: To center a line of text evenly between the margins.

Edit: To change or modify the content of the document.

Font: Type style and size.

Format: Defines how the printed document will appear; includes settings for underline, boldface, print size, margin settings, line spacing, and so on.

Grammar checker: A support feature that checks grammar, phrasing, capitalization, and other types of syntax errors.

Justified: Text that is evenly aligned on both the left and right margins.

Spelling checker: A support feature that checks words or the entire document for correct spelling.

Text data: Any number, letter, or symbol you can type on a keyboard.

Thesaurus: A support feature that displays synonyms and antonyms for words in your document.

Word wrap: The automatic adjustment of the number of characters or words on a line that eliminates the need to press the [←Enter] (or [←Return]) key at the end of each line.

Case Study for Labs 1–5

As a recent college graduate, you have accepted your first job as a management trainee for The Sports Company. The Sports Company is a chain of discount sporting goods shops located in large metropolitan areas throughout the United States. The program emphasis is on computer applications in the area of retail management and requires that you work in several areas of the company.

In this series of labs, you are working in the Southwest Regional office and are responsible for setting up the credit card enrollment program and for assisting with the monthly newsletter.

In Labs 1 and 2 you will create a letter to be sent to all new credit card recipients. You will learn how to use the Word 97 to create, edit, format, and print the letter.

In Lab 3 the regional office has decided to send a monthly newsletter to credit card customers. You have been asked to prepare several articles for inclusion in the newsletter and create a sample newsletter design using the articles.

In Lab 4 you will prepare a table that summarizes gross sales for the regional stores. You will also personalize the credit card letter by creating a form letter and merging the recipients' personal information such as name and address into the form letter.

Lab 5 demonstrates how to use Word 97 to create a home page for The Sports Company to use on their new World Wide Web site.

Before You Begin

To the Student
The following assumptions have been made:

- Microsoft Word 97 has been properly installed on the hard disk of your computer system.

- The data disk contains the data files needed to complete the series of Word 97 labs and practice exercises. These files are supplied by your instructor.

- You have completed the McGraw-Hill Windows 95 lab module or you are already familiar with how to use Windows 95 and a mouse.

To the Instructor

Please be aware that the following settings are assumed to be in effect for the Word 97 program. These assumptions are necessary so that the screens and directions in the manual are accurate.

- Language is set to English [US]. (Use Tools/Language/Set Language and set English (United States) as default.)

- Navigation keys for WordPerfect users and Help for WordPerfect users are off. (Use Tools/Options/General.)

- The ScreenTips feature is active (use Tools/Options/View).

- Toolbar ScreenTips are displayed (use Tools/Customize/Options).

- The Office Assistant is on.

- The Normal view is on. Zoom is 100 percent. (Use View/Normal; View/Zoom/100%.)

- The Wrap to Window setting is off. (Use Tools/Options/View.)

- All default settings for a normal template document are in effect.

- In addition, all figures in the manual reflect the use of a standard VGA display setting (640 x 480) and an Epson AP5000 printer. If another monitor type is used, there may be more lines of text displayed in the windows than in the figures. This setting can be changed using Windows setup. The selected printer also affects how text appears onscreen. If possible, select a printer and monitor type that will match the figures in the manual.

Microsoft Office Shortcut Bar

The Microsoft Office Shortcut Bar (shown below) may be displayed automatically on the Windows 95 desktop. Commonly, it appears in the upper right section of the desktop; however, it may appear in other locations, depending upon your setup. Because the Shortcut Bar can be customized, it may display different buttons than shown below.

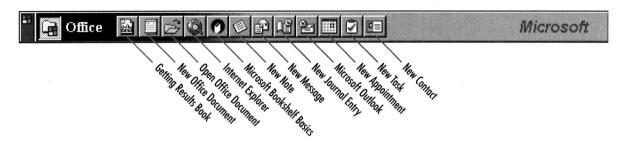

The Office Shortcut Bar makes it easy to open existing documents or to create new documents using one of the Microsoft Office applications. It can also be used to send e-mail, add a task to a to-do list, schedule appointments using Outlook, or add contacts or notes.

Instructional Conventions

This text uses the following instructional conventions:

- Steps that you are to perform are preceded with a bullet (■) and are in blue type.
- Command sequences you are to issue appear following the word "Choose." Each menu command selection is separated by a /. If the command can be selected by typing a letter of the command, the letter will appear bold and underlined.
- Commands that can be initiated using a button and the mouse appear following the word "Click." The menu equivalent and keyboard shortcut appear in a margin note when the action is first introduced.
- Anything you are to type appears in bold text.

Creating and Editing a Document

COMPETENCIES

After completing this lab, you will know how to:

1. Load Word 97.
2. Use the Office Assistant.
3. Create a new document.
4. Enter and edit text.
5. Insert and delete blank lines.
6. Move around the document window.
7. Open, close, and save files.
8. Move through a document.
9. Insert and delete text.
10. Display special characters.
11. Select text.
12. Undo editing changes.
13. Document a file.
14. Preview and print a document.
15. Exit Word 97.

CASE STUDY

As a recent college graduate, you have accepted a job in a management training program for The Sports Company, a chain of warehouse-oriented sporting goods stores. The training program emphasis is on computer applications in the area of retail management. Your current assignment is in the Southwest Regional Office, where you are responsible for setting up the new credit card program and for assisting with the monthly newsletter.

The software tool you will use while on this assignment is the word processing application Word 97. Its purpose is to help you create text documents such as letters, reports, and research papers. Specifically, you will learn about entering, editing, previewing, and printing a document while you create the first draft of a letter to be sent to all new credit card recipients. This letter is shown on the right.

Dear Preferred Customer:

Thank you for opening a new credit card account with The Sports Company and becoming one of our most valued customers. Here's your new credit card!

Please sign your new card in ink with your usual signature. If you have an old card, destroy it immediately. Always carry your new credit card with you. It will identify you as a Preferred Customer and guarantees you a quick and convenient shopping experience at any of The Sports Company stores located throughout the country.

We are the leading sports store in the Southwest with a tradition of personal, friendly service. As you use your new credit card, you will discover the many conveniences that only our credit customers enjoy.

We are very happy with the opportunity to serve you and we look forward to seeing you soon.

Sincerely,

Student Name
The Sports Company Manager

Concept Overview

The following concepts will be introduced in this lab:

1. Document Development	The development of a document follows several steps: plan, enter, edit, format, and preview and print.
2. Document Template	A document template is a document file that includes predefined settings that can be used as a pattern to create many common types of documents.
3. AutoCorrect	The AutoCorrect feature makes some basic assumptions about the text you are typing and, based on these assumptions, automatically identifies and/or corrects the entry as you type.
4. Spelling and Grammar Checkers	Word includes a Spelling Checker and a Grammar Checker that automatically advise you of misspelled words or incorrect grammar as you create and edit a document.
5. Word Wrap	The word wrap feature automatically decides where to end a line and wrap text to the next line based on the margin settings.
6. Document Preview	The Print Preview feature displays each page of your document in reduced size so you can see its layout.

Part 1

Loading Word 97

You will use Word 97 to create your letter to new credit card customers.

- If necessary, turn on your computer and put your data disk in drive A (or the appropriate drive for your system).

- Click 🏁 Start .

- Choose Programs/ 📝 Microsoft Word .

> If a shortcut to Word button Microsoft Word is displayed on your desktop, you can double-click on the button to start the program.

> If the Microsoft Office Suite is on your system and the Office Shortcut Bar is displayed, you can load Word by clicking the New Office Document button 🗔 and selecting Blank Document.

After a few moments, the Word application window is displayed. Your screen should be similar to Figure 1-1.

FIGURE 1-1

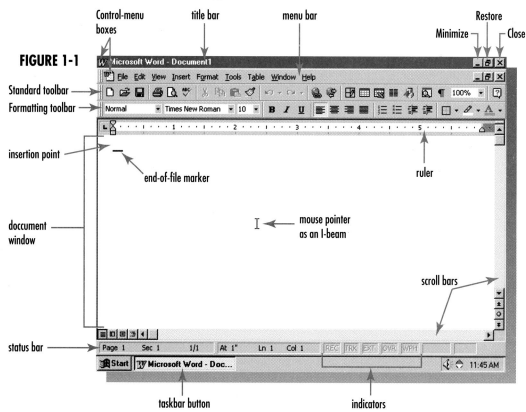

As you can see, many of the features in the Word window are the same as in other Windows 95 applications. Among those features are a title bar, a menu bar, toolbars, a document window, scroll bars, and mouse compatibility. You can move and size Word windows, select commands, use Help, and switch between files and programs, just as you can in Windows. The common user interface makes learning and using new applications much easier.

The Word window title bar displays the program name, Microsoft Word, followed by the file name Document1, the default name of the file displayed in the window. The left end of the title bar contains the ⓦ Word application window Control-menu icon, and the right end displays the ⬚ Minimize, ⬚ Restore, and ⊠ Close buttons. They perform the same functions and operate in the same way as in Windows 95.

The menu bar below the title bar displays the Word program menu, which consists of nine menus. The left end of the menu bar displays the ⬚ document window Control-menu icon, and the right end displays the document window Minimize, Restore, and Close buttons.

The two toolbars below the menu bar contain buttons that are mouse shortcuts for many of the menu items. The upper toolbar is the **Standard toolbar**. It contains buttons that are used to complete the most frequently used menu com-

If necessary, maximize the Word application window.

The mouse pointer may appear as an I-beam Ⅰ or an arrow ⮡, depending on its location in the window.

If the title bar does not display the file name, maximize the document window.

There are 13 different toolbars in Word.

mands. The bottom is the **Formatting toolbar**. It contains buttons that are used to change the appearance or format of the document.

■ To quickly identify the toolbar buttons, point to each button in both toolbars to display the button name in the ScreenTip.

The left end of both the menu and toolbar displays a move handle ▯ that when dragged moves the menu or toolbar to another location. Both menu and toolbars can be docked (as they are now) or floating. When **docked** they are fixed to an edge of the window and display the move handle. When **floating** they appear in a separate window that can be moved by dragging the title bar.

The **ruler** is displayed below the Formatting toolbar. The ruler shows the line length in inches and is used to set margins, tab stops, and indents.

The large center area of the Word application window is where documents are displayed in open windows. Currently there is one open document window, which is maximized and occupies the entire text area. The **insertion point**, also called the **cursor**, is the blinking vertical bar that marks your current location in the document. The solid horizontal line is the **end-of-file marker**. Because there is nothing in this document, the end-of-file marker appears at the first character space on the first line.

The **status bar** at the bottom of the Word window displays information about the location of the insertion point and the status of different settings as they are used.

> If the ruler is not displayed, choose Ruler from the View menu.

Using Office Assistant

The 📎 Office Assistant should also be displayed on your screen. The **Office Assistant** automatically suggests help topics as you work. It anticipates what you are going to do and then makes suggestions on how to perform a task. In addition, you can activate the Assistant at any time to get help on features in the Office application you are using. To activate the Office Assistant,

> If your Office Assistant is not displayed, click ⟨?⟩ or press ⟨F1⟩.

> The Office Assistant feature is common to all Office 97 programs.

■ Click 📎 Office Assistant.

The Office Assistant balloon displays a prompt and a text box in which you can type the topic you want help on. Then you click the Search button to display a list of related topics from which you can select. The Tips Options button displays the most recent tip and lets you scroll through tips that the Office Assistant has recently displayed. The Options button is used to change Office Assistant so it provides different levels of help.

■ Click: ⟨● **Options**⟩.

The dialog box on your screen should be similar to Figure 1-2.

FIGURE 1-2

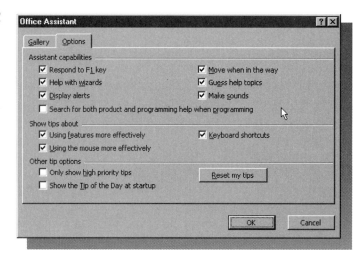

> Changes you make to these options affect the Assistant in all the Office programs.

The Options tab of the Office Assistant dialog box displays the settings. The options that appear checked are on. As you work in Word, you may want to turn on or off some of these options.

■ If necessary, turn on/off the Assistant options to reflect the same settings as in Figure 1-2.

You also want to reset the tips so that tips already seen can appear again.

■ Click Reset my tips.

■ Click OK.

Now you will ask the Office Assistant to provide help on the toolbars. While using Word, you will see that many of the toolbars open automatically as different tasks are performed. However, you can also open toolbars whenever you want. To find out how to open and close toolbars, you will use the Office Assistant.

■ Click Office Assistant.

■ Type **display toolbars**.

Close button

■ Click ● Search.

> Office Assistant displays topics related to your request.

■ Click Show or hide a toolbar.

The Help window appears, explaining how to show or hide a toolbar.

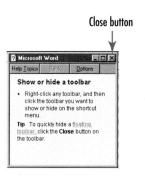

■ Click anywhere outside the Help window.

> The menu equivalent is **V**iew/**T**oolbars.

■ Right-click on any toolbar.

The Shortcut menu displays a list of 13 toolbar names. Those that are currently displayed are checked. Clicking on a toolbar from the list will display it onscreen. Likewise, clicking on a checked toolbar will hide the toolbar.

- Clear the Shortcut menu by clicking anywhere outside the menu.

- Click ☒ to close the Help window.

| Standard ✓ |
| Formatting ✓ |
| AutoText |
| Control Toolbox |
| Database |
| Drawing |
| Forms |
| Picture |
| Reviewing |
| Tables and Borders |
| Visual Basic |
| Web |
| WordArt |
| Customize... |

Developing a Document

Your first project with The Sports Company is to create a letter to be sent to all new credit card holders.

Concept 1: Document Development

The development of a document follows several steps: plan, enter, edit, format, and preview and print.

Plan	The first step in the development of a document is to understand the purpose of the document and to plan what your document should say.
Enter	After planning the document, you can begin entering the content of the document by typing the text using the word processor.
Edit	Making changes to your document is called **editing**. While typing, you are bound to make typing and spelling errors that need to be corrected. This is one type of editing. Another is to revise the content of what you have entered to make it clearer, or to add or delete information.
Format	Enhancing the appearance of the document to make it more readable or attractive is called **formatting**. This step is usually performed when the document is near completion. It includes many features such as boldfaced text, italics, and bulleted lists.
Preview and Print	The last step is to preview and print the document. Previewing displays the document onscreen as it will appear when printed, allowing you to check the document's overall appearance and make any final changes before printing.

You will find that you will generally follow these steps in order for your first draft of a document. However, you will probably retrace steps such as editing and formatting as the final document is developed.

During the planning phase, you have spoken with the regional manager regarding the purpose of the letter and the content in general. The purpose of the letter is to thank the customer for opening a new charge account with The Sports Company. The content of the letter should include instructions to the customer about how to use the card and the benefits associated with being a charge card holder.

Entering and Editing Text

Now that you understand the purpose of the letter and have a general idea of the content, you are ready to enter the text. A new Word document is like a blank piece of paper that already has many predefined settings. These settings are generally the most commonly used settings. They are called **default** settings and are stored as a document template.

Concept 2: Document Template

Every Word document is based on a document template. A document **template** is a document file that includes predefined settings that can be used as a pattern to create many common types of documents. The default document settings are stored in the Blank document template. Whenever you create a new document using this template, the same default settings are used.

There are many other template styles you can use that are designed to help you create professional-looking documents. They include templates that create different styles of memos, letters, and reports.

The Blank document template sets the top and bottom margins to 1 inch and the left and right margins to 1.25 inches. Other default settings include a standard paper-size setting of 8½ by 11 inches, tab settings at every half inch, and single-line spacing.

To verify several of the default settings, you can look at the information displayed in the status bar.

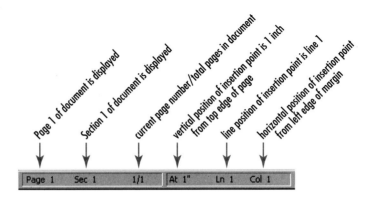

The indicators on the status bar show both the location of the text that is displayed in the document window as well as the location of the insertion point in a document. The numbers following the indicators specify the exact location in the document.

You can also look at the ruler to verify several default settings.

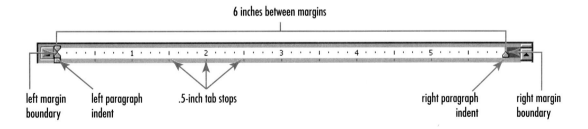

6 inches between margins

left margin boundary   left paragraph indent   .5-inch tab stops   right paragraph indent   right margin boundary

The margin boundaries on both ends of the ruler show the location of the left and right margins. The symbol at the zero position on the ruler marks the location of the left paragraph indent and the symbol on the right end of the ruler line at the 6-inch position marks the right paragraph indent. The default paragraph indent locations are the same as the margin settings. The ruler shows that the distance between the left and right margins is 6 inches. Knowing that the default page size is 8.5 inches wide, this leaves 2.5 inches for margins: 1.25 inches for equal-sized left and right margins. The ruler also displays dimmed tab marks below each half-inch position along the ruler, indicating a default tab setting of every half inch.

To create a new document, simply begin typing the text. On the first line of the letter you will enter the salutation "Dear Preferred Customer:". As you enter the text, it will include several intentional errors. Type the entries exactly as they appear.

■   Type **dear**

Notice that as you type, the character appears to the left of the insertion point. The location of the insertion point shows where the next character will appear as you type. Also, the status bar reflects the new horizontal position of the insertion point on the line. It shows the insertion point is currently positioned on column 5 of line 1.

At 1"   Ln 1   Col 5

The Office Assistant moves around the screen and changes size as you work to keep out of your way.

■   Press Spacebar.

Your screen should be similar to Figure 1-3.

automatically — capitalized word

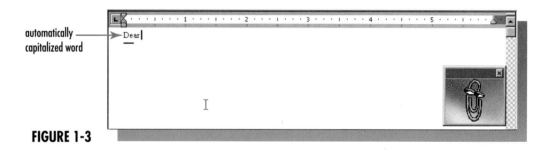

FIGURE 1-3

As soon as you complete a word, the program checks the word for accuracy. In this case, notice that Word automatically capitalized the first letter of the word. This is part of the automatic correcting feature of Word.

Concept 3: AutoCorrect

Word includes a feature called **AutoCorrect**, which makes some basic assumptions about the text you are typing and, based on these assumptions, automatically identifies and/or corrects the entry. The AutoCorrect feature automatically inserts proper capitalization at the beginning of sentences and the names of days of the week. It will also change to lowercase letters any words that were incorrectly capitalized due to the accidental use of the (Caps Lock) key. In addition, it also corrects common spelling errors automatically.

The program automatically corrects by looking for certain types of errors. This is part of Office 97's IntelliSense feature, which automatically gives you assistance while you work. For example, if two capital letters appear at the beginning of a word, Word changes the second capital letter to a lower-case letter. If a lowercase letter appears at the beginning of a sentence, Word capitalizes the first letter of the first word. If the name of a day begins with a lowercase letter, Word capitalizes the first letter.

In some cases, you may want to exclude an abbreviation or capitalized item from automatic correction. You can do this by adding the word to an exception list. Alternatively, you can add words to the list of words you want to be automatically corrected. For example, if you commonly misspell a word, you can add the word to the list and it will be automatically corrected as you type.

Word also includes **AutoText** entries, which are commonly used phrases. If Word detects you are typing one of the AutoText phrases, it automatically suggests the remainder of the phrase. You can choose to accept the suggestion or continue typing. You can also add your own entries to the AutoText list.

To continue entering the salutation,

- ■ Type **Prefered**
- ■ Press (Spacebar).

Your screen should be similar to Figure 1-4.

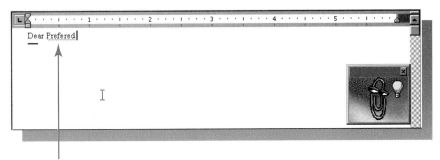

FIGURE 1-4

red wavy line indicates misspelled word

This time Word has identified the word as misspelled by underlining it with a wavy red line.

Concept 4: Spelling and Grammar Checkers

Word includes a Spelling Checker and a Grammar Checker that automatically advise you of misspelled words or incorrect grammar as you create and edit a document.

The Spelling Checker compares the word you type to a **main dictionary** of words supplied with the program. If the word does not appear in the main dictionary, it checks the **custom dictionary**, a dictionary that you can create to hold words you commonly use but that are not included in the main dictionary. If the word does not appear in either dictionary, the program identifies it as misspelled by displaying a red wavy line below the word. You can then correct the misspelled word by editing it. Alternatively, you can display a list of suggested spelling corrections for that word and select the correct spelling from the list to replace the misspelled word in the document.

Word also checks the grammar of your sentences. If Word detects grammatical errors in subject-verb agreements, verb forms, capitalization, or commonly confused words, to name a few, they are identified with a wavy green line. You can correct the grammatical error by editing it or you can display a suggested correction. Not all grammatical errors identified by Word are actual errors. Use discretion when correcting the errors.

The Spelling and Grammar status bar icon [icon] changes to [icon] when a document contains errors. Double-clicking the icon moves to the next spelling or grammar error and opens the Shortcut menu.

Because you have discovered this error very soon after typing it, and you know that the correct spelling of this word is "preferred," you can quickly correct it using ←Backspace. The ←Backspace key removes the character or space to the left of the insertion point; therefore, it is particularly useful when you are moving from right to left (backward) along a line of text. To correct this word,

■ Press ←Backspace 3 times.

The space and the letters d and e are removed. Notice the wavy underline is also cleared. This is because the word "Prefer" is spelled correctly. However, this is not the word you want to use. To complete the word and enter the last word of the salutation,

- ■   Type **red**

- ■   Press [Spacebar] twice.

- ■   Type **Custommer**

- ■   Press [Spacebar].

Again, the word is identified as misspelled. Also notice that the Office Assistant displays a light bulb, indicating there is a tip available.

- ■   Click the 💡 and read the tip.

- ■   Click (● Close).

As suggested in the tip, another way to quickly correct a misspelled word is to select the correct spelling from a list of suggested spelling corrections displayed on the Spelling Shortcut menu.

- ■   Right-click on Custommer to display the Spelling Shortcut menu.

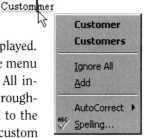

A Shortcut menu of suggested correct spellings is displayed. In this case, two correct spellings are suggested. The menu also includes several related menu options. Ignore All instructs Word to ignore the misspelling of this word throughout the rest of this session, and Add adds the word to the custom dictionary list. When a word is added to the custom dictionary, Word will always accept that spelling as correct. The AutoCorrect option adds the word to the AutoCorrect list so Word can correct misspellings of it automatically as you type. The last option, Spelling, starts the spell-checking program to check the entire document. You will learn about this feature in Lab 2.

Notice that the suggested replacements reflect the same capitalization as used in the document. Sometimes there are no suggested replacements because Word cannot locate any words in its dictionary that are similar in spelling or the suggestions are not correct. If this happens, you need to edit the word manually. The first suggestion is correct. To select it and complete the salutation,

- ■   Click Customer.

- ■   Type **:**

Inserting and Deleting Blank Lines

Next you will enter the first paragraph of the letter. The ⎱←Enter⎰ key is used to insert a blank line into text or to end a short line.

■   Press ⎱←Enter⎰.

Your screen should be similar to Figure 1-5.

insertion point   pressing ⎱←Enter⎰ starts a new line   automatic help suggestion

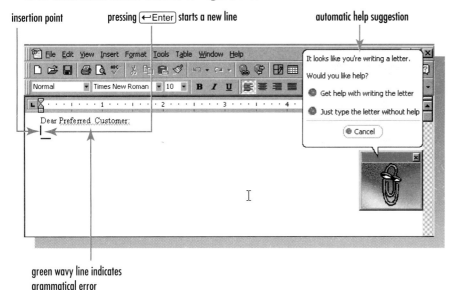

FIGURE 1-5

green wavy line indicates
grammatical error

The insertion point moves to the beginning of the next line. The status bar shows that the insertion point is positioned on line 2, column 1 of the page. Office Assistant detects that you may be typing a letter and offers help. You won't use the help to create the letter.

At 1.1"   Ln 2   Col 1

■   Click Just type the letter without help.

Also notice that there is a green line under "Preferred Customer" indicating that there is a grammatical error.

■   Right-click on Preferred Customer to display the Grammar Shortcut menu.

Dear Preferred Customer:

Preferred Customer:

Ignore Sentence

Grammar...

The Grammar Checker is very labor intensive on your computer, so the wavy green lines may not show up as quickly as the Spelling Checker.

A Shortcut menu showing a suggested correction is displayed. The second option, Ignore Sentence, instructs Word to ignore the grammatical error in this sentence. The last option, Grammar, provides an explanation of the error.

■   Choose Grammar.

Your screen should be similar to Figure 1-6.

FIGURE 1-6

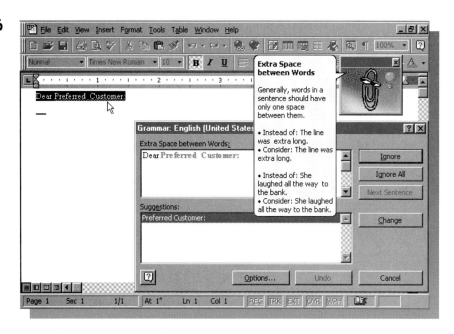

The Grammar dialog box is open and the Assistant tells you that the grammatical error is an extra space between words, in this case between the words "Preferred" and "Customer." The suggested correction is correct. To select it,

■ Click [**Change**].

You want to separate the salutation from the first paragraph with a blank line. To do this,

■ Press ⬇.

■ Press ⬅Enter.

When ⬅Enter is pressed at the beginning of a line, a blank line is inserted into the document. If the insertion point is in the middle of a line of text and you press ⬅Enter, all the text to the right of the insertion point moves to the beginning of the next line. Now you can type the text for the first paragraph of the letter. Do not worry about making typing errors as you enter the text; you will learn how to correct them next.

■ Type **Thank**

■ Press Spacebar.

The Office Assistant has anticipated what you are typing by displaying the AutoText "Thank you" above your text. Also notice that the Office Assistant displays a light bulb again, indicating there is another tip available.

Dear Preferred Customer:
Thank you,
Thank

■ Click the 💡 and read the tip.

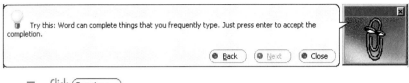

If the Office Assistant were not displayed, the light bulb would appear in the 🖼 on the toolbar.

■ Click (● Close).

If you wanted to accept the AutoText suggestion, pressing ⏎Enter would enter the text for you. However, you do not want to accept the suggested text because it includes a comma. If you keep typing, the AutoText suggestion will disappear.

■ Type **you for opening a new credit card account with The Sports Company and becoming one of our**

The line of text is very near the right margin. As you continue to type, when the text reaches the right margin, Word will automatically wrap the text to the next line.

Concept 5: Word Wrap

The **word wrap** feature automatically decides where to end a line and wrap text to the next line based on the margin settings. This saves time when entering text, as you do not need to press ⏎Enter at the end of a full line to begin a new line. The only time you need to press ⏎Enter is to end a paragraph, to insert blank lines, or to create a short line such as the salutation. In addition, if you change the margins or insert or delete text on a line, the program automatically readjusts the text on the line to fit within the margin settings. Word wrap is common to all word processors.

■ Press Spacebar.

■ Type **most valued customers.**

Your screen should be similar to Figure 1-7.

right margin boundary

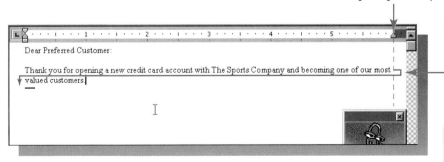

FIGURE 1-7

word wrap continues text on next line when text reaches right margin

Do not be concerned if the text on your screen wraps differently from that in Figure 1-7.

The program has wrapped the text that would overlap the right margin to the beginning of the next line. To continue the paragraph by entering a second sentence,

- Press [Spacebar].
- Type **Here's your new credit card!**

Once text is entered into a document, it is important to know how to move around within the text to correct errors or make changes. As soon as you learn about moving through a document, you will correct any errors you have made.

> Generally, when using a word processor, separate sentences with a single space rather than a double space, which was common when using typewriters.

Moving Around the Document Window

Either the mouse or the keyboard can be used to move through the text in the document window. Depending on what you are doing, the mouse is not always the quickest means of moving. For example, if your hands are already on the keyboard as you are entering text, it may be quicker to use the keyboard rather than take your hands off to use the mouse. Therefore, you will learn how to move through the document using both methods.

You use the mouse to move the insertion point to a specific location in a document. When you can use the mouse to move the insertion point, it is shaped as an I-beam. However, when the mouse pointer is positioned in the unmarked area to the left of a line (the left margin), it changes to an arrow ⌐. This area is called the **selection bar** (see Figure 1-8). When the mouse is in this area, it can be used to highlight text.

> You will learn about selecting text using this feature shortly.

- Move the mouse pointer into the selection bar. Move it back to the document text.

To move the insertion point, position the I-beam at the location in the text where you want it to be, then click the left mouse button.

- Click on the y of "you" (first line of first paragraph).
- Move the mouse pointer out of the way so you can see the insertion point better.

Your screen should be similar to Figure 1-8.

insertion point

FIGURE 1-8

selection bar

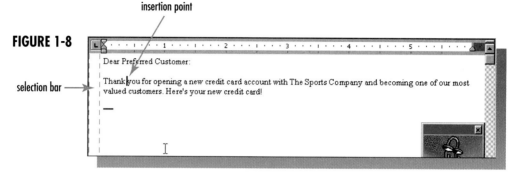

The insertion point should now be positioned on one side or the other of the y, with the status bar showing the new location of the insertion point.

At 1.3"   Ln 3   Col 7

If it is positioned to the left of the y, this means that the I-beam was positioned more to the left side of the character when you pressed the mouse button. The letter to the right of the insertion point is the selected character, in this case the y. If it is positioned to the right of the y, this means the I-beam was positioned more to the right side of the character when you clicked the mouse button. The letter to the right of the insertion point is the selected character, in this case the o.

To practice using the mouse to move the insertion point to the left side of a character,

- Move to S in Sports.

- Move to P in Preferred.

The insertion point can also be moved around the window using the arrow keys located on the numeric keypad or the directional keypad. The arrow keys move the insertion point one character space in the direction indicated by the arrow.

- Press → (10 times).

- Press ↓ (2 times).

The insertion point first moved 10 character spaces to the right, then down two lines to the o in "opening." It moved to that position because it was last located in a line containing text at that position. The insertion point will attempt to maintain its position in a line of text as you move up or down through the document.

When you hold down either → or ←, the insertion point moves quickly, character by character, along the line.

- To see how this works, hold down → until the insertion point is positioned on the C in "Company."

This saves multiple presses of the arrow key. Many of the Word insertion point movement keys can be held down to execute multiple moves.

To move word by word along a line,

- Press Ctrl + → (2 times).

- Press Ctrl + ← (3 times).

The insertion point moved two words to the right, then back three words to the left along the line.

Throughout these labs, you will be instructed to move to a specific letter in the text. This means to move the insertion point to the *left* side of the character so the character to the right is selected.

Make sure the pointer is an I-beam before clicking to move the insertion point. If text appears highlighted, click anywhere in the document where the mouse pointer is an I-beam to clear the highlighting.

If you are using the arrows on the numeric keypad, be sure the Num Lock key is off.

If you moved too far to the right along the line of text, use ← to move back to the correct position.

The [Home] and [End] keys can also be used to quickly move the insertion point to the beginning or end, respectively, of a line of text.

- ■ Press [End].

- ■ Press [Home].

- ■ Now that you know how to move within text on the window, move to any errors you may have made while entering the paragraph and correct them.

Closing and Saving Files

The rest of the letter has been entered for you and saved in a file named Credit Card Letter on your data disk. Before opening this file, you will close the current document file using the Close command on the File menu.

- ■ Choose **F**ile.

The File drop-down menu consisting of 13 commands is displayed. In addition to the commands you would expect to see in the File menu, such as Save and Exit, there are several commands that are specific to Word. At the bottom of the File menu, a list of the names of the most recently used Word document files may be displayed. Clicking on a file name opens the file.

To close the document,

- ■ Choose **C**lose.

As a precaution against losing your work, the Office Assistant displays an advisory balloon asking if you want to

save the contents of the current document to disk. As you create a new document or edit an existing document, the changes you make are immediately displayed onscreen and are stored in your computer's memory. To create a permanent copy of your document, it must be saved as a file on a disk. Selecting Yes saves the document as a file on a disk, No closes the document without saving, and Cancel returns you to the document. To save the document you have created to a file on your data disk,

- ■ Click (● Yes).

You can use [←Backspace] to delete characters to the left of the insertion point or [Delete] to delete characters to the right of the insertion point.

You can also correct misspellings and grammar errors using the Shortcut menus.

Up to nine recently used documents may be displayed.

You could also click the document window's [×] button to close the document file.

If the Office Assistant is closed, Word displays the same message in a dialog box.

The Save As dialog box on your screen should be similar to Figure 1-9.

location to save

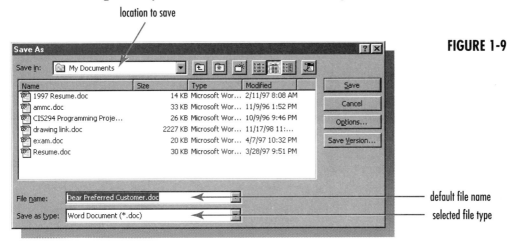

FIGURE 1-9

default file name
selected file type

This dialog box is used to specify the location to save the file and the file name. The Save In drop-down list box displays the default folder as the location where the file will be saved, and the File Name text box displays the proposed file name. First you need to change the location where the file will be saved to the drive containing your data disk.

- Select Save **In**.

- Select A: (or the drive containing your data disk).

Now the large list box displays the names of all Word files on your data disk. Only Word document files are displayed because the Save As Type list box shows that the currently selected file type is Word Document. Word document files are identified by the file extension .doc, which is automatically added to the file name when the file is saved.

Next you need to enter a file name. The File Name list box displays the default file name, consisting of the first few words from the document. You will change the name to Letter Lab 1.

- Triple-click the default file name in the File Name text box.

- Type **Letter Lab 1**

- Click [Save]

The document is saved on disk and the document window is closed. Now the Word window displays an empty text area, and the status bar indicators are blank because there are no open documents.

> Place your data disk in drive A (or the appropriate drive for your system).

> If a system error message appears, check that your disk is properly inserted in the drive.

> A Word file name can be up to 255 characters and follows standard file-naming rules.

> The file name can be entered in either uppercase or lowercase letters and will appear exactly as you type it.

Opening a File

You are now ready to open the file named Credit Card Letter. As in all Windows 95 applications, the Open command on the File menu is used to open files. In addition, the toolbar shortcut 🗁 Open can be used instead of the menu command.

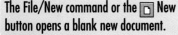

The File/New command or the ▭ New button opens a blank new document.

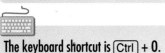

The keyboard shortcut is [Ctrl] + O.

■   Click 🗁 Open.

The Open dialog box on your screen should be similar to Figure 1-10.

location where program is looking for file

FIGURE 1-10

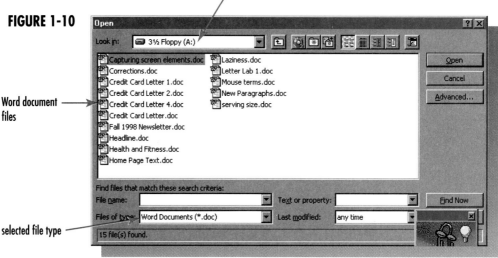

Word document files

selected file type

In the Open dialog box, you specify the location and name of the file you want to open. The Look In drop-down list box displays the drive you specified when saving as the location where the program will look for files. The location should be the drive containing your data disk. The large list box displays the names of all Word files on your data disk. Again, only Word document files are displayed because the currently selected type is Word Documents.

If the Look In location is not correct, select the appropriate location from the Look In drop-down list box.

If necessary, scroll the list box until the file name Credit Card Letter is visible. If the file name is not displayed, ask your instructor for help.

You could also double-click the file name to both select it and choose Open.

■   Select Credit Card Letter.

■   Click ⟦   Open   ⟧.

Your screen should be similar to Figure 1-11.

file name

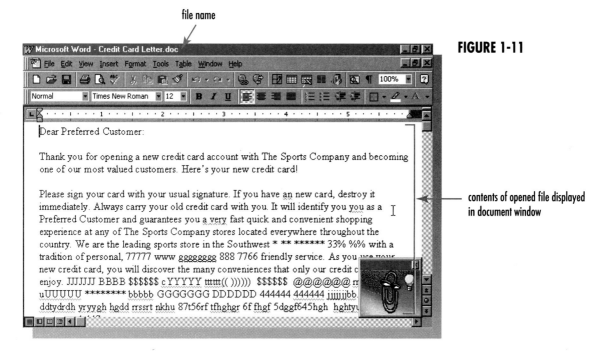

FIGURE 1-11

contents of opened file displayed
in document window

The file is loaded and displayed in the document window. This file contains the
rest of the first draft of the letter to new credit card customers. It contains many
errors that need to be edited.

Note: If you end your lab session now, close the file and follow the instructions
on page WP42 to exit the program. When you continue the lab at Part 2, load
Word and open the Credit Card Letter file.

Part 2

Moving Through a Document

As you can see, the text area is not large enough to display the entire document.
To bring additional text into view in the window, you can scroll the text using
either the scroll bars or the keyboard. Again, both methods are useful, depending on what you are doing.

- Click the ▼ in the vertical scroll bar to scroll the document until the closing is displayed in
  the window.

Your screen should be similar to Figure 1-12.

FIGURE 1-12

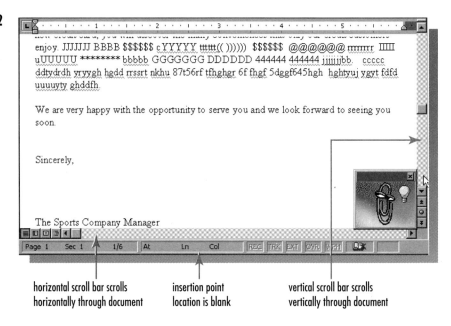

horizontal scroll bar scrolls
horizontally through document

insertion point
location is blank

vertical scroll bar scrolls
vertically through document

The text at the beginning of the letter has scrolled off the window, and the bottom of the letter is now displayed. Notice that the insertion point is no longer visible in the window, and the insertion point location information in the status bar is blank. To actually move the insertion point, you must click in a location in the window.

■   Move to T in The Sports Company Manager.

You can also scroll the document using the keyboard. While scrolling using the keyboard, the insertion point also moves. To return to the top of the letter,

■   Hold down ⬆ for several seconds until the insertion point is on the D in Dear.

You can move quickly through a document in large jumps by moving a window or a page at a time, moving to a specific page, or moving to the end or beginning of the document.

■   Press Page Down (2 times).

The insertion point moved to the bottom line of the current window and then to the bottom line of the next full window of text. You are still viewing page 1 of the

> Clicking above or below the scroll box in the vertical scroll bar also moves window by window through the document.

document. The ⬆ Previous Page and ⬇ Next Page Navigator buttons located at the bottom of the vertical scroll bar move page by page through a document. To move to the top of the next page,

■   Click ⬇ Next Page.

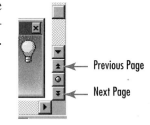

Previous Page

Next Page

The insertion point is positioned on the first line of page 2. Notice that the status bar displays "Page 2." To show where one page ends and another begins, Word displays a dotted line to mark the page break. To see this line,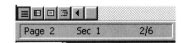

■   Press ↑.

Your screen should be similar to Figure 1-13.

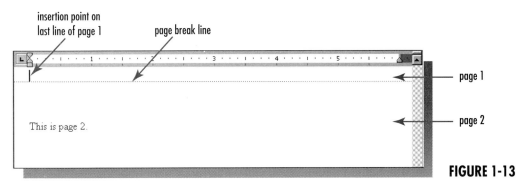

FIGURE 1-13

The insertion point is positioned on the last line of page 1, and the status bar displays "Page 1." Word automatically enters a page break line in a document when the preceding page is full to show where a new page of text begins.

Dragging the scroll box moves multiple windows forward or backward through the document. The location of the scroll box in the vertical scroll bar reflects your position in a document. When the scroll box is midway on the scroll bar, the displayed text is approximately in the middle of the document. As you drag the scroll box, a ScrollTip tells you the page that will be displayed in the window.

■   Drag the scroll box down the vertical scroll bar and release it when the ScrollTip displays "Page: 3."

You can also use the 🔘 Select Browse Object button to select the way you want to browse through the document. The method you choose changes how the ⬆ and ⬇ buttons work. Because the default is by page, using these buttons moves by page through the document,

■   Click 🔘 Select Browse Object.

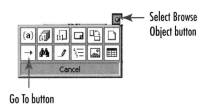

From the browser box you select the element by which you want to navigate, such as by tables or by headings instead of by page.

■   Point to each button in the browser to see the option name.

You can also move directly to a specific location in the document using the Go To option.

The menu equivalent is **Edit/Go To**, and the keyboard shortcut is Ctrl + **G**.

■   Click → Go To.

The Find and Replace dialog box on your screen should be similar to Figure 1-14.

FIGURE 1-14

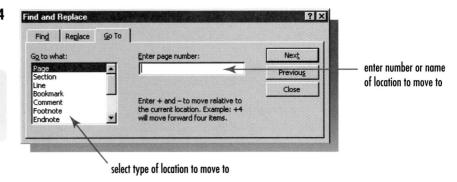

select type of location to move to

enter number or name
of location to move to

Office Assistant continues to offer tips as you work. You can choose to read the tips or ignore them.

Page is the default type of location to move to. To specify a specific page to move to, in the Enter Page Number text box,

Reminder: You can press ⏎Enter to choose the Go To command button.

■   Type **5**

■   Click   Go To

The insertion point moves directly to the first line of page 5.
    To close the dialog box,

You could also click ☒ to close the dialog box.

■   Click   Close

The biggest jump the insertion point can make is to move to the beginning or end of a document. To move to the end of this document,

■   Press Ctrl + End.

Your screen should be similar to Figure 1-15.

FIGURE 1-15

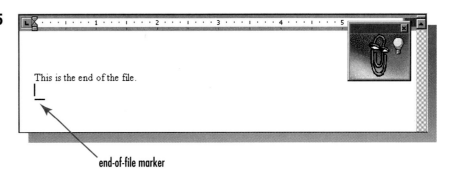

This is the end of the file.

end-of-file marker

The insertion point should be positioned on a blank line on page 6 of this document. The status bar displayss "6/6," indicating that you are viewing the sixth page of a six-page document. In addition, the end-of-file marker is displayed. This is the last line in the file.

To move quickly back to the beginning of the document,

■ Press Ctrl + Home.

To review, the following features can be used to move through a document:

You can also drag the scroll box to the bottom or top of the scroll bar to quickly move to the end or beginning of the document.

Mouse	Action
Click new location	Positions insertion point.
Click scroll arrow	Scrolls line by line or character by character in the direction of the scroll arrow.
Click above/below scroll box	Scrolls the document window by window.
Drag scroll box	Moves multiple windows up/down.
Click ⦿	Select object to browse by.
Click ⬆	Go to previous page.
Click ⬇	Go to next page.

Key	Action
→	One character to right.
←	One character to left.
↑	One line up.
↓	One line down.
Ctrl + →	One word to right.
Ctrl + ←	One word to left.
Home	Left end of line.
End	Right end of line.
Page Up	Top of window.
Page Down	Bottom of window.
Ctrl + Home	Beginning of document.
Ctrl + End	End of document.
Edit/Go To	Moves to specified location.

Inserting Characters

After entering the text of a document, you should proofread it for accuracy and completeness and modify or edit the document as needed. As you check the document, you see that the first sentence of the second paragraph is incorrect. It should read: "Please sign your new card in ink with your usual signature." The sentence is missing three words, "new," "in," and "ink." These words can easily be entered into the sentence without retyping it using either Insert or Overtype mode.

In **Insert mode** new characters are inserted into the existing text by moving the existing text to the right to make space for the new characters. To insert the word "new" before the word "card" in the first sentence,

> The default setting for Word is Insert mode.

- Move to c in card.

- Type **new**

- Press (Spacebar).

Your screen should be similar to Figure 1-16.

FIGURE 1-16

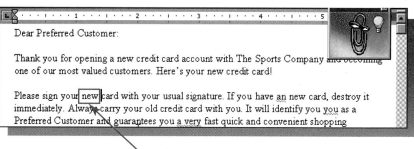

inserted text

- Continue to correct the sentence by entering the words "in ink" before the word "with."

In the second sentence, you notice that the word "new" should be "old."

- Move to n of new.

You could delete this word and type in the new word, or you can use the Overtype mode to enter text in a document. When you use **Overtype mode**, new text types over the existing characters. To switch to this mode,

> The ⊙ⱽᴿ button is in the status bar.

- Double-click ⱽᴿ.

Notice the OVR status indicator button letters appear bright. This indicates the Overtype mode is on. To change the word "new" to "old,"

- Type **old**

Your screen should be similar to Figure 1-17.

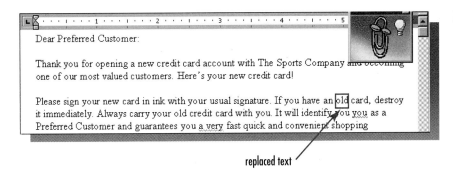

FIGURE 1-17

As each character was typed, the selected character (or space) was replaced with the character being typed.

- ■ Next replace the word "old" in the third sentence of the paragraph with "new."

- ■ Double-click OVR .

The OVR status indicator button letters are dimmed again, indicating the Overtype feature is off.

Deleting Words

As you continue to read, you find that the fourth sentence of the second paragraph contains a repeated word and several unnecessary words. The repeated word "you" has been identified by the automatic spell-checking feature.

- ■ To quickly delete a repeated word, display the Spelling Shortcut menu for the identified word "you" and select the Delete Repeated Word option.

Not all words you may want to delete, however, are repeated words. Other words may be unnecessary to the content. In the same sentence, the word "fast" is not needed because the following word "quick" conveys the same information. To delete the word "fast,"

- ■ Move to f in fast.
- ■ Press Ctrl + Delete .

Your screen should be similar to Figure 1-18.

FIGURE 1-18

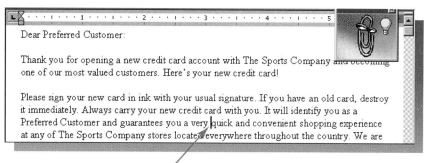

word "fast" was deleted

The characters to the right of the insertion point are deleted, including the blank space following the word. As you read the revised sentence, you also decide the word "very" is unnecessary. You can delete the character and space to the left of the insertion point using the Ctrl + ←Backspace key combination.

> When the insertion point is positioned on the beginning or end of a word, the entire word is deleted.

- Press Ctrl + ←Backspace.
- In the same sentence, use either method to delete the word "everywhere."

Displaying Special Characters

As you continue to proof the letter, you decide that the second paragraph is too long and should be divided into two separate paragraphs.

- Move to W in We (fourth line of second paragraph).
- Press ←Enter (2 times).

Each time you press ←Enter, Word inserts a special character called a **paragraph mark** at that location in the document. Word does not display these special characters because they clutter the screen, nor does it print them. However, there are times when you need to delete a special character, so you need to be able to see where it is.

> The menu equivalent is **T**ools/**O**ptions/ View/**S**paces/Paragraph **M**arks.

- Click ¶ Show/Hide.

Your screen should be similar to 1-19.

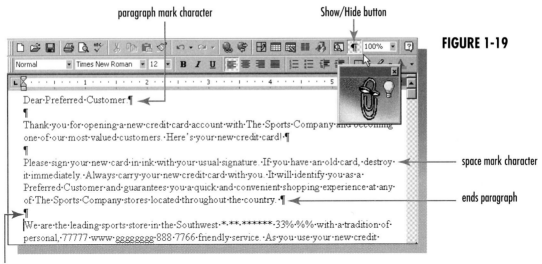

paragraph mark character

Show/Hide button

FIGURE 1-19

space mark character

ends paragraph

inserts blank line

The document now displays the special characters. A paragraph mark character ¶ is displayed wherever the [←Enter] key was pressed. Between each word, a dot shows where the [Spacebar] was pressed. The ¶ character on the line above the insertion point represents the pressing of [←Enter] that created the blank line between the second and third paragraphs. The ¶ character at the end of the line above that represents the pressing of [←Enter] that ended the paragraph and moved the insertion point to the beginning of the next line.

To delete a special character, position the insertion point on the character and press [Delete], or position the insertion point to the right of the character and press [←Backspace]. This works the same way as if you were deleting text in the document. To delete the two ¶ characters that you just inserted,

■   Press [←Backspace] (2 times).

The blank line is removed, the text moves up to fill in the blank space at the end of the previous line, and the two paragraphs return to a single paragraph. To separate the text into two paragraphs again,

■   Press [←Enter] (2 times).

In many editing situations, it is necessary to display the special characters; however, this is not needed for simple text deletions. For normal entry of text, you will probably not want the characters displayed. To hide the characters,

■   Click [¶] Show/Hide.

The screen returns to normal display. Now that you know how to turn this feature on and off, you can use it whenever you want when entering and editing text.

Selecting Text

As you continue proofreading the letter, you see that the third paragraph contains several large areas of junk characters. To remove these characters, you could use `Delete` and `←Backspace` to delete each character individually or `Ctrl` + `Delete` or `Ctrl` + `←Backspace` to delete each word. However, this is very slow. Several characters, words, or lines of text can be deleted at once by first **selecting** the text and then pressing `Delete`. Text is selected by highlighting it. To select text, first move the insertion point to the beginning or end of the text to be selected. Then select the text by dragging the mouse. You can select as little as a single letter or as much as the entire document.

The first area of characters to be removed follows the word "Southwest" in the first line of the third paragraph. To position the insertion point on the first character of the text to be selected,

- Move to * (first line of third paragraph).

- Drag the mouse until the junk text is highlighted (including the space before the word "with").

The junk text is selected. Text that is selected can then be modified using many different Word features. In this case, you want to remove the selected text. To do this,

- Press `Delete`.

- In a similar manner, select and delete the next set of junk characters following the word "personal" in this sentence.

- Scroll the window to view the entire third paragraph.

The last two sentences of the paragraph consist entirely of junk characters. You can also quickly select a standard block of text. A standard block consists of a sentence, paragraph, page, tabular column, rectangular portion of text, or the entire document. The following table summarizes the techniques used to select standard blocks.

> You can also select text with the keyboard by holding down `⇧ Shift` while using the direction keys to expand the highlight in the direction indicated. Holding down `Ctrl` + `⇧ Shift` while using the `→` or `←` keys selects word by word.

> You can also select an area of text by clicking on the beginning of the text area and then holding down `⇧ Shift` while clicking on the end of the text area.

To select a:	Procedure:
Word	Double-click in the word.
Sentence	Press `Ctrl` and click within the sentence.
Line	Click in the selection bar next to the line.
Multiple lines	Drag in the selection bar next to the lines.
Paragraph	Triple-click on the paragraph or double-click in the selection bar next to the paragraph.
Multiple paragraphs	Drag in the selection bar next to the paragraphs.
Document	Triple-click in the selection bar or press `Ctrl` and click in the selection bar.

You will select and delete the first sentence of nonsense characters in this paragraph. To do so,

- ■ Press Ctrl and click anywhere in third sentence of third paragraph.

Your screen should be similar to Figure 1-20.

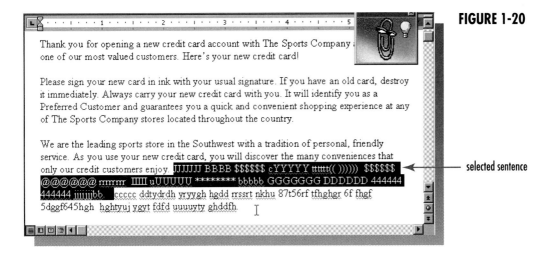

FIGURE 1-20

selected sentence

- ■ Press Delete.
- ■ In a similar manner, delete the second sentence of junk characters.

Undoing Editing Changes

Finally, you are not too pleased with the last sentence of the letter and are considering removing it.

- ■ Double-click in the selection bar next to the last sentence of the letter to select it.
- ■ Delete the selection.

After thinking about this change, you decide the last sentence may not be so bad after all. To quickly restore this sentence, you can use ⟲ Undo to reverse your last action or command.

- ■ Click ⟲ Undo.

The menu equivalent is **E**dit/**U**ndo or Ctrl + Z.

Undo returns your last deletion and restores it to its original location in the text, regardless of the current insertion point location. Notice that the Undo button includes a drop-down list button. Clicking this button displays a list of your most recent actions. When you select an action from the drop-down list, you also undo all actions above it in the list. Immediately after you Undo an action, the Redo button is available so you can restore the action you just undid.

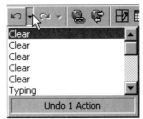

The ⟲ and ⟳ toolbar ScreenTips include the name of the feature that will be affected by their use.

The menu equivalent is **E**dit/**R**edo or [Ctrl] + Y.

If an action cannot be reversed, Can't Undo is displayed in the Edit menu.

■ Click [↶ ▾] Redo.

The sentence is removed again. To reverse this action again,

■ Click [↶ ▾] Undo.

■ Enter your name in the closing on the line above "The Sports Company Manager."

Finally, you also do not need the extra pages that were included in this document to demonstrate how to move around a document. To select and delete the text from the insertion point to the end of the file,

You could also scroll to the end of the file and hold [⇧ Shift] while clicking to select all text between the current insertion point location and the end location.

■ Move the insertion point to the line below the closing, "The Sports Company Manager."

■ Press [⇧ Shift] + [Ctrl] + [End].

■ Press [Delete].

The status bar now shows that the insertion point is positioned on page 1 of a one-page document.

Word keeps track of the last three locations where you entered or edited text. To quickly return to a previous editing location, press [⇧ Shift] + [F5].

To review, the following editing keys have been covered:

Key	Button	Action
[←Backspace]		Deletes character to left of insertion point.
[Delete]		Deletes character to right of insertion point.
[Ctrl] + [←Backspace]		Deletes word to left of insertion point.
[Ctrl] + [Delete]		Deletes word to right of insertion point.
[←Enter]		Ends a line and moves insertion point to next line or inserts a blank line.
Edit/**U**ndo	[↶ ▾]	Reverses your last action or command.
Edit/**R**edo	[↶ ▾]	Reverses the effects of the Undo.

Documenting a File

Next you will add your own documentation to the file properties. To see the information associated with this file,

- Choose File/Properties.

- If necessary, open the General tab.

The Properties dialog box on your screen should be similar to Figure 1-21.

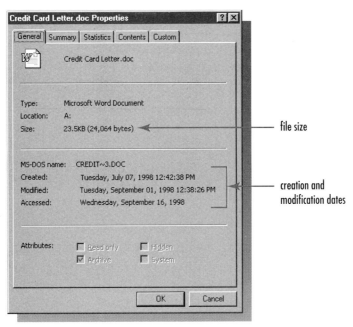

FIGURE 1-21

Each tab displays information about the document. The General tab displays basic information such as when the file was created and last modified, and the size of the file in bytes.

- Select each tab and look at the recorded information.

To make it easier to find files, you can add your own properties to the file using the Summary tab.

- Open the Summary tab.

The Summary Tab on your screen should be similar to Figure 1-22.

FIGURE 1-22

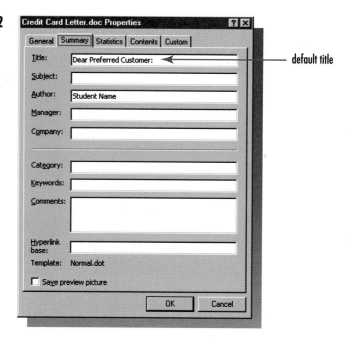

default title

The Summary tab contains text boxes that allow you to enter a title, subject, author, keywords, and comments about the file. This information helps you locate the file you want to use as well as provides information about the objectives and use of the document. First you will enter a descriptive title for the document. By default, Word displays the first few words from the document as the default title. To replace the default title with your own title,

> The title can be different from the actual file name.

- Select Dear Preferred Customer:
- Type **Credit Card Letter**
- Enter the following information in the text boxes indicated:

> Use ⌜Tab ⇆⌟ both to move and to select the entry in a text box.

Subject:	**Letter to all new credit card holders**
Author:	**[your name]**
Company:	**The Sports Company**
Comments:	**First draft - [current date]**

> The Author text box may be blank or show your school or some other name. Clear the existing contents first if necessary.

- Click   OK   .

Now you are ready to save the changes you have made to the file on your data disk using the Save or Save As commands on the File menu. The Save command or the 🔲 Save button will save the document using the same file name. The Save As command allows you to save the current file using a new file name. Because you may want to redo this lab and use the Credit Card Letter file again, you will save your edited version using a new file name.

The keyboard shortcut for File/Save is `Ctrl` + S.

■ Choose <u>F</u>ile/Save <u>A</u>s.

The file name of the file you opened, Credit Card Letter, is displayed in the File Name text box of the Save As dialog box. To save the document as Credit Card Letter 1, you can type the new file name entirely, or you can edit the existing name. In this case, it is easier to edit the file name by adding the number 1 to the end of the name.

■ Click at the end of the file name (before the file extension) to both clear the highlight and place the insertion point at the end of the name.

■ Press `Spacebar`.

■ Type 1

■ Click `Save`.

If you do not clear the highlight, the selected file name will be cleared and replaced with the new text as it is typed.

The new file name, Credit Card Letter 1, is displayed in the window title bar. The original document file is unchanged on your data disk.

Previewing and Printing a Document

Although you still plan to make several formatting changes to the document, you want to give a copy of the letter to the regional manager to get feedback regarding the content of the letter. Before printing, it is helpful to preview how the document will look when it is printed.

Concept 6: Document Preview

To save time and unnecessary printing and paper waste, it is always a good idea to preview onscreen how your document will appear when printed. The Print Preview feature displays each page of your document in a reduced size so you can see the layout. You can also make last-minute editing and formatting changes while previewing and then print directly from the Preview screen.

To preview the letter,

The menu equivalent is **F**ile/Print
Pre**v**iew.

■   Click   ▣   Print Preview.

Your screen should be similar to Figure 1-23.

Print button begins printing immediately   closes Print Preview window

FIGURE 1-23

Preview toolbar

print preview
of letter

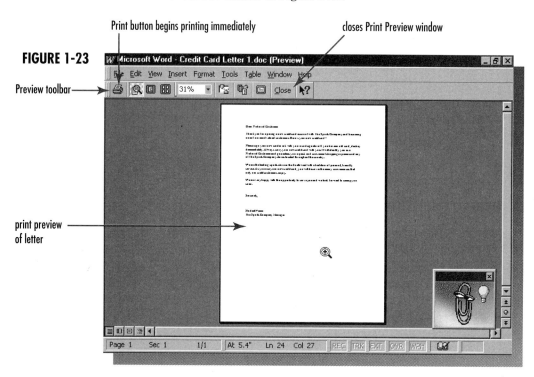

The Print Preview window displays a reduced view of how the current page will
appear when printed. This view allows you to check your page layout before
printing. The letter appears balanced within the left and right margins and does
not appear to need any further modifications immediately.

This window also includes its own toolbar. You can print the letter directly
from the Preview window using the ▣ Print button; however, this sends the
document directly to the printer. Before printing, you need to check the print
settings. To close the Print Preview window,

■   Click   Close .

The 🖨 Print button on the Standard toolbar will also send the document directly to the printer. To check the print settings, you need to use the Print command on the File menu.

■ If necessary, make sure your printer is on and ready to print.

■ Choose <u>F</u>ile/<u>P</u>rint.

The Print dialog box on your screen should be similar to Figure 1-24.

selected printer

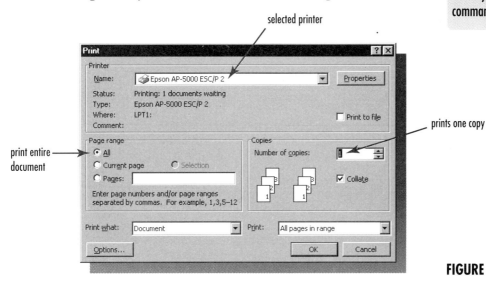

print entire document

prints one copy

FIGURE 1-24

From the Print dialog box, you need to specify the printer you will be using and the document settings. The printer that is currently selected is displayed in the Name drop-down list box in the Printer section of the dialog box.

■ If you need to change the selected printer to another printer, open the Name drop-down list box and select the appropriate printer (your instructor will tell you which printer to select).

The Page Range area of the Print dialog box lets you specify how much of the document you want printed. The range options are described in the following table:

Option	Action
All	Prints the entire document.
Current page	Prints selected page or the page the insertion point is on.
Pages	Prints pages you specify by typing page numbers in the text box.
Selection	Prints selected text only.

The default range setting, All, is the correct setting. In the Copies section, the default setting of one copy of the document is acceptable. To begin printing using the settings in the Print dialog box,

■   Click .

Your printer should be printing out the current page of the document file. The printed copy of the credit card letter should be similar to the one shown at the beginning of the lab on page WP6.

Note: Your printed copy may not match exactly if the printer you selected uses a different font size from the one used to display the document on the screen. You will learn about fonts in the next lab.

Exiting Word

The keyboard shortcut for the Exit command is [Alt] + [F4].

The Exit command on the File menu is used to quit the Word program. Alternatively, you can click the ☒ Close button in the application window title bar.

■   Click ☒ Close.

The Windows 95 desktop is visible again.

To avoid losing data, always exit Word 97 using the Exit command or the ☒ Close button.

LAB REVIEW

■ ■ ■ ■ ■ ■ ■ ■ ■ ■ ■

Key Terms

AutoCorrect   (WP14)
AutoText   (WP14)
cursor   (WP9)
custom dictionary   (WP15)
default   (WP12)
docked   (WP9)
edit   (WP11)
end-of-file marker   (WP9)
floating   (WP9)
format   (WP11)
Formatting toolbar   (WP9)
Insert mode   (WP30)
insertion point   (WP9)
main dictionary   (WP15)
Office Assistant   (WP9)
Overtype mode   (WP30)
paragraph mark   (WP32)
ruler   (WP9)
select   (WP34)
selection bar   (WP20)
Standard toolbar   (WP8)
status bar   (WP9)
template   (WP12)
word wrap   (WP19)

Command Summary

Command	Shortcut Key	Button	Action
File/**N**ew	Ctrl + N	◻	Opens new file
File/**O**pen	Ctrl + O	📂	Opens selected file
File/**C**lose		✕	Closes file
File/**S**ave	Ctrl + S	💾	Saves file using same file name
File/Save **A**s			Saves file using a new file name
File/Proper**ti**es			Shows properties of active document
File/Print Pre**v**iew		🔍	Displays document as it will appear when printed
File/**P**rint	Ctrl + P	🖨	Prints file using selected print settings
File/E**x**it	Alt + F4	✕	Exits Word program
Edit/**U**ndo	Ctrl + Z	↺ ▾	Restores last editing change
Edit/**R**edo or **R**epeat	Ctrl + Y	↻ ▾	Restores last Undo or repeats last command or action
Edit/**G**o To	Ctrl + G		Moves insertion point to specified location in document
View/**T**oolbars			Displays or hides selected toolbars
Tools/**C**ustomize/ **O**ptions			Changes display options
Tools/**O**ptions/View/ **S**paces/Paragraph **M**arks		¶	Displays or hides special characters
Help/**M**icrosoft Word Help	F1	❓	Displays Office Assistant

Matching

1. 🔍   _____ **a.** new text writes over existing text
2. document template   _____ **b.** deletes word to the right of the insertion point
3. Overtype   _____ **c.** moves to the top of the document
4. Ctrl + ←Backspace   _____ **d.** constant adjustment of text to fill in extra space in a line without exceeding the margin setting
5. .doc   _____ **e.** displays help and tips to improve your efficiency as you work
6. Ctrl + Home   _____ **f.** displays the Print Preview window
7. Office Assistant   _____ **g.** a predesigned document that is used as a pattern to create many common types of documents
8. 💾   _____ **h.** deletes word to the left of the insertion point
9. word wrap   _____ **i.** Word document file extension
10. Ctrl + Delete   _____ **j.** saves a document using the same file name

Fill-In Questions

1. Complete the following statements by filling in the blanks with the correct terms.

a. A(n) _____ indicates a potential grammar error.

b. A(n) _____ is a predesigned document.

c. Name the first three steps in developing a document: _____, _____, and _____.

d. Text can be entered in a document in either the _____ or _____ mode.

e. The _____ key erases the character to the right of the insertion point.

f. The automatic _____ feature makes entering text in a document faster than typing on a typewriter.

g. The Word document file name extension is _____.

h. The _____ displays a tip about a more efficient or alternative method directly related to the procedure you are trying to perform.

i. Word inserts hidden _____ into a document to control the display of text.

j. The _____ feature automatically identifies and corrects certain types of errors.

2. In the following Word screen, letters identify important elements. Enter the correct term for each screen element in the space provided.

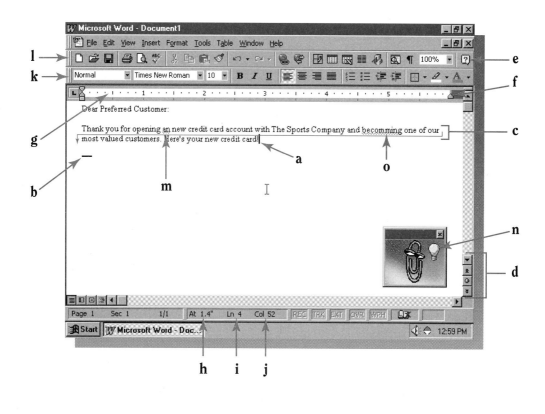

a. _____   f. _____   k. _____

b. _____   g. _____   l. _____

c. _____   h. _____   m. _____

d. _____   i. _____   n. _____

e. _____   j. _____   o. _____

3. The following screen identifies several errors and changes that need to be made to a document. From the list below, match the letter to the procedure that will make the change.

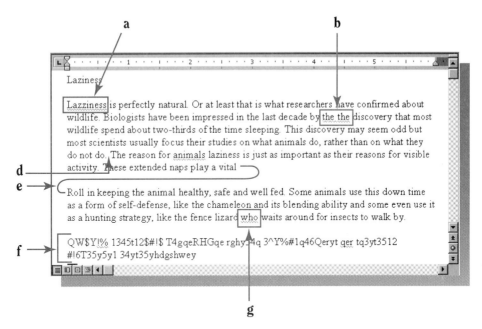

a. fix spelling

_____ Display the Grammar Shortcut menu and make necessary correction.

b. remove second "the"

_____ Display the Spelling Shortcut menu and select the correct spelling.

c. fix grammar

_____ Move to the letter "T" and press ⎰←Enter⎱ twice.

d. begin new paragraph

_____ Display the Spelling Shortcut menu and select a better word.

e. combine with previous paragraph

_____ Display the Spelling Shortcut menu and select Delete Repeated Word.

f. delete paragraph

_____ Move to the letter r and press ⎰←Backspace⎱ three times.

g. fix grammar

_____ Triple-click in the selection bar and press ⎰Delete⎱.

Discussion Questions

1. Discuss several uses you may have for a word processor. Then explain the steps you would follow to create a document.

2. Discuss how the AutoCorrect and Spelling and Grammar Checker features help you as you type. What types of corrections does the AutoCorrect feature make?

3. Discuss how word wrap works. What happens when text is added? What happens when text is removed?

4. Discuss three ways you can select text. Discuss when it would be appropriate to use the different methods.

5. Describe how the Undo and Redo features work. What are some advantages of these features?

Hands-On Practice Exercises

Step by Step

Rating System	
☆	Easy
☆☆	Moderate
☆☆☆	Difficult

1. In this problem you will use the commands and features you learned in the lab to correct a document.

a. Open the file Corrections on your data disk. Follow the directions to edit the file, and reveal a saying found on the wall of a fix-it shop.

b. When you are finished, enter your name and the current date below the document. Save the file with the same name. Preview and print the document.

c. Delete the lines of instructions to reveal only the lines of the saying, your name, and the date. Combine the first four lines to form one paragraph.

d. Document the file by adding appropriate information to the Summary tab of the Properties dialog box. Save the document as Three Kinds of Jobs on your data disk. Preview and print the saying.

2. The mouse is a standard hardware device that makes performing many tasks much quicker. In this problem you will edit a document about using a mouse.

a. Open the file Mouse Terms on your data disk. Use the editing techniques you learned in Lab 1 to correct the errors in the document.

b. Insert your name and current date below the document.

c. Document the file by adding appropriate information to the Summary tab of the Properties dialog box. Save the document as Mouse Terms 1. Preview and print the document.

You will continue this exercise as Practice Exercise 1 in Lab 2.

3. Universal Industries has banned smoking in all buildings. Mr. Biggs, the CEO, has sent a memo informing employees of this policy.

a. Create the memo shown below. Press Tab⇆ after you type colons (:) in the To, From, Date, and RE lines. This will cause information following colons to line up evenly.

To:	[Your Name]
From:	Mr. Biggs
Date:	[Current Date]
RE:	No Smoking Policy

Effective next Monday, smoking will be banned in all buildings. Ashtrays will be placed outside each door, and smoking material must be extinguished before you enter.

Thank you for your cooperation in this matter.

JBB/xxx

b. Document the file by adding appropriate information to the Summary tab of the Properties dialog box. Save the document as No Smoking Memo on your data disk. Preview then print the memo.

You will complete this exercise as Practice Exercise 1 in Lab 3.

4. You are in the process of compiling your grandmother's cookie recipes. You are going to pass the recipes on to several family members and friends who have requested them over the years. Following is a letter that you will enclose with the recipes.

a. Enter the letter as shown below, only pressing [←Enter] at the end of the paragraphs.

[Your Name]
[Street Address]
[City, State, Zip Code]
[Current Date]

Dear Friends and Family:

Enclosed, as promised, is a copy of Grandma Gertie's famous cookie recipes. We have all enjoyed them over the years, and it has been my pleasure to compile the recipes so you can continue to enjoy them for years to come.

For my next project, I would like to compile recipes from our own generation and pass them along, so we can pass them down. If you have any recipes that you would like to share with the rest of us, please send them to me at the above address.

Sincerely,

[Your Name]

b. Document the file by adding appropriate information to the Summary tab of the Properties dialog box. Save the document as Cookie Letter on your data disk. Preview then print the letter.

You will continue this exercise as Practice Exercise 3 in Lab 4.

5. Here is the first of the cookie recipes that will be included in the collection referred to in the previous exercise.

a. Enter the recipe for potato chip cookies shown below.

Potato Chip Cookies

Potato chips give these cookies a crunchy texture and eliminate the need for baking soda.

Ingredients:
2 sticks of butter (softened)
½ c. dark brown sugar (firmly packed)
½ c. crushed potato chips
1 tsp. vanilla extract
½ c. sifted flour
confectioner's sugar

Directions:
Cream the butter and brown sugar together.
Add vanilla, chips, and nuts.
Gradually add the flour. Mix thoroughly.
Cover and chill the dough for at least 1 hour.
Roll dough into 1" balls, and roll in confectioner's sugar.
Place 1" apart on greased cookie sheet.
Bake in 350 degree oven for 12–15 minutes.
This recipe makes about 3-½ dozen cookies.

b. Insert a blank line between the crushed potato chips and the vanilla extract in the Ingredients section. Add "½ c. chopped pecans" to the list of ingredients.

c. Enter your name and the current date below the recipe.

d. Document the file by adding appropriate information to the Summary tab of the Properties dialog box. Save the document as Potato Chip Cookies on your data disk. Preview and then print the recipe.

You will continue to add more recipes to your collection in Practice Exercise 3 in Lab 2.

On Your Own

6. You are about to open a bed and breakfast inn in the Pocono Mountains. You are going to advertise the B&B in a local travel guide. Type the following information to create the first draft of the ad.

Pocono Mountain Retreat
124 Mountain Laurel Trail
Pocono Manor, PA 18349

Phone: 1-717-839-5555
Host: [Your Name]

Number of Rooms: 4
Number of private baths: 1
Maximum number sharing baths: 4
Double rate for shared bath: $85.00
Double rate for private bath: $95.00
Single rate for shared bath: $65.00
Single rate for private bath: $75.00
Open: All year
Breakfast: Continental
Children: Welcome, over 12
Smoking: No
Social Drinking: Permitted

Located in the heart of the Poconos is this rustic country inn where you can choose to indulge yourself in the quiet beauty of the immediate surroundings or take advantage of the numerous activities at nearby resorts, lakes, and parks.

In the winter, shuttle buses will transport you to the Jack Frost and Big Boulder ski resorts. We have trails for cross-country skiing right on the property, and we will take you for a ride in our horse-drawn sleigh. In the summer, you can be whisked away to beautiful Lake Wallenpaupack for swimming and boating. The fall foliage is beyond compare, and you can hike our nature trails and take in the breathtaking scenery at this, or any time of year.

In the evenings, you can relax in front of a cozy fire or take advantage of the swinging nightlife in the Poconos. The choice is yours!

We have literature concerning all areas of interest in the Poconos. You can design your own custom tour, and Ed, our resident guide, will provide the transportation.

Be sure to call well in advance for reservations during the winter and summer months.

Insert the text "Pets: No" above "Children: Welcome, over 12." Enter the current date below the ad. Document the file by adding appropriate information to the Summary tab of the Properties dialog box. Save the document as B&B Ad on your data disk. Print the ad.

You will continue this exercise as Practice Exercise 4 in Lab 2.

7. Toward the end of each set of Practice Exercises in each lab, you can complete a problem that will help you prepare for a job interview. This lab's exercise helps you create a cover letter. In Lab 2 you can create a list of tips on how to prepare for an interview. In Lab 3 you can create a document that tells what should be included in a resume and cover letter. In Lab 4 you merge the cover letter and create the resume.

Much of the information contained in these exercises was extracted from *The Work Book* by Barbara N. Price, Ph.D., Director of Career Planning and Placement, Luzerne County Community College, Nanticoke, PA.

Use the format on the next page as a guide to creating a cover letter.

[Your Street Address]
[City, State, Zip Code]

[Date of Writing]

Mr. John Doe
[Job Title]
[Company]
[Street Address]
[City, State, Zip Code]

Dear Mr. Doe:

Tell why you are writing; name the position, field, or general occupational area that you are asking about; if you know of a specific job opening, mention it. When responding to an advertisement, be sure to include the name and date of the publication in which it was placed. If referred by a contact person, mention that fact and include the person's name in your opening sentence.

Mention one or two qualifications you think would be of greatest interest to the employer, slanting your remarks to his/her point of view. Tell why you are particularly interested in his/her company, location, or type of work. If you have had related experience or specialized training, be sure to point it out.

Refer the reader to the enclosed resume, application, or the medium that gives information concerning your qualifications. Close by making a specific request for an interview. Make sure your closing is not vague, but makes a specific action from the reader likely.

Sincerely,

[Your handwritten signature]

[Your Name]

ENCL.

Document the file by adding appropriate information to the Summary tab of the Properties dialog box. Save the document as Cover Letter on your data disk. Print the document.

You will continue this exercise as Practice Exercise 8 in Lab 4.

Creating and Editing a Document

Document Development

The development of a document follows several steps: plan, enter, edit, format, and preview and print.

Document Template

A document template is a document file that includes predefined settings that can be used as a pattern to create many common types of documents.

AutoCorrect

The AutoCorrect feature makes some basic assumptions about the text you are typing and, based on these assumptions, automatically identifies and/or corrects the entry as you type.

Spelling and Grammar Checkers

Word includes a Spelling Checker and a Grammar Checker that automatically advise you of misspelled words or incorrect grammar as you create and edit a document.

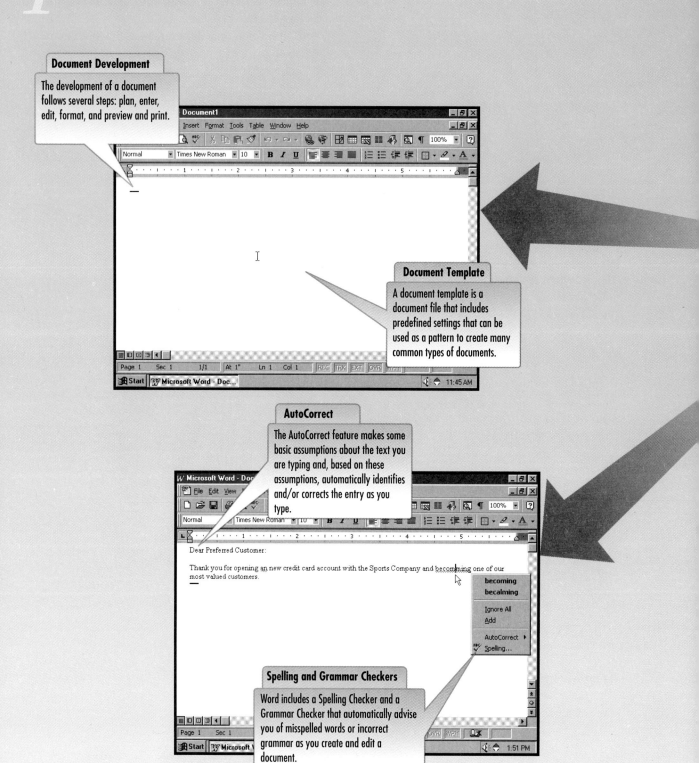

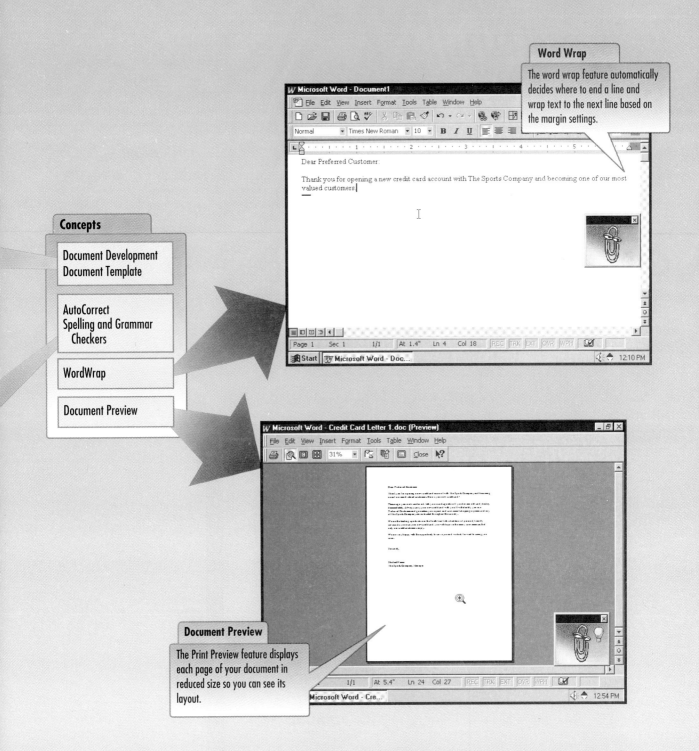

Concepts

Document Development
Document Template

AutoCorrect
Spelling and Grammar
 Checkers

WordWrap

Document Preview

Word Wrap

The word wrap feature automatically decides where to end a line and wrap text to the next line based on the margin settings.

Document Preview

The Print Preview feature displays each page of your document in reduced size so you can see its layout.

Formatting a Document

2

COMPETENCIES

After completing this lab, you will know how to:

1. Check spelling and grammar.
2. Move selected text.
3. Replace selected text.
4. Use the Find and Replace feature.
5. Use drag and drop.
6. Use the Thesaurus.
7. Use the Date and Time command.
8. Set margins.
9. Change document views.
10. Indent paragraphs.
11. Create an itemized list.
12. Change the character formatting.
13. Set paragraph alignment.
14. Edit in Print Preview.

CASE STUDY

After editing the rough draft of the credit card letter, you showed it to The Sports Company regional manager. The manager wants the letter to include information about The Sports Company newsletter and a first-purchase discount when customers use their new credit card. In addition, the manager has made several suggestions on how to improve the letter's style and appearance.

You will use many of the formatting features included in Word 97 to add style and interest to the credit card letter. You will see how using these features greatly improves the appearance and design of the letter. The result is that the letter not only looks better — it also conveys the message more clearly. The completed letter to new credit card customers is shown here.

Concept Overview

The following concepts will be introduced in this lab:

1. Move and Copy   Selections can be moved or copied to new locations in a document, saving you time by not having to retype the same information.

2. Find and Replace   To make editing easier, you can use the Find and Replace feature to find text in a document and automatically replace it with other text.

3. Thesaurus   Word's Thesaurus is a reference tool that provides synonyms, antonyms, and related words for a selected word or phrase.

4. Fields   A field is a placeholder that instructs Word to insert information into a document.

5. Margins   The margin is the distance from the text to the edge of the paper. Standard single-sided documents have four margins: top, bottom, left, and right.

6. Document Views   You can view a Word document in eight different ways. Each view offers different features for working with your documents.

7. Indents   To help your reader find information quickly, you can indent paragraphs from the margins. Indenting paragraphs sets them off from the rest of the document.

8. Bulleted and Numbered Lists   Whenever possible, use bulleted or numbered lists to organize information and make your writing clear and easy to read.

9. Fonts   A font, also commonly referred to as a typeface, is a set of characters with a specific design.

10. Character Effects   Different character effects can be applied to selections to add emphasis or interest to a document.

11. Paragraph Alignment   Alignment is how text is positioned on a line between the margins or indents. There are four types of paragraph alignment: left, center, right, and justified.

Part 1

Checking Spelling and Grammar

The regional manager noted changes to be made to the credit card letter (shown in the marked-up copy on the next page) and suggested the content for the two paragraphs about the newsletter and discount to be incorporated into the credit card letter. You hastily added the two new paragraphs to the letter.

ADD DATE

Dear Preferred Customer:

INDENT PARAGRAPHS → Thank you for opening a new credit card account with The Sports Company and becoming one of our most valued customers. Here's your new credit card!

← ADD "Sports Company"

MAKE 3 SENTENCES INTO BULLETED LIST Please sign your new card in ink with your usual signature. If you have an old card, destroy it immediately. Always carry your new credit card with you. It will identify you as a — *REWORD* Preferred Customer and guarantees you a quick and convenient shopping experience at any of The Sports Company stores located throughout the country.

ADD 2 NEW PARAGRAPHS → We are the leading sports store in the Southwest with a tradition of personal, friendly service. As you use your new credit card, you will discover the many conveniences that only | *JUSTIFY* our credit customers enjoy.

We are very happy with the opportunity to serve you and we look forward to seeing you soon.   └ *FIND A BETTER WORD*

INDENT TEXT

Sincerely,

Student Name
The Sports Company Manager

ADD CUSTOMER SERVICE TELEPHONE NUMBER

■ Load Word 97. Put your data disk in drive A (or the appropriate drive for your system).

■ Open the file Revised Credit Card Letter.

As you are reading the document, you see that Word has identified several typing and grammar errors in the new paragraphs. To correct the misspelled words and grammatical errors, you can use the Shortcut menu to correct each individual word or error, as you learned in Lab 1. However, in many cases you may find it more efficient to wait until you are finished writing before you correct any spelling or grammatical errors. Rather than continually breaking your train of thought to correct errors as you type, you can use the Spelling and Grammar tool to check and correct all the words in the document at once.

> The text will not display the Office Assistant throughout the remaining labs.

■ Click [ABC] Spelling and Grammar.

> The menu equivalent is **Tools/Spelling and Grammar**, and the keyboard shortcut is [F7].

Your screen should be similar to Figure 2-1.

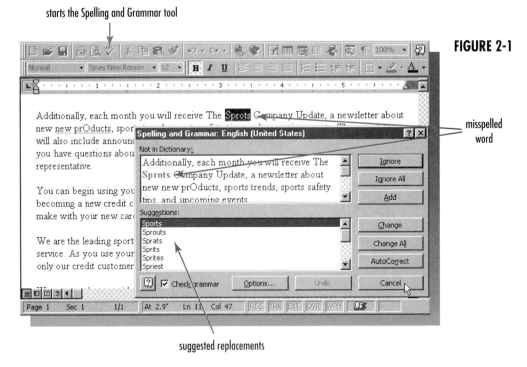

starts the Spelling and Grammar tool

FIGURE 2-1

misspelled word

suggested replacements

The Spelling and Grammar dialog box is displayed, and the Spelling and Grammar tool has immediately located the first word that may be misspelled. It displays the sentence with the misspelled word "Sprots" in red in the Not in Dictionary text box and highlights it in the document.

The Suggestions list box displays the words the Spelling tool has located in the dictionary that most closely match the misspelled word. The first word is highlighted. Sometimes the Spelling tool does not display any suggested replacements because it cannot locate any words in its dictionary that are similar in spelling. If there are no suggestions, the Not in Dictionary text box simply displays the word that is highlighted in the text.

To tell the Spelling tool what to do, you need to choose from the six option buttons. They have the following effects:

Ignore	Accepts word as correct for this occurrence only.
Ignore All	Accepts word as correct throughout the spell checking of the document.
Add	Adds word to the custom dictionary. The Spelling tool will always accept an added word as correct.
Change	Replaces word with the selected word in the suggestions box.
Change All	Replaces same word throughout the document with the word in the suggestions text box.
AutoCorrect	Adds word to the AutoCorrect list so Word can correct misspellings of it automatically as you type.

The Check Grammar check box is used to turn the grammar-check feature on or off. If it is not checked,

■   Select Chec**k** grammar.

To change the spelling of the word to one of the suggested spellings, highlight the correct word in the list and then choose [Change]. If there were no suggested replacements, and you did not want to use any of the option buttons, you could edit the word yourself by typing the correction in the Not in Dictionary box. Because "Sports" is already highlighted and is the correct replacement,

You can also press [←Enter] or double-click on the correctly spelled word in the Suggestions list to both select it and choose [Change].

■   Click [C̲hange].

The Spelling Checker replaces the misspelled word with the selected suggested replacement and moves on to locate the next error.

■   Continue to respond to the Spelling and Grammar checker by selecting the action shown below in response to the identified error:

Identified Error	Cause	Action	Result
new	Repeated word	Delete	Duplicate word "new" is deleted
prOducts	Inconsistent capitalization	Change	products
a event	Grammatical error	Change	an
received	Incorrect verb form	Change	receive
discount are	Subject-verb disagreement	Change	discount is

There should be no other misspelled words or grammatical errors. However, if the Spelling and Grammar tool encounters others in your file, correct them as needed. When no others are located, a message appears telling you that the spelling and grammar check is complete.

If the Office Assistant displays the message, it disappears automatically.

■   Click [OK].

Moving Selected Text

After looking over the credit card letter, you decide to change the order of the paragraphs. You want the paragraph about the 10 percent discount (fourth paragraph) to follow the second paragraph. To do this, you will move the paragraph from its current location to the new location.

Concept 1: Move and Copy

Selections can be moved or copied to new locations in a document, saving you time by not having to retype the same information. A selection that is moved is deleted (cut) from its original location, called the **source**, and inserted (pasted) in a new location, called the **destination**, in the document. Selections that are copied are duplicated (copied) and pasted. When you cut or copy selections, the contents are stored in the Clipboard. Then when they are pasted to the new location, the Clipboard contents are copied to the location of the insertion point in the document. You can move and copy within or between document files.

> The Clipboard is a temporary storage area in Windows 95.

There are several methods you can use to move and copy selections. One method is to use the Cut, Copy, and Paste commands on the Edit menu. You will use the Shortcut menu to select the Cut command. This menu displays options related to the current selection.

> The Cut shortcuts are ✂ or (Ctrl)+ X, the Copy shortcuts are ▣ or (Ctrl) + C, and the Paste shortcuts are ▣ or (Ctrl) + V.

- Select the paragraph beginning with "You can . . ."

- Display the Shortcut menu for the selected paragraph.

- Select ✂ Cut.

- Delete the extra blank line.

```
✂  Cut
▣  Copy
▣  Paste

A  Font...
≡  Paragraph...
≡  Bullets and Numbering...

✏  Draw Table

   Define
```

> Reminder: Drag or double-click in the selection bar next to the paragraph to select it.

> Reminder: Point to the selected text while right-clicking or press (⇧Shift) + (F10) to display the Shortcut menu.

The selected paragraph is removed from the document and copied to the Clipboard. Next you need to move the insertion point to the destination location where the text will be inserted and paste the text into the document from the Clipboard.

- Move to the A in "Additionally" (first sentence, third paragraph).

- Click ▣ Paste.

- Insert a blank line between the paragraphs.

> You can also choose Paste from the Shortcut menu.

Your screen should be similar to Figure 2-2.

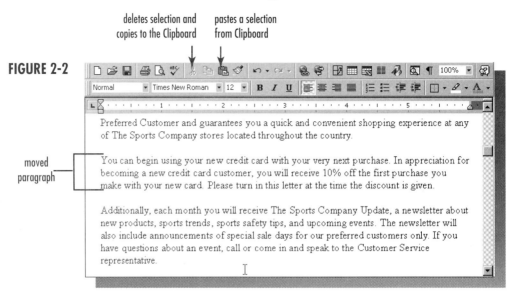

FIGURE 2-2

deletes selection and
copies to the Clipboard

pastes a selection
from Clipboard

moved
paragraph

Preferred Customer and guarantees you a quick and convenient shopping experience at any of The Sports Company stores located throughout the country.

You can begin using your new credit card with your very next purchase. In appreciation for becoming a new credit card customer, you will receive 10% off the first purchase you make with your new card. Please turn in this letter at the time the discount is given.

Additionally, each month you will receive The Sports Company Update, a newsletter about new products, sports trends, sports safety tips, and upcoming events. The newsletter will also include announcements of special sale days for our preferred customers only. If you have questions about an event, call or come in and speak to the Customer Service representative.

The deleted paragraph is reentered into the document at the insertion point location. That was a lot quicker than retyping the whole paragraph!

Replacing Selected Text

As you continue checking the letter, you want to make several text changes suggested by the regional manager. First you will reword the last sentence of the second paragraph. Instead of "It will identify you as a . . ." you would like it to say, "Your new credit card identifies you as a . . . ." Because the part you want to replace is shorter than the new text, Overtype mode will cut off some of the text you want to keep. By first selecting the text you want to remove and then typing in the new text, the part you want to keep will not be affected.

- Select "It will identify" (second paragraph, fourth sentence).
- Type **Your new card identifies**

The selected text was deleted as soon as you began to type the new text.

Using the Find and Replace Feature

The next item you want to change is to replace all occurrences of the words "new credit card" in the letter with "new Sports Company credit card" where appropriate. This process is very quick and easy using the Find and Replace feature.

Concept 2: Find and Replace

To make editing easier, you can use the Find and Replace feature to find text in a document and automatically replace it with other text. For example, suppose you created a lengthy document describing the type of clothing and equipment you need to set up a world-class home gym. You decide to change "sneakers" to "athletic shoes." Instead of deleting every occurrence of "sneakers" and typing "athletic shoes," you can use the Find and Replace feature to perform the task automatically. You can also find occurrences of special formatting, such as replacing bold text with italicized text, and special characters. This feature is fast and accurate; however, use care when replacing so that you do not replace unintended matches.

The Replace command on the Edit menu is used to find and replace text. Word will search for all occurrences of words beginning at the insertion point. If the search does not begin at the top of the document, when Word reaches the end of the document it asks if you want to continue searching from the beginning of the document. You can also highlight text to restrict the search to the selection.

To start the search at the beginning of the letter,

- ■ Press Ctrl + Home.
- ■ Choose Edit/Replace.
- ■ Click More ▾.

The Replace tab of the Find and Replace dialog box on your screen should be similar to Figure 2-3.

The Edit/Find command or Ctrl + F simply locates but does not replace specified text.

The keyboard shortcut for the Replace command is Ctrl + H.

The More ▾ button displays the advanced search and replace criteria.

You also could click ◙, then select 🔍 to open the Find and Replace dialog box.

FIGURE 2-3

enter text to locate

enter replacement text

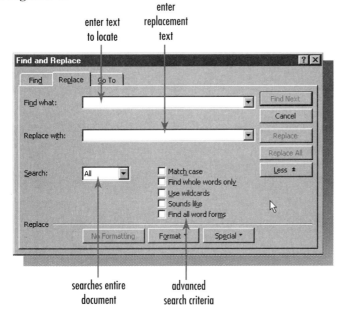

searches entire document

advanced search criteria

In the Find What text box, you enter the text you want to locate. In addition, you can use the options shown below to refine the search. These options can be combined in many ways to help you find and replace text in documents.

Option	Effect on Text
Match case	Replaces words and retains the capitalization.
Find whole words only	For example, finds "cat" only and not "catastrophe" too.
Use wildcards	Fine-tunes a search; for example, c?t finds "cat" and "cot," while c*t finds "cat" and "catastrophe."
Sounds like	Finds words that sound like the word you type; very helpful if you do not know the correct spelling of the word you want to find.
Find all word forms	Finds and replaces all forms of a word; for example, "buy" will replace "purchase" and "bought" will replace "purchased."

When you enter the text to find, you can type everything lowercase, because the Match Case option is not selected. If Match Case is not selected, the search will not be **case sensitive**. This means that lowercase letters will match both upper- and lowercase letters in the text. The text you want to replace is entered in the Replace With text box. The replacement text must be entered exactly as you want it to appear in your document.

> Word may display the last text entered in the text boxes. In addition, the four most recent text entries can be displayed by opening the drop-down lists. If the existing entry is already correct, you do not need to retype it.

- Type **new credit card** (do not press ⏎Enter).

> After entering the text to find, do not press ⏎Enter or this will choose [Find Next] and the search will begin.

- Press Tab ⭾.
- Type **new Sports Company credit card**

The default search selection is All, which means Word will search the entire document, including headers and footers. You can also choose to search up and down the document, which excludes the headers and footers. Because you want to search the entire document, All is the appropriate setting. To hide the display of the advanced criteria and begin the search,

> The [Less ▲] button hides the advanced search criteria.

- Click [Less ▲].
- Click [Find Next].

Immediately the insertion point moves to the first occurrence of text in the document that matches the Find text and highlights it.

Your screen should be similar to Figure 2-4.

located text

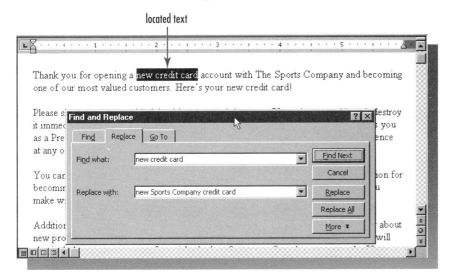

FIGURE 2-4

If necessary, move the dialog box so you can see the located text.

You do not, however, want to replace this text, because the company name would appear twice in the same sentence. To tell the program to continue the search without replacing the highlighted text,

■ Click Find Next .

Word immediately locates a second occurrence of the Find text. To replace this text with the replacement text,

Do not use Replace All, because it will replace all occurrences including the one you skipped.

■ Click Replace .

■ In the same manner, replace the rest of the located occurrences.

If you are changing all the occurrences, it is much faster to use Replace All. Exercise care when using Replace All, however, because the search text you specify might be part of another word and you may accidentally replace text you want to keep. When Word has completed the search, a message is displayed advising you that Word has finished searching the document.

When using the Find command, you can close the dialog box and use the ▲ and ▼ buttons to find the previous or next occurrence of the text.

■ If necessary, close the message box, then close the Find and Replace dialog box.

If the Office Assistant displays the message, it disappears automatically.

Using Drag and Drop

Next you want to add the telephone number of the Customer Service Department to the letter. You want it to follow the reference to the Customer Service representative in the last sentence of the fourth paragraph.

■ Enter **(1-800-555-9838)** before the period of the last sentence in the fourth paragraph.

After looking at the sentence, you decide you would like to move the telephone number to follow the word "call" in the same sentence. Word also includes a

To use drag and drop to copy a selection, hold down Ctrl while dragging. The pointer shape is ▨.

drag and drop editing feature that can be used to move or copy selections. It is most useful for copying or moving short distances in a document. To use drag and drop to move a selection, point to the selection and drag the pointer ▨ to the location where you want the selection inserted. The I-beam attached to the pointer shows you where the text will be placed.

   ■ Select the telephone number, excluding the parentheses.

   ■ Drag the selection to the space after "call" in the same sentence.

   ■ Correct the spacing as necessary around the telephone number and delete the parentheses at the end of the sentence.

Your screen should be similar to Figure 2-5.

FIGURE 2-5

text moved using
drag and drop

Using the Thesaurus

The next text change you want to make is to find a better word for "happy" in the last sentence of the letter. To help find a similar word, you will use the Thesaurus tool.

> ### Concept 3: Thesaurus
>
> Word's **Thesaurus** is a reference tool that provides synonyms, antonyms, and related words for a selected word or phrase. Synonyms are words with a similar meaning, such as "cheerful" and "happy." Antonyms are words with an opposite meaning, such as "cheerful" and "sad." Related words are words that are variations of the same word, such as "cheerful" and "cheer." The Word Thesaurus can help to liven up your documents by adding interest and variety to your text.

The keyboard shortcut is ⇧Shift + F7.

To identify the word you want looked up and to use the Thesaurus,

   ■ Move to anywhere in the word "happy" (last paragraph).

   ■ Choose Tools/Language/Thesaurus.

Your screen should be similar to Figure 2-6.

selected word

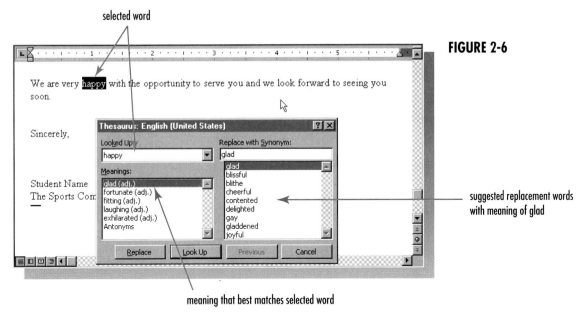

FIGURE 2-6

suggested replacement words
with meaning of glad

meaning that best matches selected word

The Thesaurus dialog box displays a list of possible meanings for the looked-up word. From this list you can select the most appropriate meaning for the word. The highlighted word "glad" is appropriate for this sentence. The words in the Replace with Synonym box are synonyms for the word "happy" with a meaning of "glad." The best choice from this list is "delighted." To replace "happy" with "delighted,"

If a synonym, antonym, or related word is not found, the Thesaurus displays an alphabetical list of entries that are similar in spelling to the selected word.

- ▦ Select delighted.

- ▦ Click ▢ Replace ▢.

- ▦ Remove the word "very" from the sentence.

Using the Date Command

The last text change you need to make is to add the date to the letter. You want to enter the date on the first line of the letter four lines above the salutation. The Date and Time command on the Insert menu inserts into your document the current date as maintained by your computer system.

- ▦ Move to the D in "Dear" at the top of the letter.

- ▦ Insert four blank lines and move to the first blank line.

- ▦ Choose Insert/Date and Time.

Reminder: Use Ctrl + Home to quickly move to the top of a document.

The Date and Time dialog box on your screen should be similar to Figure 2-7.

FIGURE 2-7

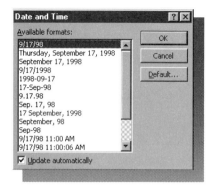

The Available Formats list box displays the format styles for the current date and time. You want to display the date in the format Month XX, 199X. This format is the third setting in the list.

You also want the date to be updated automatically whenever the letter is sent to a new credit card customer. The Update Automatically option is used to do this by entering the date as a field.

> ## Concept 4: Fields
>
> A **field** is a placeholder that instructs Word to insert information into a document. The **field code** contains the directions that tell Word what type of information to insert. The information that is displayed as a result of the field code is called the **field result**. Many field codes are automatically inserted when you use certain commands. Others you can create and insert yourself. Many fields update automatically when the document changes. Using fields makes it easier and faster to perform many common or repetitive tasks.

Alt + ⇧ Shift + D will insert the current date as a field in the format MM/DD/YY.

- ■ Select the third format setting.

- ■ If necessary, select Update Automatically.

- ■ Click ▢ OK ▢.

Although the date appears as text, it is a field. To see this,

- ■ Press ← .

Your screen should be similar to Figure 2-8.

date field result displays current date

FIGURE 2-8

The date in Figure 2-8 will be different from the date that appears on your screen.

The entire date is shaded, indicating that the insertion point is positioned on a field entry. Whenever this file is printed, Word will print the current system date using this format.

The field code can be viewed by displaying the field's Shortcut menu and choosing **T**oggle Field Codes.

Note: If you are ending your session now, replace Student Name with your name in the closing and save the file as Revised Credit Card Letter 2. Print the letter. When you begin Part 2, open this file.

Part 2

Setting Margins

Next the regional manager has suggested that you make several formatting changes to improve the appearance of the letter. The first change you will make is to reduce the size of the margins.

Concept 5: Margins

The **margin** is the distance from the text to the edge of the paper. Standard single-sided documents have four margins: top, bottom, left, and right. Double-sided documents also have four margins: top, bottom, inside, and outside.

Single-Sided Document Margins

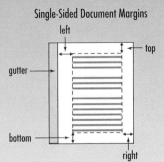

Double-Sided Document Margins

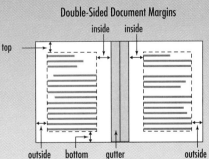

You can also set a gutter margin that reserves space in the left or inside margin to accommodate binding. There are also special margin settings for headers and footers. You will learn about these features in Lab 3. The default left and right margins are set at 1.25 inches and the top and bottom margins at 1 inch. You can set different margin widths to alter the appearance of the document.

You would like to see how the letter would look if you changed the right and left margin widths to 1 inch. The Page Setup command on the File menu is used to change settings associated with entire pages.

■   Choose File/Page Setup.

■   If necessary, open the Margins tab.

The Page Setup dialog box on your screen should be similar to Figure 2-9.

FIGURE 2-9

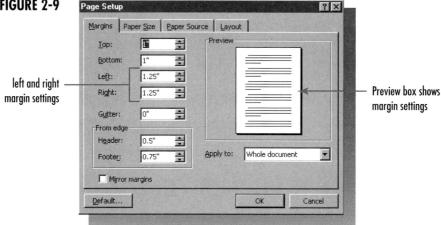

left and right margin settings

Preview box shows margin settings

The Margins tab displays the default margin settings for a single-sided document. The Preview box shows how the current margin settings will appear on a page. New margin settings can be entered by typing the value in the text box, or by clicking the [▲] and [▼] buttons or pressing the ↑ or ↓ keys to increase or decrease the setting by tenths of an inch.

> To set margins for double-sided documents, choose Mirror Margins.

■   Using any of these methods, set the left and right margins to 1 inch.

■   Click   OK   .

Your screen should be similar to Figure 2-10.

right margin not visible in window

FIGURE 2-10

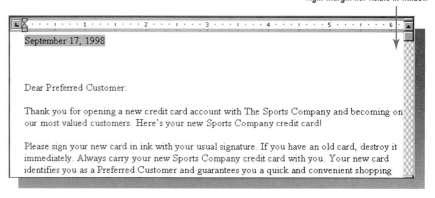

> Depending on your monitor settings, the entire line length may still be visible.

The letter has been reformatted to fit within the new margin settings. Because the margins are smaller, more text can be displayed on a line. However, now the line is too long to fit within the window.

■ Scroll the window to the right to view the end of the line.

The ruler's right margin boundary shows that the text space has increased from 6 inches to 6.5 inches.

> Dragging the margin boundaries on the ruler can also be used to change margin settings.

Changing Document Views

Because you have to scroll the window, it is difficult to see how the margins have changed the layout of the document. To make it easier to see how the document lays out on the page, you will change the document view.

Concept 6: Document Views

You can view a Word document in eight different ways. Each view offers different features for creating and editing your documents. It's best to start your document in Normal view. Then, to add finishing touches like headers, footers, and graphics, switch to Page Layout view. Finally, use Print Preview to check the document before you print.

Document View	Command	Button	Effect on Text
Normal View	**V**iew/**N**ormal		Shows text formatting but not the layout of the page. This is the best view to use when typing, editing, or formatting text.
Online Layout View	**V**iew/Onlin**e** Layout		Shows the document in the best format for online reading. Also turns on the Document Map feature, which helps you move around the document easily.
Page Layout View	**V**iew/**P**age Layout		Shows how the text and objects are positioned on the printed page. This is the view to use when adjusting margins, working in columns, drawing objects, and placing graphics.
Outline View	**V**iew/**O**utline		Shows the structure of the document. This is the view to use to move, copy, and reorganize text in a document.
Master Document	**V**iew/**M**aster Document		Shows several documents organized into a master document. This is the view to use to organize and maintain a long document that is divided into several documents.
Document Map	**V**iew/**D**ocument Map		Shows the document headings in a vertical pane along the left side of the document. Click the heading to go to that location in the document.
Full Screen	**V**iew/F**u**ll Screen		Shows the document without Word's toolbars, menus, scroll bars, and other screen elements.
Print Preview	**F**ile/Print Pre**v**iew		Shows multiple pages of a document in a reduced size. This is the view to use to check the layout of a document and make editing and format changes before you print.

Four of the View buttons are located on the left edge of the horizontal scroll bar.

To display the document in Page Layout view,

■   Click 🔳 Page Layout View.

Your screen should be similar to Figure 2-11.

Zoom button shows zoom percentage

FIGURE 2-11

1-inch top margin

September 17, 1998

vertical ruler

Dear Preferred Customer:

Page Layout view

Thank you for opening a new credit card account with The Sports Company and becoming our most valued customers. Here's your new Sports Company credit card!

Please sign your new card in ink with your usual signature. If you have an old card, destroy

Page Layout
View button

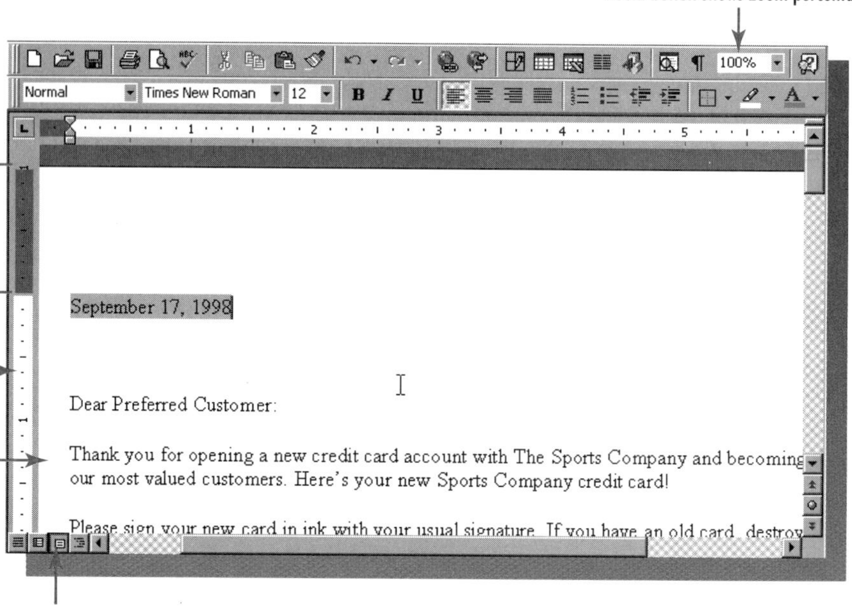

Your screen may display more or less text than is shown in Figure 2-11. This is because your zoom setting may be different. You will learn about this feature next.

This view displays the current page of your document as it will appear when printed. The text still extends off the window space to the right. In addition, the screen now displays a vertical ruler that shows the vertical position of text. Notice that the date will be printed 1 inch from the top of the paper (the default top margin setting).

To see more of the text in the window at one time, you can decrease the onscreen character size using the Zoom command.

The menu equivalent is **V**iew/**Z**oom.

■   Click [100% ▼] Zoom.

Your zoom percentage may be different than 100%. Word uses the zoom percentage that was in use when you last exited the file or program.

The default display, 100%, shows the characters the same size as they will be when printed. You can increase the character size up to five times normal display (500%) or reduce the character size to 10%.

■   Click 50%.

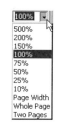

Your screen should be similar to Figure 2-12.

zoom set at 50%

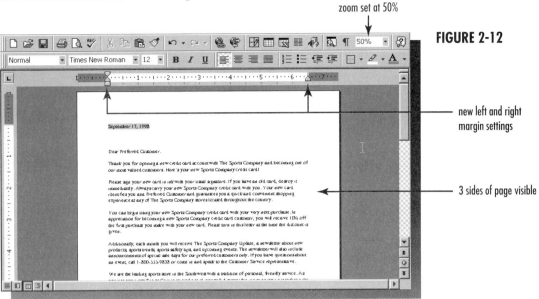

FIGURE 2-12

new left and right margin settings

3 sides of page visible

The text is fully displayed across the width of the window, and you also can see three sides of paper. You can now easily see how the change in margin width has affected the document. You would like to see what the whole page looks like.

- Click 50% Zoom.

- Click Whole Page.

The menu equivalent is **V**iew/**Z**oom/**W**hole Page.

Your screen should be similar to Figure 2-13.

whole-page zoom

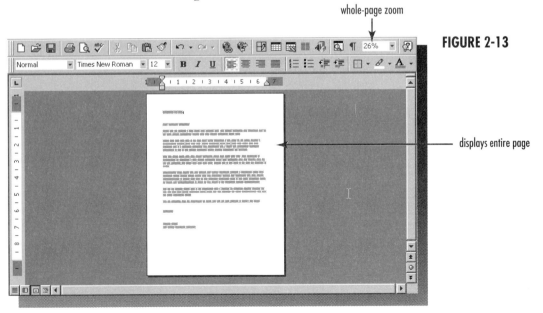

FIGURE 2-13

displays entire page

Your zoom percentage may be slightly higher.

This view is similar to Print Preview. The zoom percentage is 26% (displayed in the Zoom button). The Whole Page option automatically sets the percent value to display the entire page on the screen. Now the text is too small to read.

■ Return the zoom percentage to 100%.

You can also change the zoom in Normal view.

■ Click ▦ Normal View.

■ Click 100% ▾ Zoom.

■ Click Page Width.

Indenting Paragraphs

Next you want to change the letter style from the block paragraph style to an indented paragraph style.

Concept 7: Indents

To help your reader find information quickly, you can indent paragraphs from the margins. Indenting paragraphs sets them off from the rest of the document. There are four types of indents you can use to stylize your documents.

Indent		Effect on Text
Left		Indents the entire paragraph from the left margin. To extend the paragraph into the left margin, use a negative value for the left indent.
Right		Indents the entire paragraph from the right margin. To extend the paragraph into the right margin, use a negative value for the right indent.
First Line		Indents the first line of the paragraph. All following lines are aligned with the left margin.
Hanging		Indents all lines after the first line of the paragraph. The first line is aligned with the left margin. A hanging indent typically is used for bulleted and numbered lists.

To indent the first line of the first paragraph,

■ Move to the T in "Thank" (first sentence, first paragraph).

■ Choose F**o**rmat/**P**aragraph/**I**ndents and Spacing.

The Paragraph dialog box on your screen should be similar to Figure 2-14.

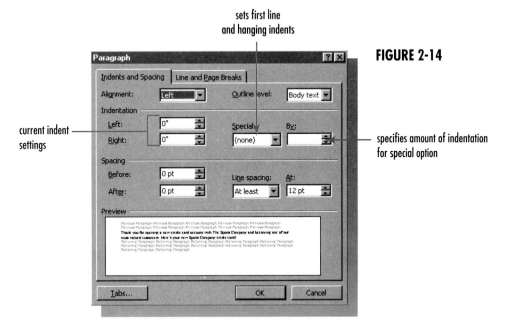

FIGURE 2-14

The Indents and Spacing tab shows that the left and right indentation settings for the current paragraph are 0. This setting aligns each line of the paragraph with the margin setting. Specifying an indent value would indent each line of the paragraph the specified amount from the margin. To indent the first line only,

■ Choose **S**pecial/First Line.

The default first line indent setting of .5" displayed in the By text box is acceptable.

■ Click .

Your screen should be similar to Figure 2-15.

first line
indent marker

FIGURE 2-15

September 17, 1998

Dear Preferred Customer:

first line indented
0.5 inch from
left margin

Thank you for opening a new credit card account with The Sports Company and becoming one of our most valued customers. Here's your new Sports Company credit card!

Please sign your new card in ink with your usual signature. If you have an old card, destroy it immediately. Always carry your new Sports Company credit card with you. Your new card identifies you as a Preferred Customer and guarantees you a quick and convenient shopping experience at any of The Sports Company stores located throughout the country.

You can begin using your new Sports Company credit card with your very next purchase. In appreciation for becoming a new Sports Company credit card customer, you will receive 10% off the first purchase you make with your new card. Please turn in this letter at the time the discount is

The first line of the paragraph indents 0.5 inch from the left margin to the first tab setting. The text in the paragraph wraps as needed. The text on the following line begins at the left margin. Notice that the upper indent marker on the ruler moved to the 0.5-inch position. This marker controls the location of the first line of text in the paragraph.

A much quicker way to indent the first line of a paragraph is to press Tab⇥ at the beginning of the paragraph. Pressing Tab⇥ indents the first line of the paragraph to the first tab stop from the left margin.

> You will learn about setting custom tab stops in Lab 3.

- ■ Move to the P in "Please."

- ■ Press Tab⇥.

You can indent the remaining four paragraphs individually, or you can select the paragraphs and indent them simultaneously by either using the Format menu or dragging the upper indent marker on the ruler.

> A dotted vertical line is displayed as you drag to show where the indent will appear in the text.

- ■ Select the remaining four paragraphs.

- ■ Drag the upper indent marker on the ruler to the 0.5-inch position.

> The lower indent marker controls the indent for all lines in a paragraph after the first line.

- ■ In the same manner, select the closing lines and indent them to the 3.25-inch position on the ruler.

- ■ Move to the top of the document.

Creating an Itemized List

Now you want to display the first three sentences in the second paragraph as a list and add a new sentence to the first paragraph to tell the reader what the list is about. The completed paragraph adjustment is shown below.

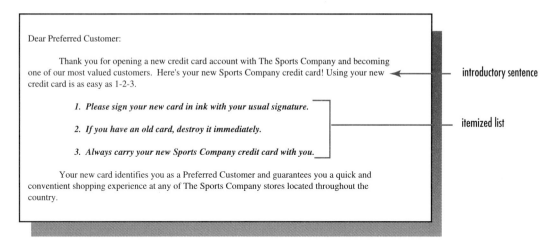

Dear Preferred Customer:

Thank you for opening a new credit card account with The Sports Company and becoming one of our most valued customers. Here's your new Sports Company credit card! Using your new credit card is as easy as 1-2-3.   ← introductory sentence

1. *Please sign your new card in ink with your usual signature.*

2. *If you have an old card, destroy it immediately.*

3. *Always carry your new Sports Company credit card with you.*   — itemized list

Your new card identifies you as a Preferred Customer and guarantees you a quick and convenient shopping experience at any of The Sports Company stores located throughout the country.

■   Add the following introductory sentence to the end of the first paragraph: **Using your new credit card is as easy as 1-2-3.**

Next you will create the itemized list using the first three sentences of the second paragraph.

Concept 8: Bulleted and Numbered Lists

Whenever possible, use bulleted or numbered lists to organize information and to make your writing clear and easy to read. A list can be used whenever you present three or more related pieces of information.

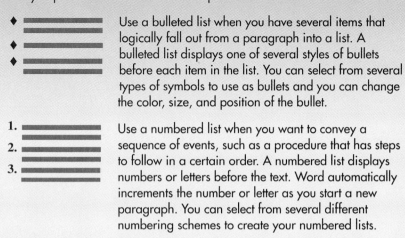

Use a bulleted list when you have several items that logically fall out from a paragraph into a list. A bulleted list displays one of several styles of bullets before each item in the list. You can select from several types of symbols to use as bullets and you can change the color, size, and position of the bullet.

Use a numbered list when you want to convey a sequence of events, such as a procedure that has steps to follow in a certain order. A numbered list displays numbers or letters before the text. Word automatically increments the number or letter as you start a new paragraph. You can select from several different numbering schemes to create your numbered lists.

You can also drag the upper indent marker to the 0 position on the ruler or press [←Backspace] to clear the indent.

First you need to remove the indent at the beginning of the second paragraph and then place each sentence that you want to be itemized in the list on a separate line. To do this,

- Move to the P in "Please."

- Press [⇧ Shift] + [Tab ⇄].

- Move to the I in "If" (second sentence, second paragraph).

- Press [←Enter] (2 times).

- In a similar manner, place the next sentence on a separate line.

- Make the last sentence, beginning with "Your new . . .", a new paragraph. (Remember to indent the first line of the paragraph.)

Your screen should be similar to Figure 2-16.

FIGURE 2-16

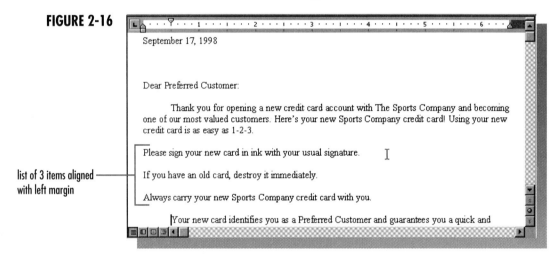

list of 3 items aligned with left margin

You should now have a list of three items, each separated with a blank line. Leaving a blank line between items in a list makes the list easier to read. Next you will add a number before each of the items.

- Select the three items.

- Choose Format/Bullets and Numbering.

- Open the Numbered tab.

The Bullets and Numbering dialog box on your screen should be similar to Figure 2-17.

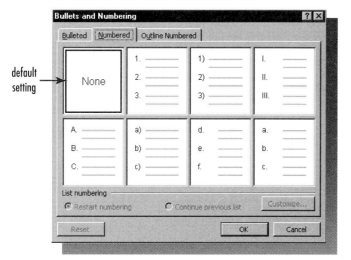

FIGURE 2-17

Seven numbered list styles are available. The document default is None. The first style to the right of None is the style you will use.

■   Select the first numbered list style.

■   Click   OK   .

Your screen should be similar to Figure 2-18.

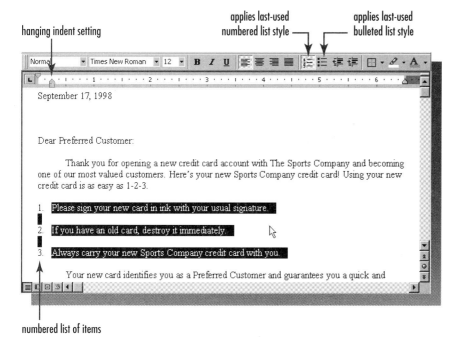

FIGURE 2-18

A number is inserted at the left margin before each sentence, and the text following the number is indented to the 0.25-inch position. The ruler displays the lower indent marker at the 0.25-inch position to show the hanging indent setting for text in the selection. If the text following each bullet were longer than a line, the text on the following lines would also be indented to the 0.25-inch position.

You can also create bulleted and numbered lists as you type. To create a bulleted list, type an asterisk (*), press [Tab ⇥], and then type the text. To create a numbered list, type a number, type a period, press [Tab ⇥], and then type the text. When you press [←Enter], Word automatically creates a list and numbers or bullets the next line. To turn off the list, press [←Enter] twice.

Finally, you want to change the indent for the three items so that the number aligns with the 0.75-inch position. The three items should still be highlighted.

> ■   If necessary, select the 3 numbered items.

> ■   Press [Tab ⇥] (2 times).

Your screen should be similar to Figure 2-19.

To remove bullets or numbers, choose F<u>o</u>rmat/Bullets and <u>N</u>umbering/<u>R</u>emove, then select the None option or click the [≣] or [≣] button again.

upper indent marker controls number placement ——

lower indent marker controls text placement following number

FIGURE 2-19

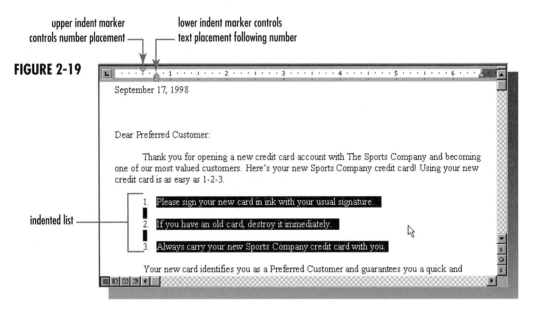

indented list ——

The numbers align with the 0.75-inch position and the text with the 1-inch position in the document. In an itemized list, the upper indent marker on the ruler controls the position of the number or bullet, and the lower indent marker controls the position of the item following the number or bullet.

Changing the Character Formatting

To make the numbered list stand out even more from the rest of the document, you will change the character format by selecting a different font and font size.

Concept 9: Fonts

A **font**, also commonly referred to as a **typeface**, is a set of characters with a specific design. The designs have names such as Times New Roman and Courier. Using fonts as a design element can add interest to your document and give readers visual cues to help them find information quickly.

There are two basic types of fonts, serif and sans serif. **Serif fonts** have a flair at the base of each letter that visually leads the reader to the next letter. Two common serif fonts are Roman and Times New Roman. Serif fonts generally are used in paragraphs. **Sans serif fonts** do not have a flair at the base of each letter. Arial and Helvetica are two common sans serif fonts. Because sans serif fonts have a clean look, they are often used for headings in documents. It is good practice to use only two types of fonts in a document, one for text and one for headers. Too many styles can make your document look cluttered and unprofessional.

Each font has one or more sizes. Size is the height and width of the character and is commonly measured in **points**, abbreviated "pt". One point equals about $1/72$ inch, and text in most documents is 10 pt or 12 pt.

Several common fonts in different sizes are shown in the following table.

Font Name	Font Type	Font Size	Font Style (Bold)
Arial	Sans serif	This is 10 pt. This is 16 pt.	Bold 10 pt. Bold 16 pt.
Courier New	Serif	This is 10 pt. This is 16 pt.	Bold 10 pt. Bold 16 pt.
Times New Roman	Serif	This is 10 pt. This is 16 pt.	Bold 10 pt. Bold 16 pt.

You would like the numbered list to be in a different font and type size than the rest of the text in the letter. To change a font setting for existing text, select the text you want to change and then use the command.

> To change the font before typing the text, use the command and then type. All text will appear in the specified font setting until another font setting is selected.

- ■ If necessary, select the 3 numbered items.
- ■ Choose Format/Font.
- ■ If necessary, open the Font tab.

The Font dialog box on your screen should be similar to Figure 2-20.

FIGURE 2-20

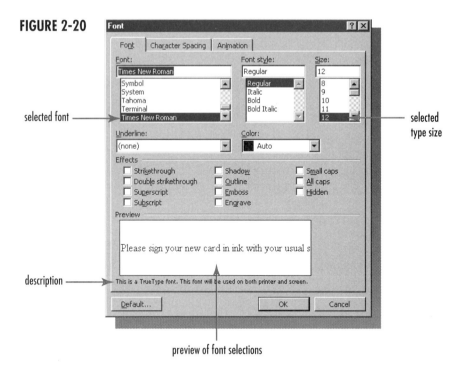

selected font

selected type size

description

preview of font selections

The Font list box displays the fonts supported by your active printer in alphabetical order. The Word default font, Times New Roman, is the currently selected font.

Notice the description of the font below the Preview box. It states that the selected font is a TrueType font. TrueType fonts are fonts that are automatically installed when you install Windows. They appear onscreen exactly as they will appear when printed. Some fonts are printer fonts, which are available only on your printer, and may look different onscreen than when printed. Courier is an example of a printer font.

You will change the font to Arial and the point size to 10. As you make the selections, the Preview box displays how your selections will appear.

■ Select Arial.

■ Select 10.

■ Click OK .

■ Clear the highlight.

> You also can select the font from the Font drop-down list and the font size from the Font Size drop-down list in the Formatting toolbar.

Your screen should be similar to Figure 2-21.

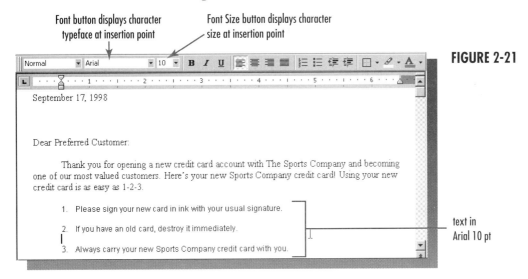

Font button displays character typeface at insertion point

Font Size button displays character size at insertion point

FIGURE 2-21

text in Arial 10 pt

The Font and Font Size buttons in the Formatting toolbar display the current font and size setting for the text at the location of the insertion point.
In addition to changing font and font size, you can apply different character effects to enhance the appearance of text.

Concept 10: Character Effects

Different character effects can be applied to selections to add emphasis or interest to a document. The table below describes some of the effects and their uses.

Format	Example	Use
Bold, italic	**Bold** *Italic*	Adds emphasis
Underline	<u>Underline</u>	Adds emphasis
Strikethrough	~~Strikethrough~~	Indicates words to be deleted
Double strikethrough	Double Strikethrough	Indicates words to be deleted
Superscript	"To be or not to be."[1]	Used in footnotes and formulas
Subscript	H_2O	Used in formulas
Shadow	Shadow	Adds distinction to titles and headings
Outline	Outline	Adds distinction to titles and headings
Small caps	SMALL CAPS	Adds emphasis when case is not important
All caps	ALL CAPS	Adds emphasis when case is not important
Hidden	Displays, but does not print	Notes or comments you do not want printed
Color	Color Color Color	Adds interest

You would like to change the itemized list to display as both bold and italic.

■ Select the three numbered items.

■ Click **B** Bold.

■ Click **I** Italic.

■ Clear the highlight.

The menu equivalent is F**o**rmat/**F**ont/
F**o**nt Style/Bold/Italic, and the
keyboard shortcuts are ⌃Ctrl + B for
bold and ⌃Ctrl + I for italic.

Your screen should be similar to Figure 2-22.

bold and italic character effects are in use

FIGURE 2-22

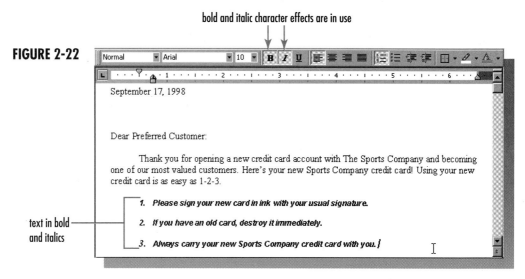

text in bold
and italics

Now you want to emphasize the information in the third paragraph about the 10 percent discount by underlining it.

■ Select the text "10% off the first purchase."

■ Click **U** Underline.

■ Clear the highlight.

The menu equivalent is F**o**rmat/**F**ont/
Underline/Single, and the keyboard
shortcut is ⌃Ctrl + U.

You could also click ↶ Undo.

The selected text appears underlined. However, you do not like how the under-line format looks. To clear any of the appearance settings, reselect the exact area of text and use the command again.

■ Remove the underline from the text.

Setting Paragraph Alignment

The final formatting change you want to make is to change the paragraph alignment.

Concept 11: Paragraph Alignment

Alignment is how text is positioned on a line between the margins or indents. There are four types of paragraph alignment: left, center, right, and justified.

Alignment		Effect on Text
Left		Aligns text against the left margin of the page, leaving the right margin ragged. This is the most commonly used paragraph alignment type and therefore the default setting in all word processing software packages.
Center		Centers each line of text between the left and right margins. Center alignment is used mostly for headings or centering graphics on a page.
Right		Aligns text against the right margin, leaving the left margin ragged. Use right alignment when you want text to line up on the outside of a page, such as a chapter title or a header.
Justified		Aligns text against the right and left margins and evenly spaces out the words. Newspapers commonly use justified alignment so the columns of text are even.

The commands to change paragraph alignment are under the Format/Paragraph menu. However, it is much faster to use the shortcuts shown below.

Alignment	Keyboard Shortcuts	Button
Left	Ctrl + L	≣
Center	Ctrl + E	≣
Right	Ctrl + R	≣
Justified	Ctrl + J	▤

You want to change the alignment of all paragraphs in the letter from the default of left-aligned to justified.

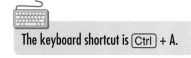

The keyboard shortcut is Ctrl + A.

The menu equivalent is Format/Paragraph/Indents and Spacing/Alignment/Justified.

■ Choose Edit/Select All.

■ Click ▤ Justify.

■ Clear the highlight and scroll through the letter to see the changes in the alignment of text on the right margin.

■ Return to the top of the document.

Your screen should be similar to Figure 2-23.

Justify button aligns text evenly along left and right margins

adding soft spaces makes even right margin

FIGURE 2-23

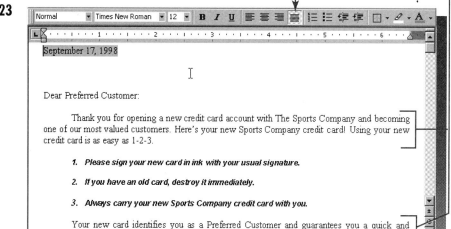

All full lines now end even with the right margin. To do this, Word inserts extra spaces between words to push the text to the right margins. These are called **soft spaces** and are adjusted automatically whenever additions and deletions are made to the text.

Next you want the date to be aligned flush against the right margin.

■ Move to the date field.

■ Click ▤ Align Right.

Your screen should be similar to Figure 2-24.

The alignment settings can also be specified before typing in new text. As you type, it is aligned according to your selection until the alignment setting is changed to another setting.

The menu equivalent is F**o**rmat/ **P**aragraph/**I**ndents and Spacing/ Ali**g**nment/Right.

Align Right button aligns text even with right margin

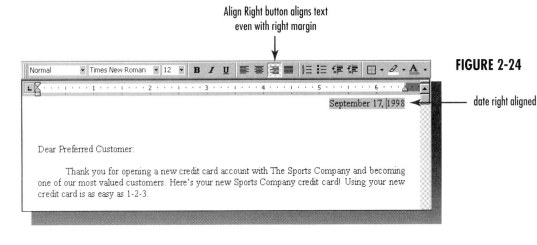

FIGURE 2-24

date right aligned

■ Return the zoom percentage to 100%.

■ Replace Student Name with your name in the closing.

Editing in Print Preview

You would like to save the edited version of the credit card letter as Revised Credit Card Letter 2. This will allow the original file, Revised Credit Card Letter, to remain unchanged in case you want to repeat the lab for practice.

■ Use the Save As command to save the file on your data disk as Revised Credit Card Letter 2.

■ Preview the letter.

Your screen should be similar to Figure 2-25.

switches between
zooming and editing

FIGURE 2-25

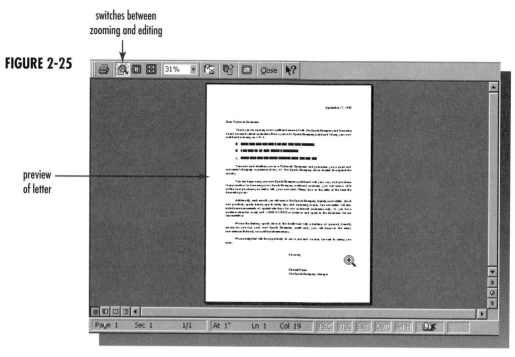

preview
of letter

Now that you can see the entire letter, you decide that the date would look better at the 3.25-inch tab position. While in Print Preview, you can edit and format text. Notice that the mouse pointer is a magnifying glass ⌕ when it is positioned on text in the window. This indicates that when you click on a document, the screen will toggle between the whole page view you currently see and 100% magnification.

■ To edit the date in the Print Preview window, point to the date and click the mouse button.

The text is displayed in the size it will appear when printed (100% zoom). Then, to switch between zooming the document and editing it,

■ Click 🔍 Magnifier.

When positioned near text, the mouse pointer changes to an I-beam and the insertion point is displayed. Now you can edit the document as in Normal view. First you need to return the date to left-aligned. Because the Formatting toolbar is not displayed, you will use the keyboard shortcut, Ctrl + L, to left-align the date. Then you will indent the date to the 3.25-inch position.

■ If necessary, move the insertion point to the date.

■ Press Ctrl + L.

■ Click 📷 View Ruler.

■ Move the upper indent marker to the 3.25-inch position.

Pointing to the top or left edge of the window will also temporarily display the ruler.

Your screen should be similar to Figure 2-26.

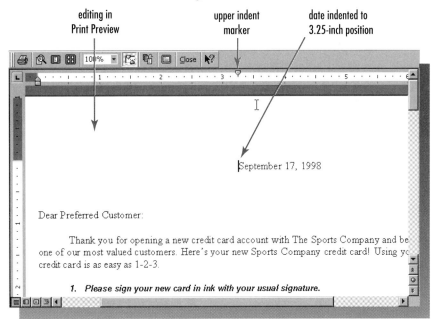

editing in
Print Preview

upper indent
marker

date indented to
3.25-inch position

FIGURE 2-26

To switch back to zooming the document and restore it to the original preview size,

- ■ Click 🔍 Magnifier.
- ■ Click the document.
- ■ Click 🗺 View Ruler.

Next, you will print a copy of the letter from the Print Preview window using the default print settings.

- ■ Click 🖨 Print.
- ■ Close the Print Preview window.
- ■ If necessary, change the view to Normal and the zoom percentage to 100%.
- ■ Choose File/Exit.
- ■ Click Yes .

The 100% Zoom button can also be used to specify the magnification.

Make sure your printer is on and ready to print.

If you need to specify a different printer, you will need to close Print Preview and use the Print command on the File menu.

LAB REVIEW

■ ■ ■ ■ ■ ■ ■ ■ ■ ■ ■ ■

Key Terms

alignment (WP83)
case sensitive (WP62)
destination (WP59)
drag and drop (WP64)
field (WP66)
field code (WP66)

field result (WP66)
font (WP79)
margin (WP67)
point (WP79)
sans serif font (WP79)

serif font (WP79)
soft space (WP85)
source   (WP59)
Thesaurus (WP64)
typeface (WP79)

Command Summary

Command	Shortcut Keys	Button	Action
File/Page Set**u**p			Changes layout of page including margins, paper size, and paper source
Edit/**C**ut	Ctrl + X	✂	Cuts selected text and copies it to Clipboard
Edit/**C**opy	Ctrl + C	📋	Copies selected text to Clipboard
Edit/**P**aste	Ctrl + V	📋	Pastes text from Clipboard
Edit/**F**ind	Ctrl + F		Locates specified text
Edit/**R**eplace	Ctrl + H		Locates and replaces specified text
View/**N**ormal		▤	Displays document in Normal view
View/Onlin**e** Layout		▣	Displays document best for onscreen reading
View/**P**age Layout		▣	Displays document as it will appear when printed
View/**O**utline		▤	Displays structure of document as an outline
View/**M**aster Document			Shows several documents organized into a master document
View/**D**ocument Map			Shows document headings along left side of document
View/F**u**ll Screen		▣	Shows document without Word's toolbars, menus, scroll bars, and other screen elements
View/**Z**oom		100% ▾	Changes onscreen character size
View/**Z**oom/**W**hole Page			Displays entire page onscreen
Insert/Date and **T**ime			Inserts current date or time, maintained by computer system, in selected format

Command	Shortcut Keys	Button	Action
Format/Font			Changes appearance of characters
Format/Font/Font Style/Italic	Ctrl + I	*I*	Makes selected text italic
Format/Font/Font Style/Bold	Ctrl + B	**B**	Makes selected text bold
Format/Font/Underline/Single	Ctrl + U	U	Underlines selected text
Format/Paragraph/Indents and Spacing/ Special/First Line			Indents first line of paragraph from right margin
Format/Paragraph/Indents and Spacing/ Alignment/Left	Ctrl + L	≣	Aligns text to left margin
Format/Paragraph/Indents and Spacing/ Alignment/Centered	Ctrl + E	≣	Centers text between left and right margins
Format/Paragraph/Indents and Spacing/ Alignment/Right	Ctrl + R	≣	Aligns text to right margin
Format/Paragraph/Indents and Spacing/ Alignment/Justified	Ctrl + J	▦	Aligns text equally between left and right margins
Format/Bullets and Numbering		≣ ≣	Creates a bulleted or numbered list
Tools/Spelling and Grammar	F7	✓	Starts Spelling and Grammar tool
Tools/Language/Thesaurus	⇧Shift + F7		Starts Thesaurus tool

Matching

1. justified   _____   **a.** suggests synonyms and antonyms

2. date field   _____   **b.** allows you to select the entire document

3. Edit/Select All   _____   **c.** shortcut for bold command

4. margins   _____   **d.** used to copy or move a selection

5. Ctrl + B   _____   **e.** text that has even left and right margins

6. ≣   _____   **f.** white space between printed text and edge of paper

7. drag and drop   _____   **g.** removes text from the document and stores it in the Clipboard

8. Thesaurus   _____   **h.** quickly locates specified text

9. ✂   _____   **i.** creates bulleted list

10. Find   _____   **j.** a code that instructs Word to insert the current date in the document using the selected format whenever the document is printed

Fill-In Questions

1. Complete the following statements by filling in the blanks with the correct terms.

   a. The white space between the text and the edge of the paper is the _____ .

   b. Use a(n) _____ list to convey a sequence of events.

   c. The _____ text format is used to indicate words to be deleted.

   d. The _____ and _____ views show how text will appear on the printed page.

   e. Use the _____ to find synonyms for common words.

   f. When text aligns evenly against the right and left margins, it is _____ .

Discussion Questions

1. What is the purpose of formatting a document? What criteria would you suggest for a professional document?

2. Discuss the differences between serif and sans serif fonts. When would it be appropriate to combine font styles? How does a font's point size affect the display of characters?

3. Discuss the different ways information can be moved within a document. When would it be appropriate to use either method?

4. Discuss the different document views. When would it be appropriate to switch to a different view?

5. Discuss the problems that can be associated with finding and replacing text. What can you do to avoid some of these problems?

Hands-On Practice Exercises

Step by Step	Rating System		
		☆	Easy
		☆☆	Moderate
		☆☆☆	Difficult

1. To complete this exercise, you must have first completed Practice Exercise 2 in Lab 1. Open the file Mouse Terms 1 on your data disk. *(Note*: You can only complete step a if you have Wingdings in your font collection. If you do not have Wingdings, select and change the title to Arial 16 pt, and go to step b.)

   a. Wingdings are a set of icons that can be used to add fun and flair to your documents. A "Wingding" 7 is a keyboard; a "Wingding" 8 is a mouse. In this portion of the exercise, you will replace the word "Mouse" with a picture of a mouse. Replace the word "mouse" in the title with the number 8. Select the number 8, and change the font to Wingdings 18 pt. Change the font of the word "Terms" in the title to Arial 16 pt.

   b. Bold and italicize the terms ("Point," "Click," "Double-click," etc.).

   c. Find all occurrences of the word "thing" and replace them with the word "object."

   d. Use the Thesaurus to find synonyms for the words "often" and "several" in the last sentence of the Click paragraph. Then use the Thesaurus to find a synonym for "location" in the Drag and Drop paragraph.

   e. Set the paragraph alignment to justified, and center and bold the title. Change all margins to 1.5 inches.

   f. Bullet the five terms and their definitions.

   g. Save the document as MOUSE TERMS 2. Print the document.

2. You have been accepted at Metropolitan Community College, and have received a letter from the Director of Admissions informing you of the orientation that you will be required to attend. You will create that letter in this exercise.

a. Before you type the letter (shown below), change all margins to 1.5 inches, and set the alignment to justified. Type the letter as shown except use the Date and Time command to insert the date as a field, and substitute information that pertains to you in the bracketed areas. *(Note:* only press ⏎Enter at the end of heading text or to end paragraphs.)

Metropolitan Community College
123 Metropolitan Blvd.
Anytown, USA

[Current Date]

[Your Name]
[Street Address]
[City, State Zip Code]

Dear [Your Name]:

Congratulations on your acceptance into the [Your Major] program at Metropolitan Community College.

Orientation for new students will be held next Friday morning from 9:00 - Noon. It is imperative that you attend this session prior to your enrollment at Metropolitan Community College.

Student leaders from the [Your Major] program will be there to give you a guided tour of the Metropolitan Community College campus with an emphasis on your course of study.

We will initially meet in the Student Center, where you will be introduced to the [Your Major] program coordinator. Light refreshments will be served at this time while you become acquainted with others in your major field as well as faculty members in attendance.

After the orientation ends at 12:00, you are encouraged to join us for a luncheon in the cafeteria.

Once again, [Your Name], congratulations on your acceptance, and we hope to see you next Friday.

If you are unable to attend, please call me at 1-800-555-1622.

Sincerely,

Joseph K. College
Director of Admissions

JKC/xxx

b. Add documentation to the file. Save the document as Acceptance Letter. Print the letter.

c. Search for all occurrences of Metropolitan Community College. Replace all but the first occurrence (in the address) with M.C.C.

d. Italicize and bold the word "imperative" in the second paragraph. Then use the Thesaurus to replace the word with an appropriate synonym.

e. Reverse the order of the third and fourth paragraphs.

f. Center and bold the return address. Right-align the date.

g. Indent the three closing lines to the 3-inch position on the ruler.

h. Save the document again with the same name. Print the letter.

You will complete this exercise as Practice Exercise 4 in Lab 4.

3. In this problem you will continue creating Grandma Gertie's cookie recipes cookbook. To complete this exercise, you must have completed Practice Exercise 5 in Lab 1. Open the file Potato Chip Cookies from your data disk.

a. Bold the name of the cookie at the top of the document. Bold and italicize the headings Ingredients: and Directions:.

b. Indent the instructions from "2 sticks of butter" to "Confectioner's sugar" 0.5 inch from the left. Bullet the directions from "Cream the butter. . ." to "Bake in 350 degree oven. . . ." Indent the bulleted directions 0.5 inch from the left.

c. Copy the entire file to the Clipboard. Save the file using the same name. Close the document.

d. Open the file More Recipes on your data disk. Paste the Potato Chip Cookies file from the Clipboard to the end of the More Recipes file.

e. Center and bold the title at the top of the document. Italicize the note at the top of the document, and justify that paragraph only.

f. The Cut-Out Sugar Cookies have their Ingredients and Directions sections mixed up. Reverse the order of these two sections. "Makes about 5 dozen 2" cookies" should be the last line in the recipe.

g. Change the font to Times New Roman 12 pt for the entire document. Then change the title to a 14 pt font of your choice.

h. Bold the names of the first two cookies. Bold and italicize the headings Ingredients: and Directions: for the first two cookies.

i. Indent the instructions for the first two cookies 0.5 inch from the left. Bullet the directions for the first two cookies, and indent the bulleted directions 0.5 inch from the left.

j. Document the file. Save the document as Updated Cookie Recipes. Print the document.

You will complete this exercise as Practice Exercise 5 in Lab 3.

4. To complete this exercise, you must have completed Practice Exercise 6 in Lab 1. Open the file B&B Ad from your data disk.

a. Bold and center the first three lines. Italicize the two lines that contain the host's phone number and name.

b. Bullet the lines from "Number of Rooms" to "Social Drinking" and indent them to the 1-inch position on the ruler.

c. Reverse the order of the third and fourth paragraphs.

d. Set the alignment of the five paragraphs to justified, and change all margins to 1.3 inches.

e. Search for all occurrences of "Poconos" and replace them with "Pocono Mountains."

f. Use the Thesaurus to find synonyms for "rustic" and "numerous" in the first paragraph and "breathtaking" in the second paragraph.

g. Select the five paragraphs below the indented items, and increase the font size to 11 pt.

h. Save the document as B&B Ad Part 2. Print the ad.

You will complete this exercise as Practice Exercise 4 in Lab 3.

On Your Own

5. Many people create lists of things they need to do each day or each week. In this problem you will create a list of things you need to do for the week.

Create a numbered "to do" list of all the things you have to do this week (or all the things you would like to do this week) either in order of importance or in chronological order.

Add a title that includes your name and the current date. Use the formatting techniques you have learned to improve the appearance of the list.

Document the file. Save the document as To Do List. Print the document.

6. In this exercise you will modify a document containing tips on how to prepare for a job interview.

Open the file Preparing for the Interview on your data disk. Center and bold the title and change the font to Arial 16 pt. Bold the heading Helpful Tips.

Bullet the four Helpful Tips from "Know the exact place and time of the interview" to "Dress for success." Indent the bulleted list to the 0.5-inch position.

Italicize and bold the first sentence in each of the four tips. In the second tip, emphasize the sentence "Failure to do homework can be the kiss of death." In the last tip, emphasize the text "only one" in the seventh sentence. In the same section, emphasize the last sentence, "Call attention to what you say, not what you wear." Italicize the reference "CPC Annual 1990-91 Edition" below the list of tips.

Justify all lines below the title. Increase the margins to 1.5 inches all around.

Insert your name and the current date below the document. Document the file. Save the document as Interview Tips. Print the document.

7. In this exercise you will format a document that tells how to redisplay screen elements that have, for one reason or another, disappeared!

Open the file Capturing Screen Elements on your data disk. This document tells how to hide and display toolbars and how to return the document from full-screen view to the last view you used. Spell- and grammar-check the document.

Enter the following text above the Toolbars section:

The Ruler

The ruler is usually displayed below the toolbars. You can use the ruler to conveniently set margins or tabs with a click of the mouse. If the ruler is not displayed, here's how to get it back.

Open the View menu. The Ruler command is just below Toolbars. Clicking a checked Ruler turns it off, and clicking an unchecked Ruler turns it on.

Add appropriate text formatting to emphasize the title, Capturing Screen Elements At Large, and the headings The Ruler, Toolbars, and Help! All I Have Is This Big White Screen! In the line Choose: View/Toolbars, bold and underline the V in View and the T in Toolbars.

Move The Ruler section below the Toolbars section. Adjust spacing as needed.

Change the alignment to justified for the document, and center the title.

Locate all occurrences of Ruler Bar and replace them with Ruler.

Adjust margins until the document just fits on one page. What settings did you use?

Indent the three lines of instruction (Choose: View/ Toolbars, Choose: OK when you are finished, and Press: Esc!) to the 0.5-inch mark on the ruler.

Document the file and save it as Capturing Screen Elements 2. Print the document.

Move and Copy

Selections can be moved or copied to new locations in a document, saving you time by not having to retype the same information.

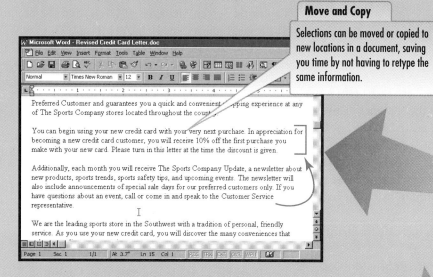

Concepts

Move and Copy

Find and Replace

Thesaurus

Fields
Margins
Indents

Document Views

Bulleted and Numbered Lists
Fonts
Character Effects
Paragraph Alignment

Thesaurus

Word's Thesaurus is a reference tool that provides synonyms, antonyms, and related words for a selected word or phrase.

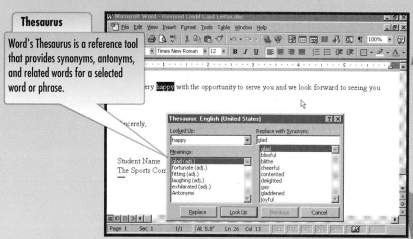

Document Views

You can view a Word document in eight different ways. Each view offers different features for working with your documents.

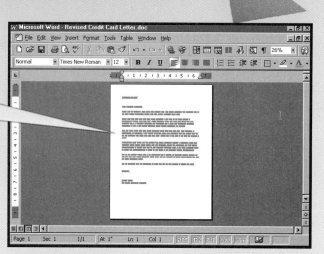

Find and Replace

To make editing easier, you can use the Find and Replace feature to find text in a document and automatically replace it with other text.

Fields

A field is a placeholder that instructs Word to insert information into a document.

Indents

To help your reader find information quickly, you can indent paragraphs from the margins. Indenting paragraphs sets them off from the rest of the document.

Margins

The margin is the distance from the text to the edge of the paper. Standard single-sided documents have four margins: top, bottom, left, and right.

Bulleted and Numbered Lists

Whenever possible, use bulleted or numbered lists to organize information and make your writing clear and easy to read.

Character Effects

Different character effects can be applied to selections to add emphasis or interest to a document.

Fonts

A font, also commonly referred to as a typeface, is a set of characters with a specific design.

Paragraph Alignment

Alignment is how text is positioned on a line between the margins or indents. There are four types of paragraph alignment: left, center, right, and justified.

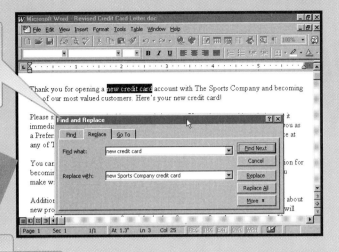

Creating a Report and a Newsletter

3

COMPETENCIES

After completing this lab, you will know how to:

1. Create a page break.
2. Format headings.
3. Use the Document Map.
4. Create and update a table of contents.
5. Center a page vertically.
6. Add footnotes.
7. Set tab stops.
8. Insert and size graphic objects.
9. Add captions and cross-references.
10. Add headers and footers.
11. Create and enhance a WordArt object.
12. Create horizontal rules.
13. Create newspaper columns.
14. Use hyphenation.
15. Insert text boxes.
16. Add a drop cap.

CASE STUDY

The Southwest regional manager is very pleased with your work so far, and has asked you to help with the development of the first monthly newsletter.

You have been asked to develop several topics to be used as articles in the newsletter. In this lab you will use many features of Word 97 that make it easy to create a well-organized and attractive report. The first two pages of your report are shown here.

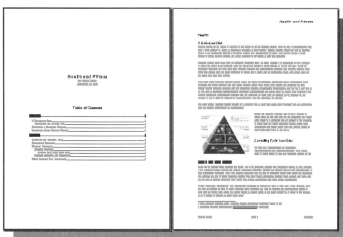

In addition you are to create a sample newsletter design using several of the topics from your report. In a newsletter, information must be easy to read and, most importantly, be visually appealing. In this lab you will use some of the desktop publishing tools in Word 97 to create a newsletter. The first page of the newsletter is shown here.

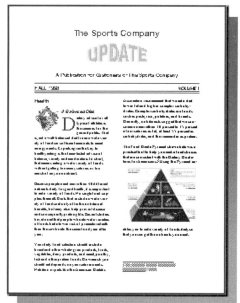

Concept Overview

The following concepts will be introduced in this lab:

1. Document Breaks There are three types of breaks that can be inserted into a document: page, column, and section.

2. Styles A style is a set of formats that is assigned a name.

3. Footnotes and Endnotes Footnotes are source references or text offering additional explanation that are placed at the bottom of a page. Endnotes are also source references or long comments that typically appear at the end of a document.

4. Tab Stops A tab stop is a stopping point along a line to which text will indent when you press (Tab ⇥).

5. Graphics A graphic is a non-text element or object, such as a picture or drawing, that can be added to a document.

6. Captions and Cross-References A caption is a title or explanation for a table, picture, or graph. A cross-reference is a reference from one part of your document to related information in another part.

7. Headers and Footers A header is a line or several lines of text at the top of each page just below the top margin. A footer is text at the bottom of every page just above the bottom margin.

8. WordArt The WordArt feature is used to enhance your documents by changing the shape of text, adding 3-D effects, and changing the alignment of text on a line.

9. Special Effects Word 97 includes many commands that add special effects, such as shadows and 3-D effects, to enhance drawing objects, including WordArt.

10. Hyphenation The hyphenation feature inserts a hyphen in long words that fall at the end of a line to split the word between lines.

Part 1

Creating a Page Break

You have just attended the first planning session for the newsletter, during which it was decided that the purpose of the newsletter would be two-fold: to promote The Sports Company and to provide information related to a healthy, active lifestyle.

After several days of research, you have organized your notes and written a brief report on topics related to nutrition and fitness using information from many sources including books, magazine articles, and the World Wide Web.

■ To see the report, load Word 97 and open the file Newsletter Research from your data disk.

■ If necessary, maximize the document window and switch to Normal view.

Your screen should be similar to Figure 3-1.

FIGURE 3-1

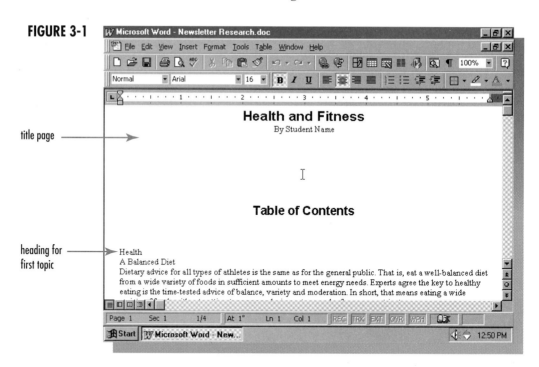

title page

heading for
first topic

The first page of the report is the title page. This page commonly includes information such as the report title, the name of the author, and the date. In addition, you have decided to include a brief table of contents on this page.

- ▪ Replace Student Name with your name.

- ▪ Enter the current date below your name.

Notice that the text for the first topic currently begins on the same page as the title. You want the title page to print on a page by itself. To force a new page to begin at a specified location, you need to insert a page break. A page break is one of several types of document breaks.

- ▪ Move to the H in "Health."

Concept 1: Document Breaks

There are three types of breaks that can be inserted into documents: page, column, and section. Page and column breaks start a new page or column beginning with the next line. Normally Word inserts "soft" page and column breaks automatically into a document whenever the text fills the page or column. Entering a **manual** (or "hard") **page break** or column break instructs Word to begin a new page or column regardless of the amount of text on the previous page or column.

Section breaks divide a document into sections that can be formatted differently. The section break stores the format settings associated with that section of the document. The type of section break selected controls whether the following text begins on the next page, on the next even or odd page, or continues on the same page.

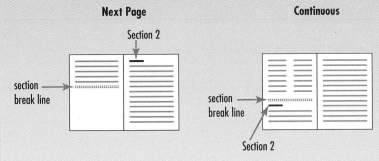

Word automatically inserts section breaks for you if you change the formatting of selected text, such as inserting columns or centering selected text vertically on a page.

- Choose Insert/Break.

- If necessary, select Page Break.

- Click OK.

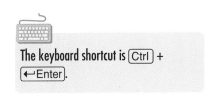

The keyboard shortcut is Ctrl + ←Enter.

Your screen should be similar to Figure 3-2.

FIGURE 3-2

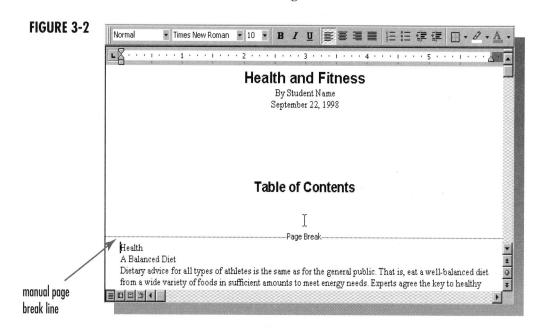

manual page
break line

A dotted Page Break line appears above the heading indicating that a manual page break was entered at that position. All soft page breaks following the insertion of a manual page break are immediately adjusted.

Formatting Headings

Next you would like to improve the appearance of the document by adding formatting to the headings. Although you could apply different fonts, sizes, and character effects to each heading, it is easier to use Word's built-in formatting styles.

Concept 2: Styles

A **style** is a set of formats that is assigned a name. Word includes 75 predefined styles, or you can create your own custom styles. Many styles are automatically applied when certain features, such as footnotes, are used. Others must be applied manually to selected text.

Styles can be applied to characters or paragraphs. **Character styles** consist of a combination of any character formats in the Fonts dialog box that affect selected text. **Paragraph styles** are a combination of any character formats and paragraph formats that affect all text in a paragraph. A paragraph style can include all the font settings that apply to characters as well as tab settings, indents, and line settings that apply to paragraphs. The default paragraph style is Normal, and it includes character settings of Times New Roman 10 pt and paragraph settings of left indent to 0, single line spacing, and left alignment. The Styles drop-down list box in the Formatting toolbar displays the style of the current selection.

In addition, many paragraph styles are designed to affect specific text elements such as headings, captions, and footnotes. One of the most commonly used styles is a **heading style**, which is designed to identify different levels of headings in a document. Heading styles include combinations of fonts, type sizes, bold, and italics. The first four heading styles and the formats associated with each are shown below:

Heading Level	Appearance
Heading 1	**Arial 14 pt bold**
Heading 2	***Arial 12 pt bold, italic***
Heading 3	Arial 12 pt
Heading 4	**Arial 12 pt bold**

The most important heading in a document should be assigned a Heading 1 style. This style is the largest and most prominent. The next most important heading should be assigned the Heading 2 style, and so on. Headings give your reader another visual cue about how the information is grouped in your document.

This document contains four levels of headings that you would like to identify with different heading styles. The two main headings are Health at the beginning of page 2 and Fitness on page 4. You will apply a Heading 1 style to these headings.

- If necessary, move to anywhere in the Health heading on page 2.
- Choose F_ormat/_Style.
- If necessary, select All Styles from the _List drop-down list box.

The Style dialog box on your screen should be similar to Figure 3-3.

FIGURE 3-3

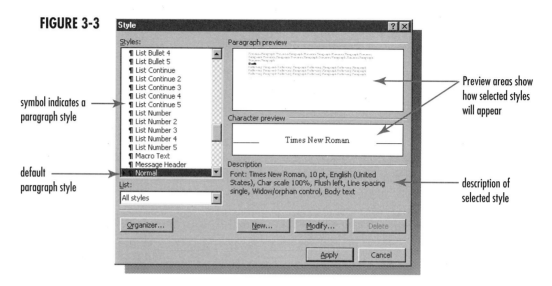

symbol indicates a
paragraph style

default
paragraph style

Preview areas show
how selected styles
will appear

description of
selected style

A character style is preceded with the
letter a.

The Styles list box displays the names of all the preset styles that are included in the Word program in alphabetical order. The default style, Normal, is highlighted. Notice the ¶ symbol preceding the style. This indicates it is a paragraph style. The format settings included in the currently selected style of Normal are displayed in the Description box, and the Preview areas show how text formatted in this style will appear. To apply the Heading 1 style to the text,

■ Select Heading 1.

■ Click **Apply** .

Your screen should be similar to Figure 3-4.

Style box shows
style of selection

format characteristics associated
with Heading 1 style

FIGURE 3-4

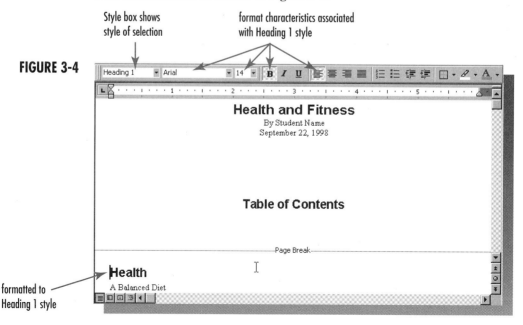

formatted to
Heading 1 style

Notice that the entire heading appears in the selected style. This is because a Heading 1 style is a paragraph style and it affects the entire paragraph that the insertion point is on. Also notice that the Styles drop-down list box in the Formatting toolbar now displays Heading 1 as the style applied to the selected paragraph.

Word 97 will apply the Heading 1 style automatically to text as you type if you end a sentence without punctuation and press ⏎Enter twice.

Using the Document Map

Next you want to apply the same heading style to the second main topic heading, Fitness, located on page 4. To help you locate and move through the document, you can use Online Layout view. This view is designed for reading online.

The menu equivalent is **V**iew/Onli**n**e Layout.

■ Click 🔲 Online Layout View.

Your screen should be similar to Figure 3-5.

Document Map pane
displays headings

shows/hides the
Document Map

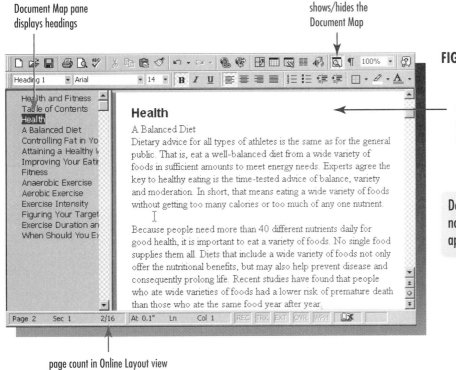

FIGURE 3-5

document pane in Online Layout view
displays text larger and wrapped to
fit window

Do not be concerned if your screen does
not display all the headings. They will
appear as you apply heading styles.

page count in Online Layout view

The workspace is divided vertically into two sections or **panes**. The **document pane** on the right displays the document in Online Layout view. In this view the character size is displayed at 12 pt to make the text easier to read, and the text automatically wraps to fit the window space, rather than the way it would actually print. This causes the page numbering shown in the status bar to adjust based on the new size and length of the document.

Both panes can be scrolled
independently and can be resized.

The **Document Map pane** on the left displays the headings in your document. All text that is formatted with a heading style is displayed in this pane. When your document does not contain any headings formatted with heading styles, the program automatically searches the document for paragraphs that

If the Document Map is not displayed on
your screen, click 🔲 or choose **V**iew/
Document Map to display it.

> If your Document Map does not display the headings, scroll to page 9 and move the insertion point to the Fitness heading.

> The Repeat command displays the last action performed following the command. If you cannot repeat the last action, the Repeat command displays "Can't Repeat."

> The keyboard shortcut is Ctrl + Y.

> The Styles list displays the most commonly used styles.

> The menu equivalent is F**o**rmat/**S**tyle/**S**tyles/Heading 2/⎡ Apply ⎤.

look like headings (for example, short lines with a larger font size) and displays them in the Document Map. If it cannot find any such headings, the Document Map is blank. The highlighted heading shows your location in the document. Clicking on a heading in the Document Map quickly jumps to that location in the document.

■ Click Fitness (in the Document Map).

Rather than reselecting the same style from the menu again, you can quickly repeat your last action. To do this,

■ Choose **E**dit/**R**epeat Style.

The Fitness heading is formatted to the Heading 1 style. The next heading to be formatted is the title of the first article in the Health section of the report. To quickly move back to the Health section heading,

■ Click Health (in the Document Map).

The insertion point moves to the beginning of the Health heading. The article title is a subheading below the main topic heading. Because it is one level lower than the heading above it, the Heading 2 style will be used. Another way to select a style is from the Style button.

■ Move the insertion point to anywhere in the heading "A Balanced Diet" on page 2.

■ Open the Style drop-down list box.

■ Choose Heading 2.

Your screen should be similar to Figure 3-6.

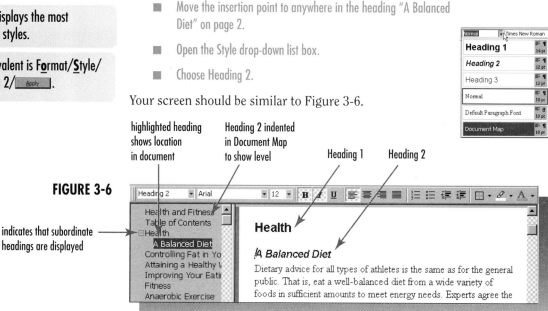

FIGURE 3-6

highlighted heading shows location in document

Heading 2 indented in Document Map to show level

Heading 1

Heading 2

indicates that subordinate headings are displayed

Notice the ▬ symbol to the left of the Health heading in the Document Map; this indicates that all subordinate headings are displayed. A ▥ symbol would indicate that subordinate headings are not displayed.

■ Apply the heading styles in the table below to the remaining headings in the document:

Page #	Heading	Style
4	Controlling Fat in Your Diet	Heading 3
6	Attaining a Healthy Weight	Heading 2
7	Improving Your Eating Habits	Heading 2
9	Exercise and Weight Loss	Heading 2
10	Anaerobic Exercise	Heading 2
11	Aerobic Exercise	Heading 2
12	Exercise Intensity	Heading 3
13	Figuring Your Target Heart Rate	Heading 4
14	Exercise Duration and Frequency	Heading 3
16	When Should You Exercise?	Heading 2

To display the Heading 4 style in the Styles drop-down list, hold down ⟨⇧ Shift⟩ while clicking to open the list. All available styles are displayed.

If you accidentally apply the wrong heading style, reselect the text and select the correct style. To return the style to the default, select Normal.

■ When you are done, use the Document Map to quickly return to the top of the document.

■ Return to Normal view.

Creating a Table of Contents

Now you are ready to create the table of contents to appear on the title page. A table of contents is a listing of the topics that appear in a document and their associated page references. It shows the reader at a glance what topics are included in the document and makes it easier for the reader to locate information. A table of contents can be generated automatically by Word once you have applied heading styles to the document headings.

You want the table of contents listing to be displayed several lines below the heading Table of Contents on the title page. To create the table of contents,

■ Move to the second blank line below the Table of Contents heading (page 1).

■ Choose Insert/Index and Tables.

■ If necessary, open the Table of Contents tab.

The Index and Tables dialog box on your screen should be similar to Figure 3-7.

FIGURE 3-7

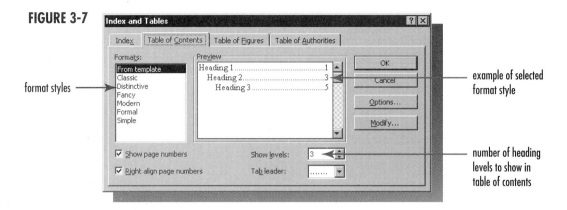

First you need to select the format or design of the table of contents. The Formats list box displays the names of the available formats, and the Preview box displays an example of the selected format, From Template. This format option is used to design your own table of contents and save it as a template by modifying the existing format.

■   Highlight each format option to preview the different table of contents formats.

■   Select the Formal format.

This style will display the page numbers flush with the right margin, and with a series of dots called **tab leaders** between the heading and the page number. The Show Levels text box shows that Word will create a table of contents for three levels of headings. Your document has four levels of headings.

■   Change the Show Levels to 4.

■   Click [OK].

Your screen should be similar to Figure 3-8.

FIGURE 3-8

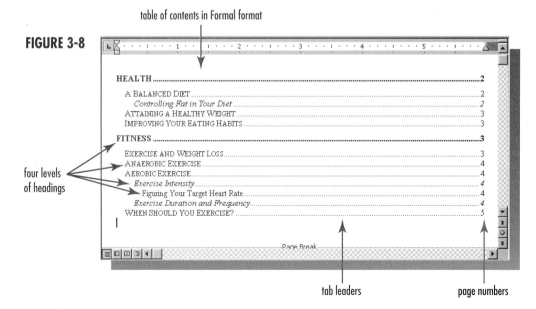

Word searches for headings with the specified styles, sorts them by heading level, references their page numbers, and displays the table of contents in the document. The headings that were assigned a Heading 1 style are aligned with the left margin, and subordinate heading levels are indented as appropriate.

■ Click anywhere within the table of contents.

Notice that the text in the table of contents is shaded, indicating it is a field. This means it can be updated to reflect changes you may make at a later time in your document. Also notice that the Styles box displays "TOC" followed by a number. Each line in the table of contents is formatted using the appropriate table of contents style.

Centering a Page Vertically

Finally, you want the information on the title page to be centered vertically. To do this,

■ Select all text on the title page.

■ Choose **F**ile/Page Set**u**p.

■ If necessary, open the **L**ayout tab.

The Page Setup dialog box on your screen should be similar to Figure 3-9.

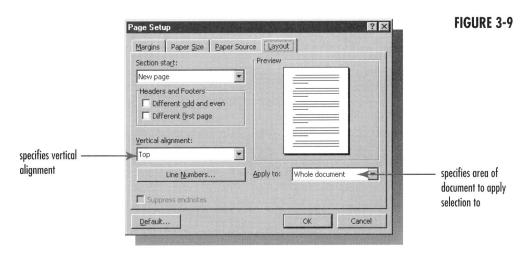

specifies vertical alignment

specifies area of document to apply selection to

FIGURE 3-9

From the Vertical Alignment list box you specify how the text is to be aligned on the page vertically. In addition, in the Apply To list box you need to specify what part of the text you want to be aligned to the new setting. To center the selected text vertically on the page,

■ From the Vertical Alignment drop-down list, select Center.

■ From the Apply To drop down-list, select Selected Text.

■ Click [OK].

■   Clear the selection.

■   Switch to Page Layout view and set the zoom to Whole Page.

Your screen should be similar to Figure 3-10.

FIGURE 3-10

text centered
vertically on page

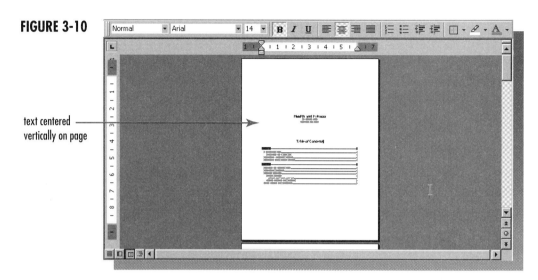

Now you can see the text on the title page is centered vertically between the top and bottom margin.

■   Return to Normal view and scroll to the bottom of page 1.

Notice that, in addition to the page break line, a section break line is displayed. Word automatically inserts a section break whenever different page formats are used within the same ┄┄┄┄┄┄Section Break (Next Page)┄┄┄┄┄┄ document. In this case, a section break was inserted because the title page now has a different vertical alignment than the rest of the document. This type of section break starts the next page of the document on a new page. Therefore the page break you added earlier, if left in the document, would cause a blank page to be printed.

■   Delete the manual page break.

■   If necessary, delete any blank lines above the Health heading.

> To remove a manual page break, select the page break line and press ⟨Delete⟩.

Adding Footnotes

Next you need to add several footnotes to the document.

Concept 3: Footnotes and Endnotes

Footnotes are source references or text offering additional explanation that are placed at the bottom of a page. **Endnotes** are also source references or long comments that typically appear at the end of a document. You can have both footnotes and endnotes in the same document.

Footnotes and endnotes consist of two parts, the note reference mark and the note text. The **note reference mark** is commonly a superscript number appearing in the document at the end of the material being referenced (for example text[1]). It can also be a character or combination of characters. The **note text** for a footnote appears at the bottom of the page on which the reference mark appears. The footnote text is separated from the document text by a horizontal line called the **note separator**. Endnote text appears as a listing at the end of the document.

The Footnote command on the Insert menu will automatically number and place footnotes and endnotes in a document. The first reference that needs to be footnoted is the text in the second paragraph on page 2. Before using the Footnote command, the insertion point must be positioned where the footnote number is to be displayed. To quickly move to that location in the document, you can use the Document Map.

- ■ Click 📖 Document Map.

> Document Map can be displayed in all views.

Notice that the text in the right window is not adjusted in size as it is when in Online Layout view, and the text does not wrap to fit the window.

- ■ Click A Balanced Diet (in the Document Map).

- ■ Move to the end of the second paragraph after the word "year."

- ■ Choose <u>I</u>nsert/Foot<u>n</u>ote.

> The keyboard shortcut to insert a footnote using the default setting is
> [Alt] + [Ctrl] + F.

In the Footnote and Endnote dialog box, you specify whether you want to create footnotes or endnotes and the type of reference mark you want to appear in the document: a numbered mark or a custom mark. A custom mark can be any nonnumeric character, such as an asterisk, that you enter in the text box. You want to create numbered footnotes, so the default settings of Footnote and AutoNumber are acceptable.

Footnote and Endnote `? X`

Insert
- ● <u>F</u>ootnote — Bottom of page
- ○ <u>E</u>ndnote — End of document

Numbering
- ● <u>A</u>utoNumber — 1, 2, 3, ...
- ○ <u>C</u>ustom mark: [　　　　] ◄— use to specify a custom mark

[Symbol...]

[OK] [Cancel] [Options...]

- ■ Click  .

Your screen should be similar to Figure 3-11.

FIGURE 3-11

style to be used in footnotes

document pane

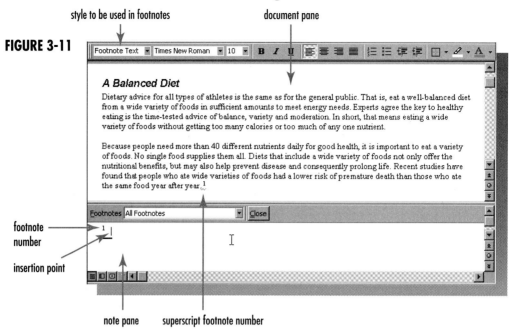

footnote number

insertion point

note pane   superscript footnote number

The Document Map is cleared, and the workspace is now horizontally divided into an upper document pane and a lower **note pane**. The footnote number, 1, appears as a superscript in the document at the location of the insertion point. The note pane displays the footnote number 1 and the insertion point. This is where you enter the text for the footnote. When you enter a footnote, you can use the same menus, commands, and features as you would in the document window. Any commands that are not available are dimmed.

> If necessary, choose Ignore All for all names that are identified as misspelled words as they occur when you enter the note text.

■ Type **Sally Squires, "Expand Your Palate."** *Weight Watchers*, **Nov/Dec 1996, p. 16.** (Do not press ⊣Enter.)

The note pane on your screen should be similar to Figure 3-12.

FIGURE 3-12

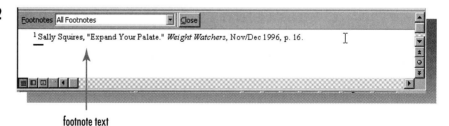

footnote text

The second footnote will provide the source for information located on page 3. To move to this location and insert a second footnote,

- Click [Document Map button] Document Map.
- Click Attaining a Healthy Weight.
- Move to after the sentence ending "woman 22%."
- Choose Insert/Footnote/ OK .

The footnote number 2 is entered at the insertion point location. The note pane is active again, so you can enter the text for the second footnote.

- Type **Covert Bailey, *The New Fit or Fat* (Boston: Houghton Mifflin Company), p. 18.**

Now you realize that you forgot to enter a footnote earlier in the text, on page 2.

- Display the Document Map and click A Balanced Diet.
- Set the zoom to Page Width.
- Move to the end of the first line of paragraph 5 on page 2 (following the word "need").
- Insert a footnote at this location.

The note pane on your screen should be similar to Figure 3-13.

To delete a footnote or endnote, highlight the reference mark and press Delete. The reference mark and associated note text are removed, and the following footnotes are renumbered.

You may need to scroll the window to see the end of the sentence.

A footnote or endnote can be copied or moved by selecting the marker and using cut or copy and paste. You also can use drag and drop to copy or move a note.

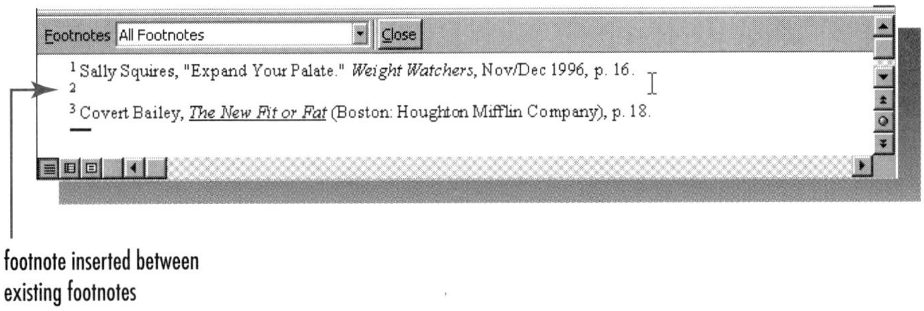

FIGURE 3-13

Notice that this footnote is now number 2 in the document, and a blank footnote line has been entered in the note pane for the footnote text. Word automatically adjusted the footnote numbers when the new footnote was inserted. This footnote reference is to a site on the World Wide Web. It will include the URL to the site. A **URL** (**Uniform Resource Locator**) is the address that indicates the location of a document on the World Wide Web.

- Type **American Dietetic Association. http://www.eatright.org (9/16/98).**

If you click on a URL hyperlink, Word tries to start the program on your system that accesses the Internet and the World Wide Web.

You'll learn more about URLs and the Word Wide Web in a later lab.

The text of the URL appears in blue and underlined. This indicates Word has changed the text to a hyperlink. A **hyperlink** is a connection to a location in the current document, another document, or to a WWW site. It allows the reader to jump to the referenced location by clicking on the hyperlink when reading the document on the screen.

■   Add the following two footnotes to the document:

Section	Paragraph	Following	Footnote
Improving Your Eating Habits	2nd	"frustrating"	Squires, p. 20.
Anaerobic Exercise	2nd	"long"	Daryn Eller, "The Energy Edge." *Health*, Nov/Dec 1996, p. 93.

Additional footnotes will be added to the report as a practice exercise.

Now that you are finished entering footnotes, to close the note pane, move to the first article and turn off the Document Map.

■   Click Close.

■   Click Health (in the Document Map).

You can also hide and display the footnote pane any time by using the **V**iew/Foot**n**otes command or by double-clicking on a footnote reference mark.

■   Click Document Map.

In Normal view you can see the footnote associated with a note reference mark by pointing to the reference mark. The footnote will be displayed as a Screen Tip.

If your Screen Tip does not display, use **T**ools/**O**ptions/View/Sc**r**een Tips to turn on this feature.

■   Point to note reference mark 1 in the document.

Finally, you want to see how the footnotes will actually appear when the document is printed.

more than 40 different nutrients daily for go
Sally Squires, "Expand Your Palate."
Weight Watchers, Nov/Dec 1996, p. 16.

If the zoom percentage is too small, the footnote numbers will not display correctly.

■   Switch to Page Layout view and set the zoom percentage to 75 percent.

■   Scroll to the bottom of page 2 to see the footnotes.

Your screen should be similar to Figure 3-14.

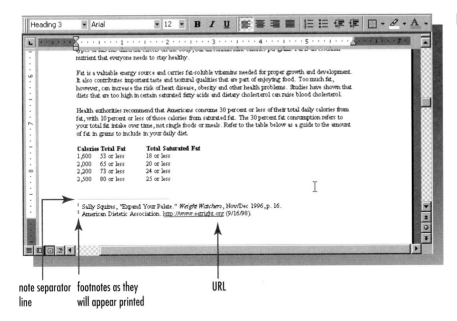

FIGURE 3-14

note separator footnotes as they   URL
line   will appear printed

The footnotes are displayed immediately above the bottom margin separated from the text by the note separator line.

■ Scroll to the bottom of the next page to see the third and fourth footnotes.

While looking at the third footnote, you see that you forgot to include the publication date. While in Page Layout view, you can edit and format footnotes just like any other text.

■ Insert a comma and the year 1991 after the word "Company" in footnote 3.

■ Check the other footnotes. If you see any other errors, correct them.

Setting Tab Stops

Next you want to improve the appearance of the calorie data on the bottom of page 2.

■ Move to the information on calories located near the bottom of page 2.

The first column of data is aligned with the left margin. The second and third columns of data have been indented to tab stops. However, because the default tab stops are set at every 0.5 inch, the columns are not evenly spaced. To improve the appearance of the data, you will create custom tab stops that will align the data in evenly spaced columns.

Concept 4: Tab Stops

A **tab stop** is a stopping point along a line to which text will indent when you press [Tab⇆]. The default tab stops of every 0.5 inch are visible on the ruler as light vertical lines below the numbers. As with other default settings, you can change the location of tab stops in the document. You can also select from five different types of tab stops that control how characters are positioned or aligned with the tab stop. The five tab types, the alignment tab mark that appears on the ruler, and the effects on the text are explained in the following table.

default tab stop markers

Alignment	Tab Mark	How It Affects Text	Example
Left	⌊	Extends text to right from tab stop	left
Center	⊥	Aligns text centered on tab	center
Right	⌟	Extends text to left from tab stop	right
Decimal	⊥.	Aligns text with decimal point	35.78
Bar	I	Draws a vertical line through text at the tab stop	text

When setting new tab stops, the new settings affect the current paragraph or selected paragraphs. When you insert custom tab stops, all default tab stops to the left of the custom tab stop are deleted. You can quickly specify custom tab stop locations and types using the ruler. To select a tab stop type, click the **tab alignment selector box** on the left end of the ruler to cycle through the types. Then, to specify where to place the selected tab stop type, click on the location in the ruler.

tab alignment selector box

Setting different types of tab stops is helpful for aligning text or numeric data vertically in columns. Using tab stops ensures that the text will indent to the same set location. Setting custom tab stops instead of pressing [Tab⇆] or [Spacebar] repeatedly is a more professional way to format a document, as well as faster and more accurate. It also makes editing easier because you can change the tab stop settings for several paragraphs at once.

To align the calorie data, you will place two left tab stops at the 1-inch and 2.25-inch positions on the ruler.

- Select the table heading line and the four lines of data.
- If necessary, click the tab alignment selector box until the left tab icon ⌊ appears.
- Click the 1-inch position on the ruler.
- Click the 2.25-inch position on the ruler.

The menu equivalent is F**o**rmat/**T**abs/ 1.0/2.25/Left.

Your screen should be similar to Figure 3-15.

tab alignment selector   left tab stops

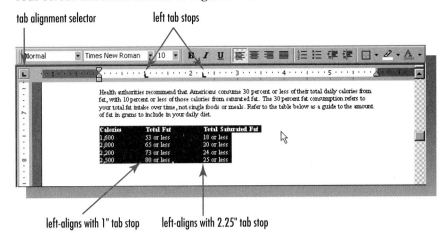

FIGURE 3-15

left-aligns with 1" tab stop   left-aligns with 2.25" tab stop

The two tabbed columns appropriately align with the new tab stops. All default tabs to the left of the new tab stops are cleared. After looking at the columns, you decide the third column heading would look better centered over the column of data. To make this change,

- Move to anywhere in the heading line.

- Drag the 2.25 tab stop mark off the ruler.

- Click the tab alignment selector box until the center tab icon ▣ appears.

- Set a center tab stop at the 2.5-inch position.

The menu equivalent is F**o**rmat/**T**abs/ 2.5/Center.

Your screen should be similar to Figure 3-16.

center tab stop

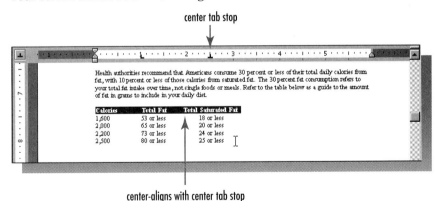

FIGURE 3-16

center-aligns with center tab stop

Inserting and Sizing Graphics

Next you want to add a picture of the Food Guide Pyramid to the report that will complement the subject of the first article. A picture is one of several different graphic objects that can be added to a Word document.

Concept 5: Graphics

A **graphic** is a non-text element or object, such as a drawing or picture, that can be added to a document. An **object** is an item that can be sized, moved, and manipulated. A graphic can be a simple **drawing object** consisting of shapes such as lines and boxes that can be created using the Drawing toolbar. A **picture** is an illustration such as a scanned photograph.

Each graphic object is surrounded by a **frame**, which is an invisible box or container. The frame keeps the items it contains together and lets you place the graphic object anywhere on the page, including in the margins or on top of or below other objects, including text.

When you insert or draw a graphic object, it is attached or **anchored** to a paragraph. However, sometimes the graphic and the paragraph may not appear on the same page. To keep the graphic and paragraph together on a page, you can **lock** the anchor. The text in the paragraph may wrap around the object in different ways. The five wrapping styles are shown below.

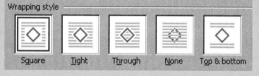

A graphic object can be manipulated in many ways. You can change its size, add captions, borders or shading, or move it to another location. In most cases you can simply drag a graphic to move it. If you have several graphics that you would like to manipulate as one unit, you can **group** them together as if they were a single object. You can then format and manipulate all the objects of a group at the same time. One way to group text and graphics is to include them inside a text box. A text box is a mini-document that acts as an object in that it is surrounded by a frame.

As objects are added to a document, they stack in layers and may overlap. You can move objects up or down within a stack.

Triangle is on top of stack

Triangle is sent to the back

Square is brought to the front

Add graphics to your documents to help the reader understand concepts, to add interest, and to make your document stand out from others.

> Graphic files commonly have file extensions such as .wmf, .bmp, .tif, .pcx, .wpg, .pic, and .cgm.

> The only places you cannot place a graphic object are into a footnote, endnote, or caption.

> If you "lose" an object in a stack, you can press [Tab ⇄] to cycle forward (or [⇧ Shift] + [Tab ⇄] to cycle backward) through the objects until the one you want is selected.

You would like the picture of the Food Guide Pyramid to appear after the fourth paragraph on page 2.

- Move to the beginning of the fifth paragraph on page 2, which begins, "Using the Pyramid. . . ."

- Choose Insert/Picture/From File.

- Change the Look In location to the drive containing your data disk.

- Select Pyramid.pcx.

- Click [Insert].

The picture of the Food Guide Pyramid is inserted in the document at the insertion point (see Figure 3-17). However, the graphic is very large and you would like to reduce its size. To do this you must first select the object.

- Click on the pyramid picture.

Your screen should be similar to Figure 3-17.

> The Preview box displays the selected picture. If the Preview box is not displayed, click 🔳 Preview in the toolbar.

> Graphic objects are not displayed in Normal view. If you insert a graphic in Normal view, Word automatically changes the view to Page Layout.

FIGURE 3-17

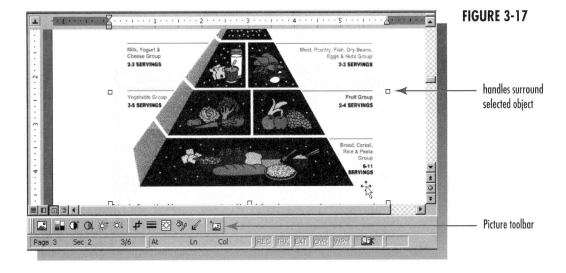

handles surround selected object

Picture toolbar

The picture is surrounded by eight boxes, called **handles**, indicating it is a selected object and can now be sized and moved anywhere in the document. The Picture toolbar is also automatically displayed. Its buttons (identified below) are used to modify the selected picture object. Your Picture toolbar may be floating or docked along an edge of the window, depending on where it was when last used.

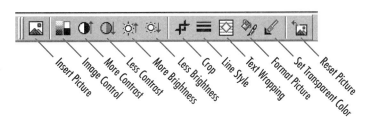

> Refer to Toolbars in Lab 1 for information on this feature.

- If necessary, move the Picture toolbar to the left end of the status bar as in Figure 3-17.

The handles are used to size the object, much as you would size a window. You want to reduce the image to approximately 3 inches wide by 2.25 inches high.

■ Point to the lower right corner handle.

■ Drag the mouse to reduce the size of the picture to approximately 3 x 2.25 inches.

Now that the picture is much smaller, you decide to have the text wrap around the graphic object.

■ Click ⊠ Text Wrapping.

■ Choose ⊠ Square.

■ Resize the picture until the text wraps around it as in Figure 3-18.

■ Clear the selection by clicking anywhere outside the graphic object.

Your screen should be similar to Figure 3-18.

> The mouse pointer changes to ↖, just as it does when resizing a window.

> Use the rulers as a guide and refer to Figure 3-18 for size reference.

> Dragging a corner handle maintains the original proportions of the picture.

> The menu equivalent is Format/Picture/Wrapping/Square.

FIGURE 3-18

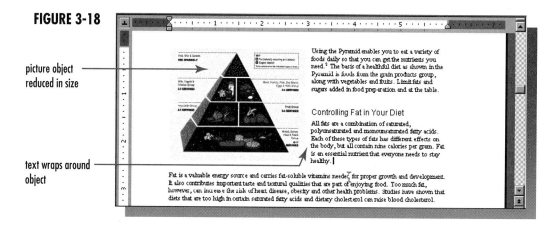

picture object reduced in size

text wraps around object

Because the picture object is aligned with the left margin, the text wraps to the right side of the object. If the object were centered between the margins, the text would wrap around the object on both sides.

Adding Captions and Cross-References

Next you want to add a caption to the pyramid figure, and a cross-reference to the figure in another part of the document.

Concept 6: Captions and Cross-References

A **caption** is a title or explanation for a table, picture, or graph. Captions aid the reader in quickly finding information in a document. Word can automatically add captions to graphic objects as they are inserted, or you can add them manually. The caption can be changed to reflect the type of object to which it refers, such as a table, chart, or figure. In addition, Word automatically numbers graphic objects and adjusts numbering when objects of the same type are added or deleted.

Once you have captions you can also include cross-references. A **cross-reference** is a reference from one part of your document to related information in another part. For example, if you have a graph in one part of the document that you would like to refer to in another section, you can add a cross-reference that tells the reader what page the graph is on. A cross-reference can also be inserted as a hyperlink, allowing you to jump to another location in the same document or in another document.

First you will add a caption below the Food Guide Pyramid picture.

■ Move to the blank line below the Food Guide Pyramid picture.

■ Choose Insert/Caption.

The Caption dialog box on your screen should be similar to Figure 3-19.

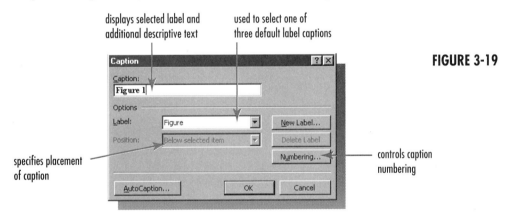

displays selected label and additional descriptive text

used to select one of three default label captions

FIGURE 3-19

specifies placement of caption

controls caption numbering

The options in this box are described below.

Option	Description
Label	Select from one of three default captions: Table, Figure, or Equation.
Position	Specify the location of the caption, either above or below a selected item. When an item is selected, the Position option is available.
New Label	Create your own captions.
Numbering	Specify the numbering format and starting number for your caption.
AutoCaption	Turns on the automatic insertion of a caption (label and number only) when you insert selected items into your document.

The most recently selected caption label and number appear in the Caption text box. You want the caption to be Figure 1, and you want to add additional descriptive text.

■ If necessary, select Figure from the Label drop-down list.

■ In the Caption text box, type **: Food Guide Pyramid** following "Figure 1."

■ Click [OK].

Your screen should be similar to Figure 3-20.

FIGURE 3-20

style used

caption added below figure

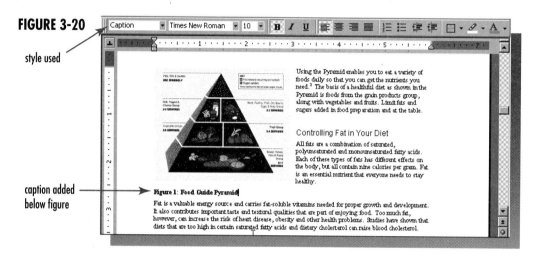

Later in the report, you have included a reference to information provided in the Food Guide Pyramid. To clarify this reference, you will use the cross-reference feature.

■ Move to page 4, to the space following "recommended number of servings" in the first paragraph below the heading Improving Your Eating Habits.

■ Type **in**

■ Press [Spacebar].

■ Choose Insert/Cross-reference.

The Cross-reference dialog box on your screen should be similar to Figure 3-21.

FIGURE 3-21

specifies type of item to be referenced

creates hyperlink cross-reference

displays list of selected reference types

specifies information to include in the cross-reference

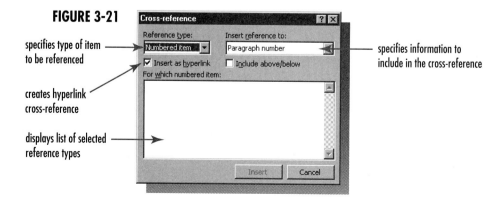

You need to specify the type of item you are referencing and how you want the reference to appear. You want to reference the Food Guide Pyramid figure, and you only want the label "Figure 1" entered in the document.

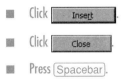

- From the Reference Type drop-down list box, select Figure.

- From the Insert Reference To list box, select Only label and number.

Because there is only one figure in this document, the Refers To list box correctly selects the figure to refer to. If there were multiple figures in the document, you would need to select the appropriate figure. Notice that the Insert as Hyperlink option is selected by default. This option creates a hyperlink between the cross-reference and the caption. The default setting is appropriate.

- Click Insert.

- Click Close.

- Press Spacebar.

Your screen should be similar to Figure 3-22.

cross-reference hyperlink

FIGURE 3-22

To improve your eating habits, you first have to know what's wrong with them. Write down everything you eat for three days. Then analyze your diet to see where you are eating foods that are high in fat and calories. Compare what you usually eat to the recommended number of servings in Figure 1 and make modifications to your diet that are consistent with healthy eating.

If your favorite foods are high in fat, salt or sugar, don't eliminate them. Instead, moderate how much of these foods you eat and how often you eat them. If you keep portion sizes reasonable, it's easier to eat the foods you want and stay healthy. It has been found that adhering to a rigid diet plan can be too restrictive and can set you up for failure. This is because the rate at which your body burns calories slows by about 15% on rigid weight-loss plans, making it even more difficult and frustrating.[4]

When eating "forbidden" foods that are high in fat or calories, select other foods during the day that are low in these ingredients. Your food choices over several days should fit together into a healthy pattern. Using this strategy, you won't feel deprived of the foods you enjoy.

A cross-reference is entered into the document as a field. Therefore, if you insert another picture, the captions and cross-references will renumber automatically. When you are working on a long document with several figures, tables, and graphs, this feature is very helpful.

To use a cross-reference hyperlink to jump to the source it references, simply click on it.

- Click on the Figure 1 cross-reference.

The document automatically jumps to the caption beneath the Food Guide Pyramid. The Web toolbar is automatically displayed because many hyperlinks are to items on the World Wide Web.

- Close the Web toolbar.

The mouse pointer shape changes to a 🖑 when pointing to a hyperlink to show that the cross-reference is a hyperlink.

Adding Headers and Footers

Next you want to add a header to the report.

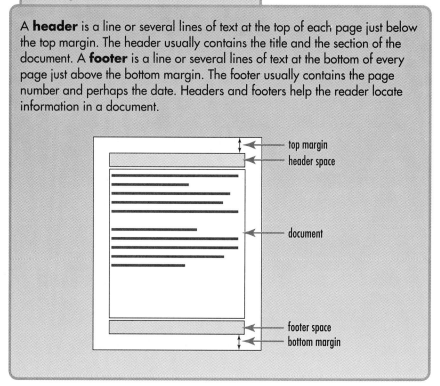

Concept 7: Headers and Footers

A **header** is a line or several lines of text at the top of each page just below the top margin. The header usually contains the title and the section of the document. A **footer** is a line or several lines of text at the bottom of every page just above the bottom margin. The footer usually contains the page number and perhaps the date. Headers and footers help the reader locate information in a document.

You want to add the title of your document to the header. To do this,

■ Choose **V**iew/**H**eader and Footer.

Your screen should be similar to Figure 3-23.

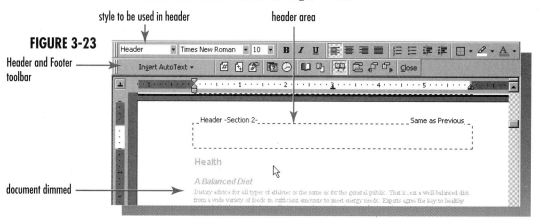

FIGURE 3-23

style to be used in header

header area

Header and Footer toolbar

document dimmed

The document dims, the header area becomes active, and the Header and Footer toolbar is displayed. Its buttons are identified below.

You could also double-click in the header or footer area to activate it.

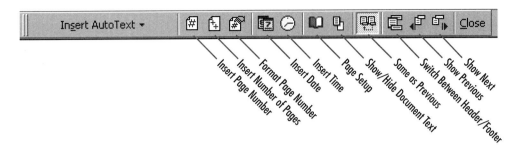

■ If necessary, dock the Header and Footer toolbar below the Formatting toolbar.

Notice that you are in the header for Section 2. Section 1 is the title page. In the upper right corner is the message, "Same as Previous." This means that the Section 2 header will be the same as Section 1. Since the title page does not have a header, you need to turn off the Same as Previous option.

If ▦ Same as Previous is on, the header in the sections before and after the section in which you are entering a header will have the same header.

■ Click ▦ Same as Previous.

You type in the header as if it were a mini-document. The header and footer text can be formatted just like any other text. In addition, you can control the placement of the header and footer text by specifying where it should appear: left-aligned, centered, or right-aligned in the header or footer space.

■ Set the format to Arial 14 pt, bold, italic, and right-aligned.

■ Type **Health and Fitness**

Next you will insert your name, a page number, and today's date in the footer. To quickly add this information, you will use an AutoText entry. These are common entries that are stored in Word that can be selected and used multiple times.

You can create your own AutoText entries using Insert/AutoText.

■ Click ▣ Switch between Header and Footer.

■ Turn off the Same as Previous option.

■ Click Insert AutoText ▾ .

■ Choose Author, Page#, Date.

AutoText entry ⟶

■ Replace Student Name with your name in the footer.

The page number displayed in the footer is the current page, 2. The title page is counted as page 1 of the document. You want to begin page numbers with the first page of Section 2. To make this change,

> You can also add and format page numbers using Insert/Page Numbers.

■ Click 🔢 Format Page Number.

The Page Number Format dialog box on your screen should be similar to Figure 3-24.

FIGURE 3-24

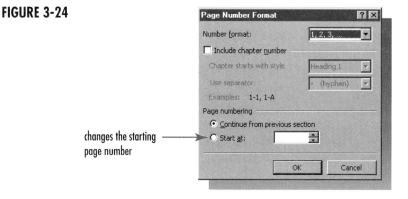

changes the starting page number ⟶

This dialog box is used to change the format of page numbers, include chapter numbers, and to change the page numbering sequence. The default page numbering setting continues the numbering from the first section. To reset the page number sequence to begin Section 2 with page 1,

> The default starts the current section (2) with page 1. You could enter any number as the starting number for a section.

■ Choose Start At.

■ Click   OK .

The footer now displays page 1 as the current page.

■ Close the Header and Footer toolbar.

■ Scroll down to see the top of page 2 and the bottom of page 1.

Your screen should be similar to Figure 3-25.

FIGURE 3-25

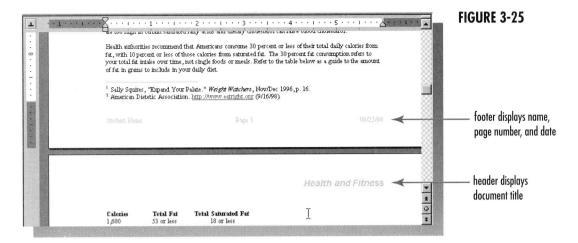

footer displays name, page number, and date

header displays document title

The document area is active again, and the header and footer text appears dimmed.

Updating the Table of Contents

You have made many modifications to the report since generating the table of contents, so you want to update the page references in the listing. Because the table of contents is a field, if you add or remove headings, rearrange topics, or make other changes that affect the table of contents listing, you can quickly update the table of contents using the Update Field command on the Shortcut menu.

The keyboard shortcut to the Update Field command is F9.

Right-click the table of contents to display the Shortcut menu.

- Move to anywhere in the table of contents and display the Shortcut menu.

- Choose Update Field.

From the Update Table of Contents dialog box, you specify the part of the table of contents that needs updating. You need to update the page references.

- If necessary, choose Update Page Numbers Only.

- Click OK.

Your screen should be similar to Figure 3-26.

FIGURE 3-26

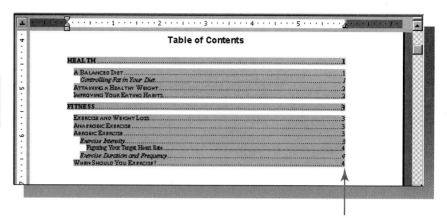

You can click a table of contents page number to quickly move to that page in a document.

page numbers updated to reflect new locations of headings in document and page numbering

You are now ready to print the complete report.

■ Preview, then print the entire document.

■ Save the edited document as Newsletter Topics and close the file.

Note: If you are ending your lab session now, exit Word. To begin Part 2, load Word.

Part 2

Using WordArt

The topics in your report were well received by your manager. Now you will create a sample newsletter design using several of the topics from your report.

A newsletter commonly consists of two basic parts: the headline and the body. (See the figure on the next page.) The headline, also called the nameplate or banner, is the top portion of the newsletter that generally contains the name, issue identification, and publication date. It may also include a company logo, a line that announces the main subject or article included in the newsletter and a brief table of contents. The body, which is the text of the newsletter, is commonly displayed in two- or three-column format. Article headings often include subheadings that help organize the newsletter topics. The headline is often visually separated from the body by horizontal lines, called rules. The sample newsletter you will create will include many of these features.

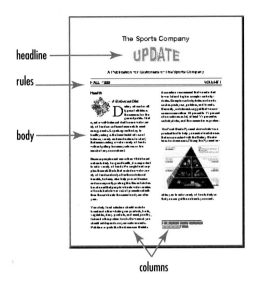

headline
rules
body

columns

The first thing you want to do is to create a headline for the newsletter. The headline will display the name of the newsletter, The Sports Company Update, and issue identification information that includes the date of publication and volume number. The headline you will create is shown here.

The text for the headline has already been entered for you.

■ To see the headline text, open the file Headline from your data disk.

Your screen should be similar to Figure 3-27.

FIGURE 3-27

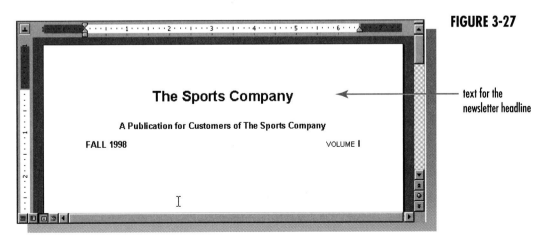

text for the
newsletter headline

You need to complete the newsletter name by entering the word Update below the company name. To make this word unique and more interesting, you will use the WordArt feature to enter it.

Concept 8: WordArt

The **WordArt** feature is used to enhance your documents by changing the shape of text, adding 3-D effects, and changing the alignment of text on a line. The text that is added to the document using WordArt is a graphic object that can be edited, sized, or moved to any location in the document.

Use WordArt to add a special touch to your documents. Its use should be limited to headlines in a newsletter or to a single element in a flyer. You want the WordArt to capture the reader's attention. Here are some examples of WordArt.

The Drawing toolbar is used to access the WordArt feature. To display this toolbar,

■   Click [image] Drawing.

The Drawing toolbar is displayed by default above the status bar. Its buttons (identified below) are used to add and enhance drawing objects in your documents.

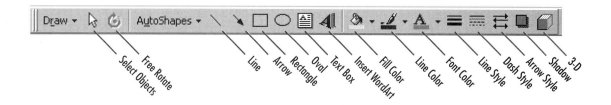

To create a WordArt object of the newsletter name below the company name,

■ Move to the blank line below the company name.

■ Click [4] Insert WordArt.

The WordArt Gallery dialog box on your screen should be similar to Figure 3-28.

FIGURE 3-28

gallery of
30 WordArt styles →

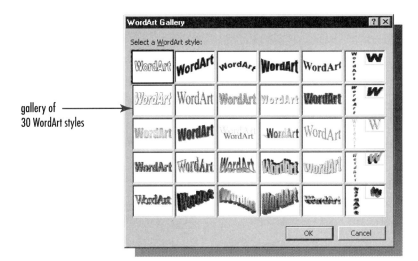

The first step is to select one of the 30 styles or designs of WordArt for the headline. These styles are just a starting point. As you will see, you can alter the appearance of the style by selecting a different color, shape, and special effect.

■ Click [WordArt] (third column, second shape).

■ Click [OK].

The Edit WordArt Text dialog box on your screen should be similar to Figure 3-29.

FIGURE 3-29

enter text to display as WordArt

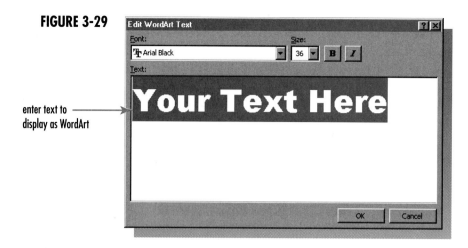

Next you need to enter the text you want displayed using the selected WordArt design.

■ Type **UPDATE**.

■ Click [OK].

Your screen should be similar to Figure 3-30.

FIGURE 3-30

WordArt object inserted into document

WordArt toolbar

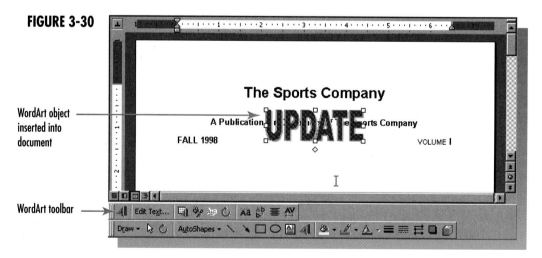

Refer to Concept 5: Graphics to review these features.

Now the word you entered is displayed in the selected WordArt style in the document. When a WordArt object is first inserted in the document, it is displayed at the location of the insertion point. The object is centered because the paragraph alignment to which it is associated is centered. It also floats over the text on the page. This is because the default wrapping style for WordArt objects is None.

The handles surrounding the WordArt object indicate that it is selected. Whenever a WordArt object is selected, the WordArt toolbar is displayed. The WordArt toolbar buttons (identified below) are used to modify the WordArt.

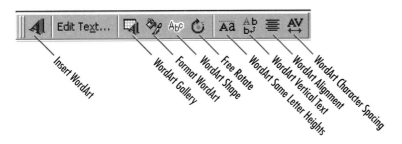

■ If necessary, move and dock the WordArt toolbar above the Drawing toolbar (see Figure 3-30).

You want to change the wrapping style of the object so the text appears above and below it.

■ Click 📎 Format WordArt.

■ Open the Wrapping tab if necessary.

The Format WordArt dialog box on your screen should be similar to Figure 3-31.

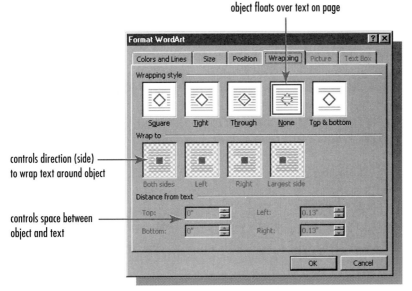

FIGURE 3-31

Depending on the wrapping style you select, you can also specify the space between the object and the text by entering values in the Distance from Text option boxes. The default of 0 places the object as close to the text above and below it as possible. You want text in the headline to wrap above and below the WordArt object. To make this change,

■ Click ◇ Top & bottom.

■ Click OK.

Your screen should be similar to Figure 3-32.

FIGURE 3-32

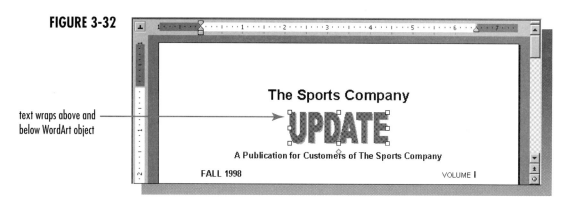

text wraps above and below WordArt object

The object can still be moved anywhere on the page, but text will always appear above and below the object, not to the sides or underneath it.

Changing the WordArt Shape

Now you want to change the appearance of the WordArt object to have a curved top. You select shapes from the WordArt palette.

■ Click Abc WordArt Shape.

■ Choose ⬟ Inflate Top (fifth column, fourth row).

Your screen should be similar to Figure 3-33.

FIGURE 3-33

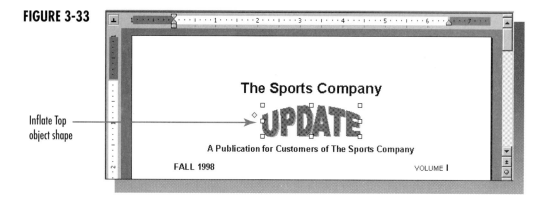

Inflate Top object shape

Changing the Fill and Line Color

Next you want to change the color of the WordArt characters to reflect the corporate colors used in the company logo. You can easily do this using many of the special effects options that can be applied to graphic objects.

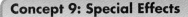

Concept 9: Special Effects

Word 97 includes many commands that add special effects, such as shadows and 3-D effects, to enhance drawing objects, including WordArt. When you draw an object, a border is drawn around the object automatically. You can change the thickness and color of the border. You also can fill a drawing object with a solid color, gradient color, texture, or a picture. Adding shadows or 3-D effects gives depth to an object.

Fill and line colors

Shadows

Patterns and textures

3-D effects

Use these effects in moderation. You want to capture the reader's interest with your graphics, not detract from your message.

- Click 🖉 Format WordArt.

- Open the Colors and Lines tab.

The Format WordArt dialog box on your screen should be similar to Figure 3-34.

FIGURE 3-34

applies fill color to selected object

makes fill color partially transparent

applies color to line surrounding WordArt shape

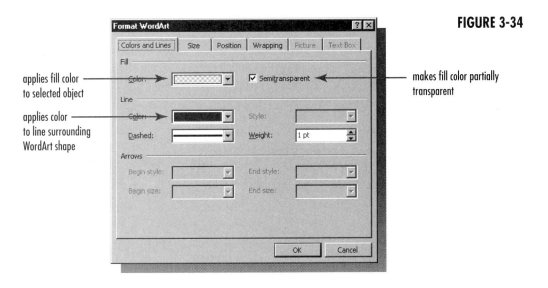

The color and line settings for the selected WordArt design style is a light gray semitransparent fill color with a blue line. The Semitransparent option when selected makes the selected fill color partially transparent, allowing the shadow color to bleed through. When not selected, the color is solid or opaque. You want to use the corporate colors of light green and medium blue in your newsletter. You also do not want the background shadow color of gray to bleed through the letters, so you will turn off the semitransparent selection. To make these changes,

> The fill color is used to fill the object, and the line color is applied to the outline surrounding the ⬚UPDATE⬚ shape.

- Open the Fill Color drop-down list box.

- Select ▢ Light Green (fourth column, fifth color).

- Clear the Semitransparent check box.

- Click [OK].

Creating Horizontal Rules

Next you want the issue identification information to be displayed between two horizontal rules. Rules can be added to any side of a paragraph or object using the Borders toolbar. The paragraph or object must be selected first.

- Move to anywhere within the issue identification text.

- Choose Format/Borders and Shading/Borders.

The Borders and Shading dialog box on your screen should be similar to Figure 3-35.

FIGURE 3-35

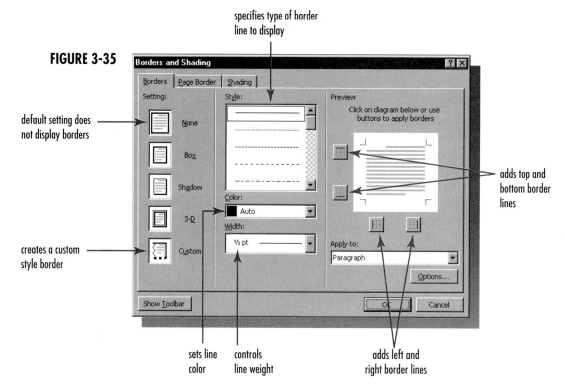

specifies type of border line to display

default setting does not display borders

creates a custom style border

adds top and bottom border lines

sets line color

controls line weight

adds left and right border lines

You want to add a 1½ pt single-line border in blue above the text and a 3 pt double-line border in blue below the text. As you specify the border line settings, the Preview area will reflect your selections.

- Click ▤ Custom.

- From the Width drop-down list box, select 1½ pt.

- From the Color drop-down list box, select Blue.

- Click ▦ Top Border.

- From the Line Style drop-down list, select ▭.

- From the **W**idth drop-down list, select 3 pt.

- From the Color drop-down list, select Blue.

- Click ▦ Bottom Border.

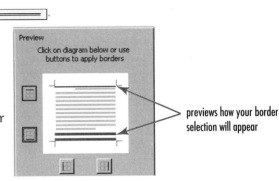

previews how your border selection will appear

The Preview area of the dialog box shows how your selections will appear.

- Click OK .

Your screen should be similar to Figure 3-36.

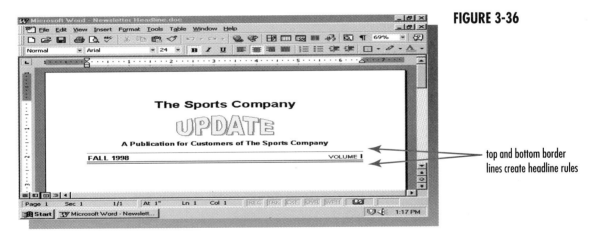

FIGURE 3-36

top and bottom border lines create headline rules

The horizontal border lines extend between the margins above and below the text in the color, style, and point size you specified. The newsletter headline is now complete and can be used with any newsletter.

- Save the headline as Newsletter Headline.

You also can create border lines automatically as you type. To create a single line, press ⊟ three times and press ⏎Enter. To create a double line, press ═ three times and press ⏎Enter.

Now you are ready to copy the headline for the newsletter into the file containing the newsletter text. Following your manager's suggestions, you shortened the topic coverage and divided the topics into several short articles on the same theme that could be continued to the next newsletter. In addition, you revised the text so that footnote references were not needed. The only footnote you kept was to the figure of the Food Guide Pyramid. To see the revised document,

- Open the file Newsletter Articles.

- Scroll through the text to view the contents of the two articles you selected for the sample newsletter. When you are done, return to the top of the document.

You now have two document files open in two separate document windows. Although you can have multiple document windows open at one time, only one can be active. The **active window** is the window you can work in and that is affected by any commands you use. To make a window active, you switch to the window of your choice from the Window menu.

You can also press Ctrl + F6 to cycle forward through all open documents, or Ctrl + ⇧Shift + F6 to cycle backward.

- Switch to the Newsletter Headline window and use the Select All command on the Edit menu to select the entire file.

- Copy the selection text to the Clipboard.

- Make the Newsletter Articles window active. If necessary, move the insertion point to the top of the file (Ctrl + Home).

- Paste the selection from the Clipboard to this location in the file.

Your screen should be similar to Figure 3-37.

FIGURE 3-37

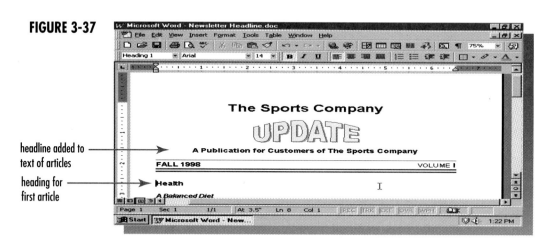

headline added to text of articles

heading for first article

The newsletter headline is displayed at the top of the document. The Health heading should be separated from the bottom border line by one blank line.

- If necessary, insert or delete blank lines above it to position it there.

Creating Newspaper Columns

You want the articles in the newsletter to be displayed in newspaper style columns. **Newspaper columns** display text so that it flows from the bottom of one column to the top of the next. The Normal template has one column the full width of the margins, so the text appears to flow continuously from one page to the next. On occasion, the layout for your document may call for two or more columns on a page. A common application for this is a newsletter.

The optimum column width for reading comfort is 4.5 inches. In a newsletter, narrower columns help the reader read the articles more quickly, and you as the writer can fit more information on a page in a visually pleasing arrangement. It is not wise to use more than four columns on an $8\frac{1}{2}$ by 11-inch page. The columns will be too narrow and the page will look messy.

The Columns command on the Format menu is used to set the text format of a document to columns. When using the column feature, the text in the entire document is changed to the new format. To affect only a portion of a document, the document must be divided into sections. Because you do not want the headline to appear in column format, you will create a section break below the headline.

■ Move to the blank line under the bottom border line.

■ Choose Insert/Break/Continuous/ OK .

Although section break lines do not display in Page Layout view, the status bar shows that the insertion point is positioned in Section 2. The new section continues to the end of the document unless another section break is inserted. To change the Section 2 format to newspaper columns,

■ Choose Format/Columns.

The Columns dialog box on your screen should be similar to Figure 3-38.

column styles →

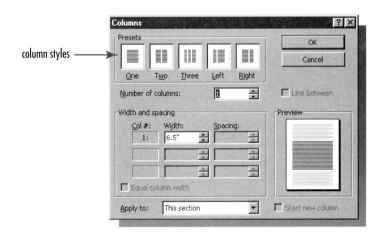

FIGURE 3-38

The Presets area displays five preset column styles and shows the default style is one column the full width of the page. Using the Presets area you can select up to three evenly spaced columns or two unevenly spaced column formats. If none of the preset styles is appropriate, you can enter a number in the Number of Columns text box to create up to 13 columns. You want the newsletter to have two columns of text on the first page. From the Presets area,

■ Select T**wo**.

The Number of Columns text box now displays 2. Based on the number of columns you specify and your document's left and right margin settings, Word automatically calculates the size of columns and the spacing between columns. Using the default setting, the two columns will be 3 inches wide, separated by 0.5 inch. The Preview box shows how text will appear on the page using the specified column settings.

■ Click [OK].

■ If necessary, set the zoom to 75 percent. Scroll the window to display more of the first article in the two-column format.

Your screen should be similar to Figure 3-39.

FIGURE 3-39

column widths   space between columns

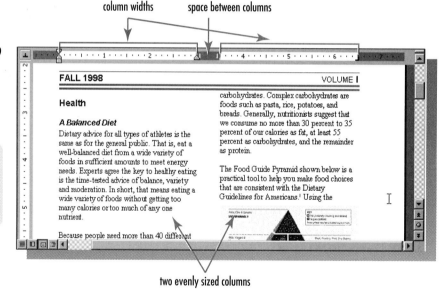

two evenly sized columns

Do not be concerned if the text in your columns wraps differently than in Figure 3-39. This is a function of the selected printer on your system.

The text is displayed as two evenly sized newspaper columns, with 0.5 inch of space between. The text at the bottom of the first column continues at the top of the second column. The column markers on the horizontal ruler show the size and spacing of each column.

You would like the second page of the newsletter to be in three-column format. Rather than inserting a section break first, you can select the area of the text to be affected before setting the format to columns and Word will automatically insert the section break at the beginning (and end if necessary) of your selection. Another way to specify columns is to use the ▦ Columns button on the Standard toolbar. It allows you to specify up to six columns using the default column definitions.

- ■ Select the text from the Fitness heading to the end of the document.

- ■ Click ▦ Columns.

- ■ Click on the third column.

- ■ Move to the Fitness heading at the beginning of the three-column section.

The menu equivalent is F**o**rmat/ Columns/**N**umber of Columns/3.

Your screen should be similar to Figure 3-40.

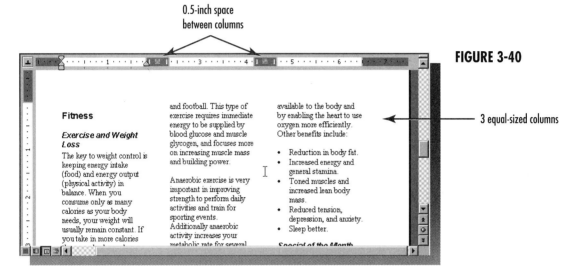

0.5-inch space between columns

FIGURE 3-40

3 equal-sized columns

The default width of 0.5 inch between the columns was appropriate for two columns, but seems too wide for three columns. To reduce the space between columns to 0.3 inch and maintain equal column widths,

- ■ Choose F**o**rmat/**C**olumns.

- ■ In the Width and Spacing section of the dialog box, set the spacing to 0.3 for Column 1.

- ■ Select **E**qual Column Width.

- ■ Click OK .

You can also drag the column marker in the ruler to adjust the column size and spacing between columns.

Using Hyphenation

Now that the layout is in columns, you notice that many of the lines have very uneven right margins, especially in the three-column layout. On lines of text where there are several short words, the wrapping of text to the next line is not a problem. However, on lines that contain long words, the long word is wrapped to the next line, leaving a large gap on the previous line. To help solve this problem you will use the hyphenation feature.

Concept 10: Hyphenation

The **hyphenation** feature inserts a hyphen in long words that fall at the end of a line to split the word between lines. Because word processors automatically wrap long words that fall at the end of a line to the beginning of the next line, uneven right margins or large gaps of white space commonly occur in a document. Using hyphenation reduces the amount of white space and makes line lengths more even to improve the appearance of a document. The program inserts **optional hyphens**, which only break the word if it appears at the end of a line. Then, as you edit the document, the hyphenation is adjusted appropriately.

To hyphenate the document,

■   Choose **T**ools/**L**anguage/**H**yphenation.

Word generally proposes accurate hyphenation. If you do not agree with how a word is hyphenated after it has been done, you can select the word and hyphenate it manually.

The Hyphenation dialog box is displayed. The Automatically Hyphenate Document option lets Word set hyphenation for the entire document. You can also specify the size of the **hyphenation zone**, an unmarked space along the right margin that controls the amount of white space in addition to the margin that Word will allow at the end of a line. Making the hyphenation zone narrower (a smaller number) reduces the unevenness of lines by hyphenating more words, while making the zone wider (a larger number) hyphenates fewer words.

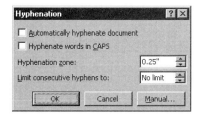

Use the Manual command button only if you want to be able to accept, reject, or change the proposed hyphenation of each word that Word is considering hyphenating.

■   Select Automatically Hyphenate Document.

■   If necessary, specify a hyphenation zone setting of 0.25".

■   Click   OK   .

Your screen should be similar to Figure 3-41.

FIGURE 3-41

Depending on your printer, different words may be hyphenated.

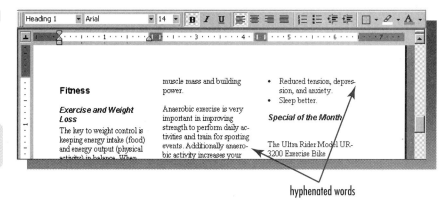

hyphenated words

Word has examined each line and determined where it is possible to hyphenate a word. Hyphenating the newsletter has made the column margins much less uneven.

■ To save the changes you have made to the document to this point, save the document as Fall 1998 Newsletter.

If the text in three-column format now begins at the bottom of page 1, insert a continuous section break before the Fitness heading.

Inserting Text Boxes

To make certain elements in your newsletter stand out, you decide to put them into text boxes. **Text boxes** are graphic objects, so you can place them on the page as you would a picture or WordArt. You can also add drawing features to text boxes to enhance their appearance. You want to create a text box for the information about the special of the month and include a picture of the item from the catalog.

■ Select the text located at the end of column 3 on page 2 beginning with the heading Special of the Month and ending with "description."

■ Click  Text Box.

The menu equivalent is Insert/Text Box.

The selected text is placed in a text box, and the Text Box toolbar is displayed. Its buttons (identified below) are used to link text boxes together so text flows from one to the next. You can use this feature to place text into a newsletter and have it automatically flow from one page to another page later in the newsletter.

■ If necessary, adjust the size of the text box so it is the same width as the column.

■ Fill the text box with the Light Green color.

■ Change the line color to Blue.

Use the Drawing toolbar buttons to make these changes.

Next you want to add a picture of the exercise bike to the text box.

■ Move to the blank line beneath the heading Special of the Month.

■ Choose Insert/Picture/From File.

■ Change the Look In location to the drive containing your data disk.

■ Select Exercise Bike.jpg.

■ Click   Insert   .

■ Increase the length of the text box to fully display the text.

■ Select the Exercise Bike object and increase the size of the object to nearly the full width of the text box as in Figure 3-42.

■ Add a blue border around the exercise bike graphic.

■ Move the text box down the column slightly to separate it from the end of the text in the column.

Use the ▢ button to draw a border, then use ✐▾ to apply the color.

Reminder: Drag the corner handle when resizing to maintain proportions.

When you are done, your screen should be similar to Figure 3-42.

FIGURE 3-42

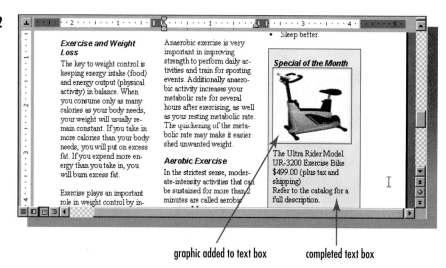

graphic added to text box   completed text box

Notice that when you moved the text box, all the objects inside the text box moved too. This is because the text box is a grouped object and is considered one graphic element. However, you can still format the text and size the graphic as separate items.

You also want to add two more pictures to the newsletter. The first will be a picture that will complement the Health topic area and the second the Fitness topic area.

■ Move to the heading A Balanced Diet on page 1.

■ Insert the picture file Foodgrps.wmf from your data disk.

■ Select the picture and reduce its size to about a 1-inch square (see Figure 3-43).

■ Change the wrapping style to Tight and the direction to wrap to Right.

Office 97 comes with many clip art images that are located in the Clip Gallery.

You can also purchase clip art packages to add to your collection.

The text in the paragraph now wraps tightly around the object to the right. The food groups object is a clip art image. **Clip art** is a term used to describe a collection of graphics that usually is bundled with a software application.

- Add the picture Jogger.wmf from your data disk to the first paragraph below Fitness on page 2. Size the graphic to approximately 1 x 3 inches.

- Set the wrapping to Tight Both Sides.

- Move the graphic to the location shown in Figure 3-43.

Now you need to check the newsletter layout and move text and graphic elements around on the page until the newsletter has an orderly yet interesting appearance.

- Set the zoom to Two Pages.

- Position all the graphic elements in the newsletter so they are similar to those shown in Figure 3-43.

Your screen should be similar to Figure 3-43.

object wrapped tight right   clip art wrapped tight both sides

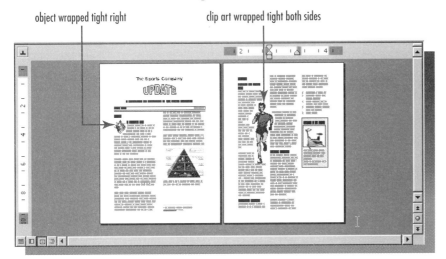

FIGURE 3-43

Adding a Drop Cap

Finally, you would like to make the first letter of the first paragraph of the newsletter a drop cap. A **drop cap**, used most often with the first character in a paragraph, appears as a large, uppercase character with the top part of the letter even with the line and the rest of the letter extending into the paragraph below it. The character is changed to a graphic object in a frame and the text wraps to the side of the object. To create a drop cap,

- Change the zoom to Page Width.

- Select the D in "Dietary" (first letter on the first page where the columns start).

- Choose Format/Drop Cap/Dropped/2/ OK .

■ Move the graphic object to the right of the picture as shown here.

■ Deselect the object.

■ Insert a blank line above the second column to separate the text from the bottom headline rule.

Health

A Balanced Diet

Dietary advice for all types of athletes is the same as for the general public. That ↓ eat a well-balanced diet

drop cap

The drop cap effect emphasizes the beginning of the paragraph and makes the columns appear more like those in a magazine.

■ Add the same style and size drop cap to the T of "The" at the beginning of the first article under Fitness.

■ Preview the newsletter. Set the Print Preview window to display two pages by selecting View/Zoom/Many Pages or by clicking [⊞] Multiple Pages and then selecting 1x2 pages.

Your screen should be similar to Figure 3-44.

FIGURE 3-44

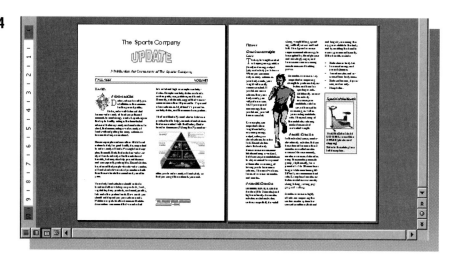

■ Close the Preview window.

■ Add your name at the bottom of page 2 only.

■ Save the formatted newsletter.

■ If necessary, select the appropriate printer for your computer system.

■ Because the text is reformatted to the font and graphic capabilities of your printer, scroll through the document to see the changes that were made.

■ Adjust the text wherever necessary to produce a newsletter as similar as possible to the one you created in this lab.

■ Preview your changes, then resave the document.

You may need to insert a blank line or two below the last column of text to add space to enter your name.

■ Print the newsletter.

■ Set the Page Layout view zoom back to 100 percent, set the view back to Normal, and turn off the Drawing toolbar.

■ Close all the open files and Exit Word.

> To close all open documents at the same time, hold down ⇧Shift while you select File, then choose Close All.

LAB REVIEW

■ ■ ■ ■ ■ ■ ■ ■ ■ ■ ■

Key Terms

active window   (WP136)
anchor   (WP116)
caption   (WP119)
character style   (WP101)
clip art   (WP142)
cross-reference   (WP119)
Document Map pane   (WP103)
document pane   (WP103)
drawing object   (WP116)
drop cap   (WP143)
endnote   (WP109)
footer   (WP122)
footnote   (WP109)
frame   (WP116)
graphic   (WP116)
group   (WP116)
handle   (WP117)
header   (WP122)
heading style   (WP101)
hyperlink   (WP112)
hyphenation   (WP140)
hyphenation zone   (WP140)
lock   (WP116)

manual page break   (WP99)
newspaper column   (WP137)
note pane   (WP110)
note reference mark   (WP109)
note separator   (WP109)
note text   (WP109)
object   (WP116)
optional hyphen   (WP140)
pane   (WP103)
paragraph style   (WP101)
picture   (WP116)
style   (WP101)
tab alignment selection box   (WP114)
tab leaders   (WP106)
tab stop   (WP114)
text box   (WP141)
URL (Uniform Resource Locator)   (WP111)
WordArt   (WP128)

Command Summary

Command	Shortcut	Button	Action
File/Page Set**u**p/**L**ayout/**V**ertical Alignment			Aligns text vertically on a page
View/**H**eader and Footer			Displays header and footer areas
View/Foot**n**otes			Hides or displays note pane
Insert/**B**reak/**P**age Break	Ctrl + ←Enter		Inserts manual page break
Insert/**B**reak/**C**ontinuous			Starts next section on same page as current section
Insert/Page N**u**mbers			Specifies page number location
Insert /Foot**n**ote	Alt + Ctrl + F		Inserts footnote reference at insertion point
Insert/**C**aption			Inserts caption at insertion point
Insert/Cross-**r**eference			Inserts cross-reference at insertion point
Insert/Inde**x** and Tables			Inserts index or table, such as table of contents
Insert/**P**icture/**F**rom File			Inserts picture from file
Insert/Te**x**t Box		▣	Inserts text box
F**o**rmat/**B**orders and Shading			Adds borders and shadings to selection
		▭	Adds top border
		▭	Adds bottom border
F**o**rmat/**C**olumns		▦	Specifies number, spacing, and size of columns
F**o**rmat/**T**abs			Inserts tab stops
F**o**rmat/**D**rop Cap/**D**ropped			Changes character to drop cap
F**o**rmat/**S**tyle			Applies, creates, or modifies styles
F**o**rmat/Pi**c**ture			Changes picture scaling, size, wrapping, position, and cropping information
Tools/**L**anguage/**H**yphenation			Specifies hyphenation settings

Matching

1. note pane	_____	**a.**	text that appears at the bottom of each page above the bottom margin
2. tab leaders	_____	**b.**	dots that separate table of contents headings from page numbers
3. footer	_____	**c.**	source reference displayed at the bottom of a page
4. caption	_____	**d.**	lower section of workspace that displays footnote text
5. footnote	_____	**e.**	instructs Word to begin a new page at that location regardless of the amount of text on the previous page
6. manual page break	_____	**f.**	a title or explanation for a table, picture, or graph
7. tight wrap	_____	**g.**	a graphic object that contains text or other graphic objects
8. text box	_____	**h.**	text closely follows contours around a graphic
9. WordArt	_____	**i.**	non-text element that adds visual interest to a document
10. graphic	_____	**j.**	applies shapes and special effects to text

Discussion Questions

1. Discuss the differences between footnotes and endnotes. Why is it necessary to add notes to a document?

2. Discuss how you can move and place graphic objects in a document. Use Help to learn more about anchors and locked anchors. Discuss the different wrapping options.

3. How can newspaper columns enhance the look of a document? What types of documents are columns best suited for? How can the adjustment of widths, spacing, and hyphenation affect the layout?

Fill-In Questions

1. Complete the following statements by filling in the blanks with the correct terms.

a. A(n) _____ is a named group of formats.

b. _____ are useful for aligning text or numeric data vertically in columns.

c. The _____ displays the headings in your document, making it easier to navigate.

d. A(n) _____ can be displayed below a graphic to identify the object.

e. A(n) _____ can be placed within a document to refer back to a figure or other reference in the document.

f. A(n) _____ allows you to jump to another location in a document, another document, or the WWW.

g. A(n) _____ is used to apply different formats to different parts of a document.

h. The _____ feature changes the shape of text.

i. _____ divides words to allow more text to be displayed on each line.

j. Non-text elements such as drawings and pictures are called _____.

Hands-On Practice Exercises

Step by Step

Rating System	
☆	Easy
☆☆	Moderate
☆☆☆	Difficult

1. To complete this exercise, you must have completed Practice Exercise 3 in Lab 1. Open the file No Smoking Memo on your data disk.

a. Change the font to Arial 12 pt. Set a left-aligned tab at 0.75 inch, and set the alignment to Justified. Change all margins to 1.5 inches.

b. Enter the current date following "Date."

c. Go to the beginning of the first paragraph and insert the picture Nosmoke.wmf from your data disk. Size the picture and wrap the text until it fits perfectly to the left of the two paragraphs.

d. Save the file as Revised No Smoking Memo. Print the memo.

2. In this exercise you will create a letterhead for yourself using a WordArt image for your name.

a. Enter your name as a WordArt object. Apply a shape and a shadow to the image.

b. Size the object appropriately and center it between the margins.

c. Enter your address, centered, below your name. Change the font and size of the address.

d. Place the object 0.5 inch from the top of the page. Two lines below the address, enter a date that will update automatically when the letter is printed. Right-align the date, and change its font to Times New Roman 12 pt.

e. Use the AutoShapes button to add a drawing object to the left of the address. It should display the text "New Address!". (Use Help for information on this feature.)

f. Document the file. Save the letterhead as Letterhead. Print the letterhead.

3. To complete this problem, you must have completed the Newsletter Topics document in Lab 3. Open the Newsletter Topics document from your data disk.

a. Turn on the Document Map and add the following footnotes to the document:

Section	Paragraph	Following Word	Footnote
Aerobic Exercise	1st	"rate"	Lisa Balbach, "What is Aerobic Exercise and Why Should I do it?" http://k2.kirkland.cc.mi.us/~balbach/fitness.htm#Aerobics (current date)
Exercise Intensity	1st	"maximum"	Bailey, p. 161.
Exercise Duration and Frequency	1st	"week"	Nordictrac, "Too Much. . . Too Little. . . How Do I Know How Much is Enough?" *Designing an Aerobic Exercise Program.* http://www.nordictrack.com/aerobic_program.html (current date)
Exercise Duration and Frequency	3rd	"days"	"Physical Activity and Health: A Report of the Surgeon General." http://www.cdc.gov/needphp/sqr/ataglan.htm (current date)

b. You want to add another illustration to the document. Move to the blank line after the fourth paragraph in the Controlling Fat in Your Diet section. Insert another blank line. Insert the picture file Nutrition Label.bmp.

c. Size the picture to 3 x 2.5 inches.

d. Add the figure caption, "Figure 2: Nutrition Label."

e. Save the file as Newsletter Topics Revised. Print the document.

4. To complete this exercise, you must have completed Practice Exercise 4 in Lab 2. Open the file B&B Ad Part 2.

a. Change the name of the inn (Pocono Mountain Retreat) to a WordArt object. Use a shape of your choice. Explore and use several additional special effects such as shadows, 3-D, and colors to enhance your WordArt object.

b. Select the five paragraphs below the indented items, and enclose them in a text box. Apply a color line and fill to the text box.

c. Surround the page in a colored border. (Use Help for information on page borders.)

d. Update the documentation to indicate that this is the final ad. Save the file as Camera Ready B&B Ad. Print the ad.

5. To complete this problem, you must have completed Practice Exercise 3 in Lab 2. Open the file Updated Cookie Recipes from your data disk.

a. Enter your name on the line below the title and the current date on the next line. Make sure they are 12 pt and centered.

b. Insert the picture Cookie from your data disk centered above the title. Size the picture appropriately.

c. Enter the heading Table of Contents three lines below the date. The heading should be 16 pt and centered. Insert a section break below the note on this page.

d. Insert a hard page break between each cookie recipe so that each page will contain just one recipe. Insert page numbers that will print at the bottom center of each page, beginning with the first cookie recipe page.

e. Apply the Heading 1 style to the names of the cookies at the top of each recipe. Use the Formal format to create a table of contents of the cookie recipes on the second blank line below the Table of Contents heading. Increase the font size of the table of contents to 12 pt. Make sure there are two or three blank lines between the table of contents and the note.

Center the table of contents on the page.

f. Next you will insert three footnotes to add information to some of the recipes.

■ Go to the Cut-Out Sugar Cookies recipe on page 1. Move to the end of the line that displays the ingredient "1 1/2 tsp. vanilla extract." Insert the following footnote: **You can substitute pure anise extract for vanilla.**

■ Go to the Cut-Out Gingerbread People recipe on page 2. Move to the end of the line that displays the ingredient "1 tsp. allspice." Insert the following footnote: **Add a bit more of each spice to give the cookies an extra kick.**

■ Go to the Peanut Butter Surprise recipe on page 4. Move to the end of the line that reads "Double Peanut Butter Cookie recipe . . ." Insert the following footnote: **Use smooth peanut butter for this recipe.**

g. Remove your name and date from below the Potato Chip Cookie recipe. Save the file as Completed Cookie Recipes. Print the document.

h. Optional: Open the file Updated Cookie Recipes and modify the document using layouts of your own choice. Save the file with a new name, and print the document.

6. You have written an article for your travel newsletter on scenic drives in your state. You want to enhance the appearance of the article. Open the file Top 10 Scenic Drives from your data disk.

a. Insert six blank lines at the top of the document. Create a centered WordArt report title that displays "Top 10 Scenic Drives" on the first line. Center your name and the current date on lines 2 and 3 below the title. Add a section break below the date. Center the page vertically.

b. Zoom the title page to full page and drag the WordArt title so that it is centered just above your name.

c. On page 2, insert a picture of a car (from the Clip Gallery or your data disk). Display the picture to the left of the first paragraph and size the picture appropriately.

d. Create a drop cap as the first character in the first paragraph. Justify the first three paragraphs only. Bold each of the numbered locations.

e. Add the following footnote at the end of the first sentence of the third paragraph: **This top 10 list was obtained from the Weissmann Travel Reports in the America Online Traveler's Corner.**

f. Change the format to two columns for the 10 locations. Change the spacing between columns to 0.6 inch. Make the columns evenly sized and check the Line Between box to draw a line between the columns of text. Hyphenate the document.

g. Insert the picture of a 1st place award (from the Clip Gallery or your data disk) at the beginning of the Rocky Mountains paragraph. Size it to fit to the left of the first five lines of the paragraph.

h. Number the pages, excluding the cover page.

i. Check the layout of your document and make adjustments to the text as necessary.

j. Document the file. Save the document as Scenic Drives Newsletter. Print the document.

k. Optional: Open the file Top 10 Scenic Drives and modify the document using layouts of your own choice. Save the file with a new name, and print the document.

On Your Own

7. Create a flier to announce an event (party, garage sale, bake sale, auction, and so on) or advertise something you have for sale (used car, used books, and so on), a service you are offering, or a service you need (babysitting, tutoring, car pool, dog walking, and so on).

Integrate any or all of the following features into the flier:

> Borders, shading, colors
>
> Bullets and/or numbering
>
> Indents
>
> Different fonts in different sizes, colors, and styles
>
> WordArt
>
> Pictures (you can use the images from the Clip Gallery or you can create your own with the Paint program)
>
> Different alignment options
>
> Anything else you can think of!

Document and save the file. Print the flier.

8. Prepare a brief research paper (or use a paper you have written in the past) on a topic of interest to you. The paper must include the following features:

- A title page that displays the report title, your name, the current date (using the Date and Time command), and a table of contents.

- The body of the paper should include at least two levels of headings and a minimum of three footnotes.

- The report layout should include page numbers on the top right corner of every page (excluding the title page). The title page should be vertically aligned.

- Include at least one graphic object with a caption.

9. The Career Services department is presenting a series of discussions on how to find a job. You have prepared a document for distribution to participants on how to write an effective resume and cover letter. You want to make a few enhancements to the document. Open the file How to Write a Resume on your data disk.

■ Justify the entire document. Center the report title, and apply a font and font size of your choice. Center the name and date lines below the title. Enter the heading "Table of Contents" below the date. Center the heading and increase the point size. Insert a page break at the beginning of The Resume title line on page 1.

■ Apply the Heading 1 style to the Overview of Resumes and Overview of Cover Letters headings. Apply the Heading 2 style to the Basic Principles of Resume Construction and Organizing Your Resume headings.

■ Create a table of contents on the title page. Use any format you wish. Adjust the spacing and overall layout of the title page any way you wish.

■ In the Overview of Resumes section, bullet and indent the five lines from "Who you are" to "What kind of job you would like." In the Overview of Cover Letters section, bullet and indent the four measures that are needed for the cover letter. Number the eight Basic Principles of Resume Construction in the resume section and the four "abilities you have developed in school" at the end of the cover letter section.

■ Arrange the paragraphs so they are in the following order: Name, Address, and Phone Number, Career Objective, Education, Work Experience, Activities, Honors and Awards, Special Skills, and References.

■ Below the first sentence of the Overview of Resumes on page 1, insert the following footnote: **This information was obtained from *The Work Book* by Barbara N. Price, Ph.D., Director of Career Planning and Placement, Luzerne County Community College, Nanticoke, PA.**

■ Insert page numbers in any position, excluding the title page.

■ Adjust the layout of the document so that the pages contain the following information:

Page 0: The report title, your name, the current date, and the table of contents.

Page 1: The Overview, all eight Basic Principles of Resume Construction, and the footnote.

Page 2: All of the Organizing Your Resume information.

Page 3: All of The Cover Letter information.

■ Document the file. Save the file as Resume Tips. Print the document.

Optional: Open the file How to Write a Resume and modify the document using layouts of your own choice. Save the file with a new name, and print the document.

Creating a Report and a Newsletter

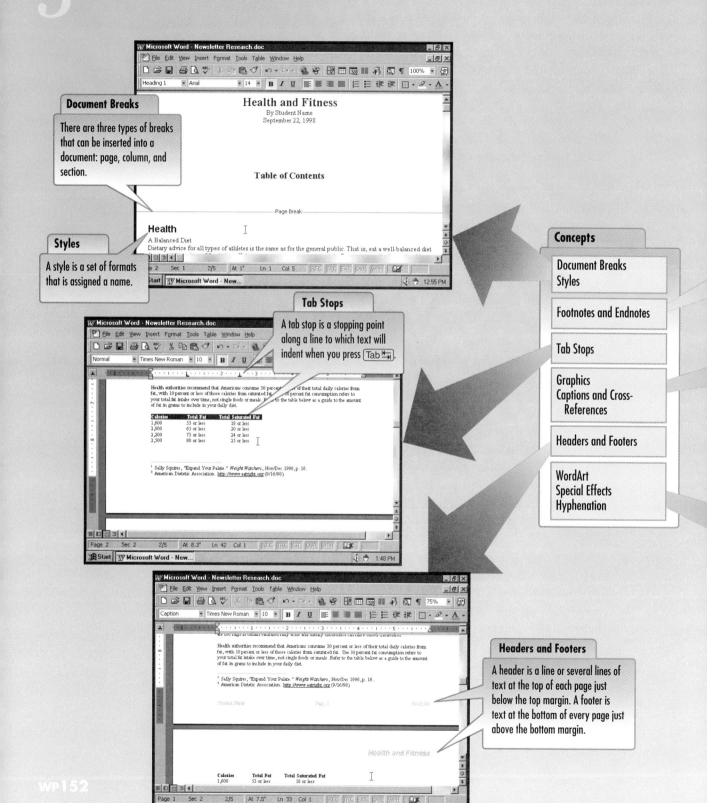

Document Breaks

There are three types of breaks that can be inserted into a document: page, column, and section.

Styles

A style is a set of formats that is assigned a name.

Tab Stops

A tab stop is a stopping point along a line to which text will indent when you press Tab.

Concepts

Document Breaks
Styles

Footnotes and Endnotes

Tab Stops

Graphics
Captions and Cross-References

Headers and Footers

WordArt
Special Effects
Hyphenation

Headers and Footers

A header is a line or several lines of text at the top of each page just below the top margin. A footer is text at the bottom of every page just above the bottom margin.

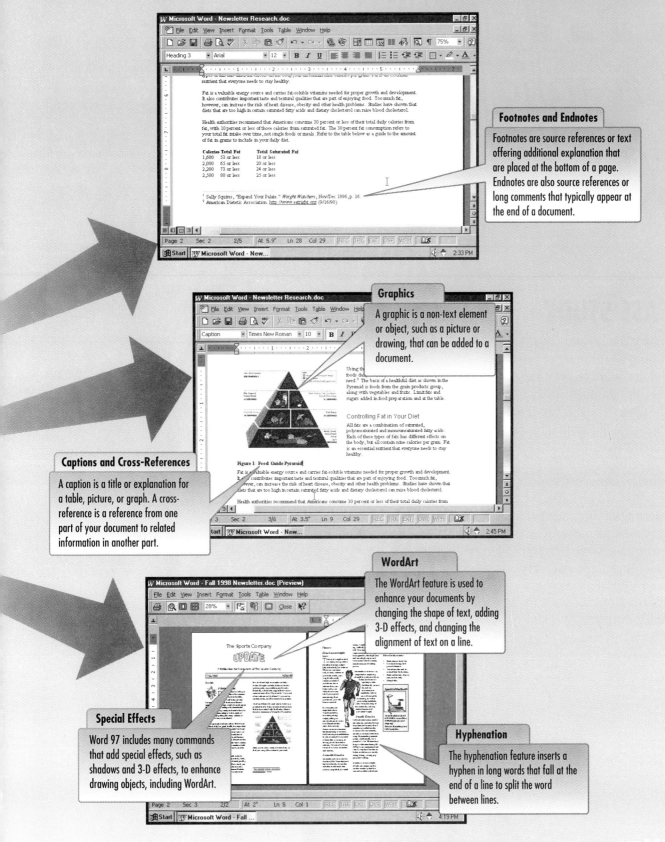

Footnotes and Endnotes

Footnotes are source references or text offering additional explanation that are placed at the bottom of a page. Endnotes are also source references or long comments that typically appear at the end of a document.

Graphics

A graphic is a non-text element or object, such as a picture or drawing, that can be added to a document.

Captions and Cross-References

A caption is a title or explanation for a table, picture, or graph. A cross-reference is a reference from one part of your document to related information in another part.

WordArt

The WordArt feature is used to enhance your documents by changing the shape of text, adding 3-D effects, and changing the alignment of text on a line.

Special Effects

Word 97 includes many commands that add special effects, such as shadows and 3-D effects, to enhance drawing objects, including WordArt.

Hyphenation

The hyphenation feature inserts a hyphen in long words that fall at the end of a line to split the word between lines.

Creating a Table and Merging Documents

CASE STUDY

Your latest project with The Sports Company is to prepare a memo containing a summary of gross sales for the four metropolitan stores. You will use Word to create a table of this data. Tables are an effective way to present complicated data in an orderly format. The table helps the reader compare data and eliminates a lot of text that makes the document more difficult to read.

You have also been asked by the regional manager to make the credit card form letter more personalized by including the name and address information for each preferred customer in the inside address as well as their first name in the salutation. To do this you will create a form letter. Form letters are common business documents used when the same information needs to be communicated to many different people.

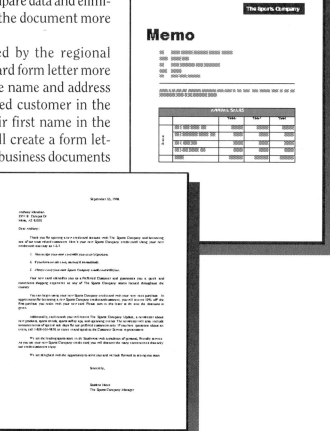

> ### Concept Overview
>
> The following concepts will be introduced in this lab:
>
> **1. Tables** A table is used to organize information into an easy-to-read format.
>
> **2. Formulas and Functions** Formulas and functions are used to perform calculations in tables.
>
> **3. Mail Merge** The Mail Merge feature combines a list of data (typically a file of names and addresses) with a document (commonly a form letter) to create a new document.
>
> **4. Field Names** Field names are used to label each data field in the data source.

Part 1

Using a Template

Your next project is to prepare a summary of gross sales for the four metropolitan area stores for the past three years. You want to include the data in a brief memo to the regional manager. You would like to create the memo using one of the predesigned document templates included with Word. The templates are designed to help you create professional-looking business documents such as letters, faxes, memos, reports, brochures, press releases, manuals, newsletters, resumes, invoices, purchase orders, and weekly time sheets. Once created, you can change different elements to give the document your own personal style.

- Load Word.

- Choose File/New.

- Open the Memos tab.

- Select (highlight) Contemporary Memo.

The New dialog box on your screen should be similar to Figure 4-1.

FIGURE 4-1

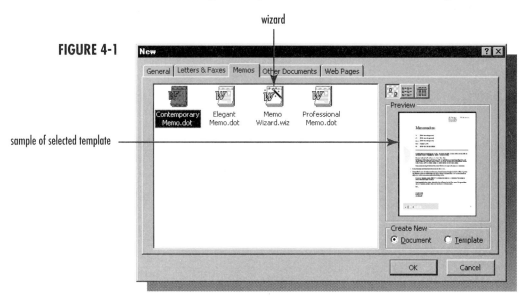

.dot is the file extension associated with a template document.

Word has several memo templates and a Memo Wizard that guides you step by step through creating a memo. The Preview area displays how the selected memo template looks. You will use the Professional Memo template to create your memo.

■   Select Professional Memo.

■   Click   OK   .

Your screen should be similar to Figure 4-2.

FIGURE 4-2

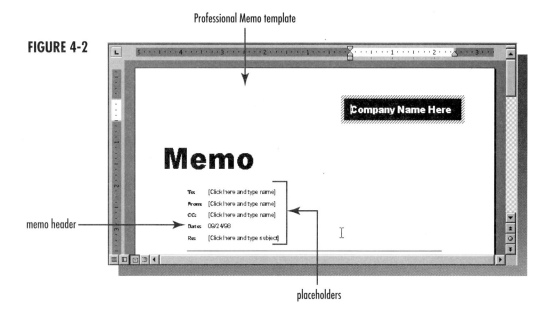

The memo template is displayed in Page Layout view. The insertion point is in the box displaying "Company Name Here." You need to replace the text in the box with your company name.

■ Select Company Name Here.

■ Type **The Sports Company**

The next area in the memo template you need to modify is the memo header, which includes the name of the recipient, sender's name, a carbon copy (CC) recipient, the date, and a subject line. Notice that the date is the current system date. The text in brackets is a **placeholder** that tells you what information to enter. To replace the placeholder, click on it to select it and type the information you want to include in your document. This **click and type** feature is found in most templates.

You can delete any items you do not want from the memo template.

■ Click the To: placeholder.

Notice that the Style button displays "Message Header" as the default style; this sets the font to Arial and 10 pt.

■ To make it easier to read, zoom the document to 85%.

■ Replace the placeholders with the following:

Type the zoom percent directly in the Zoom button.

To:	**Ramon Martinez, Southwest Regional Manager**
From:	**Your name**
CC:	**Donna Blackcloud, Sales Coordinator**
Re:	**Gross Sales Summary**

Next you want to enter the body of the memo. The memo template also includes instructions on how to use the template in the body of the memo. To enter your memo text, you replace the template instructions with your own memo text.

■ Scroll the window to see the paragraph of template instructions in the body of the memo.

■ Select the instructions and enter the following text: **Below is the data you requested comparing gross sales for the years 1996 through 1998 for the four metropolitan stores in the Southwest region.**

■ Press [←Enter] (2 times).

Your screen should be similar to Figure 4-3.

FIGURE 4-3

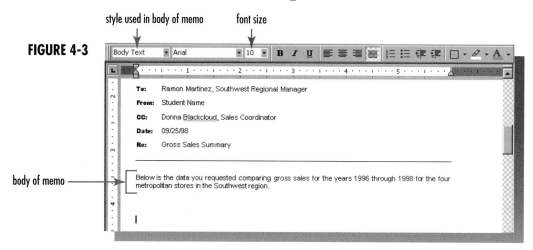

style used in body of memo   font size

body of memo

Notice that the Style button now shows the style as Body Text and the font as Arial 10 pt.

Creating a Table

Next you want to enter the sales data as a table.

Concept 1: Tables

A **table** is used to organize information into an easy-to-read format. A table displays information in horizontal **rows** and vertical **columns**. The insertion of a row and column creates a **cell** in which you can enter data or other information.

Cells in a table are identified first by a letter and number, called a **table reference**. Columns are identified from left to right beginning with the letter A, and rows are numbered from top to bottom beginning with the number 1. The table reference of the top leftmost cell is A1 because it is in the first column (A) and first row (1) fo the table. The second column is cell B2. The fourth cell in column 3 is C4.

column B

	A	B	C	D
1	Cell A1			
2		Cell B2		Cell D2
3				
4			Cell C4	
5				
6				

row 3

Tables are a very effective method for presenting information. The table layout organizes the information for the reader and greatly reduces the number of words they have to read to interpret the data. Use tables whenever you can to make your documents easier to read.

The table you want to create will display the data for the three years in the columns. The rows will display the data for the four stores and a total. Your completed table will be similar to the one shown below.

ANNUAL SALES			
	1996	**1997**	**1998**
#48 -- Metro Center Mall	$719,590	$761,000	$782,205
#55 -- Superstition Springs Mall	544,900	589,800	592,800
#57 -- Fiesta Mall	620,700	633,800	631,700
#62 -- Park Central Mall	578,900	569,400	565,300
TOTAL	$2,464,090	$2,554,000	$2,572,005

Word includes several different methods you can use to create tables. One method (Table/Convert Text to Table) will quickly convert existing text that is separated into columns using separators such as tabs into a table. Another method uses the Table/Insert Table command or the ⊞ button to create a simple table consisting of the same number of rows and columns. The last method, called Draw Table, is used to create any type of table, but is most useful for creating complex tables that contain cells of different heights or a varying number of columns per row. You will use the Draw Table feature to create this table.

■ Click ⊞ Tables and Borders.

The menu equivalent is T**a**ble/Draw Ta**b**le.

The Tables and Borders toolbar appears, and the mouse pointer changes to a pen when positioned in the text area. The Tables and Borders toolbar buttons (identified below) are used to modify table settings.

If the Assistant is on, directions on how to draw a table are displayed.

Using Draw Table to create a table is similar to the way you would use a pen to draw a table. First you define the outer table boundaries, then you draw the column and row lines. A dotted line appears to show the boundary or lines you are creating as you drag. When creating row or column lines, drag from the beginning boundary to the end to extend the line the distance you want.

If necessary, move and dock the Tables and Borders toolbar below the Formatting toolbar.

■ Drag downward and to the right to create an outer table boundary of approximately 2 inches by 6 inches (refer to Figure 4-4).

■ Add four vertical column lines at positions 0.5, 2.25, 3.5, and 4.5 on the ruler (see Figure 4-4 on the next page).

■ Then draw five horizontal lines to create the rows as shown in Figure 4-4. Lines 2, 3, and 4 begin at the first column.

If you make an error, click or click Eraser and drag over the line.

Your screen should be similar to Figure 4-4.

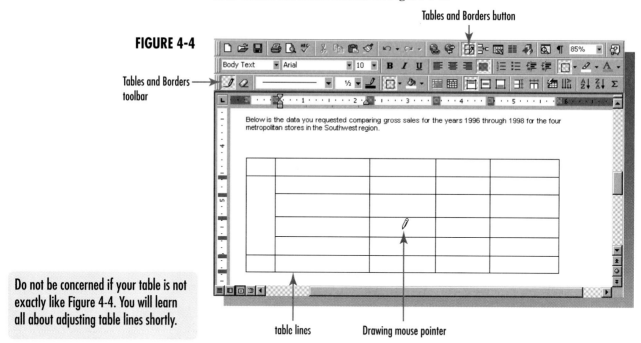

FIGURE 4-4

Tables and Borders button

Tables and Borders toolbar

table lines

Drawing mouse pointer

Do not be concerned if your table is not exactly like Figure 4-4. You will learn all about adjusting table lines shortly.

Entering Data in a Table

Now you are ready to enter information in the table. Each cell contains a single line space where you can enter data. You can move from one cell to another by using the arrow keys or by clicking on the cell. In addition, you can use the keys in the table below to move around a table.

To move to:	Press:
Next cell in a row	Tab
Previous cell in row	Shift + Tab
First cell in row	Alt + Home
Last cell in row	Alt + End
First cell in column	Alt + Page Up
Last cell in column	Alt + Page Down
Previous row	↑
Next row	↓

The mouse pointer may also appear as an arrow when positioned in the table. When it is an arrow and you click on a cell, the entire cell is highlighted, indicating that it is selected. You will learn more about this feature shortly.

You will begin by entering the year column headings 1996 through 1998 in cells C1 through E1. Typing in any cell will turn off the Draw Table feature and allows you to type in the cell as you would anywhere in a normal document.

- Click C1.

- Type **1996**

- Press Tab.

- In the same manner, continue entering the years 1997 and 1998 in cells D1 and E1.

1996	1997	1998

- Next enter the store names and a Total label as row headings and the sales data as shown below.

	Col B	Col C	Col D	Col E
Row 2	#48 – Metro Center Mall	$719,590	$761,000	$782,205
Row 3	#55 – Superstition Springs Mall	544,900	589,800	592,800
Row 4	#57 – Fiesta Mall	620,700	633,800	631,700
Row 5	#62 – Park Central Mall	578,900	569,400	565,300
Row 6	TOTAL			

Your screen should be similar to Figure 4-5.

You can also click at any time to turn on or off the Draw Table feature.

By default, entries in cells are left-aligned horizontally and top-aligned vertically in the cell space.

Include the currency symbol as shown in row 2.

FIGURE 4-5

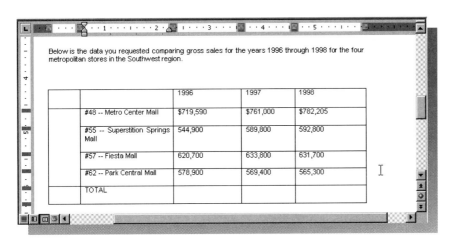

Entering a Formula

Now you are ready to enter the data for the totals. Rather than adding the values for each column of data and entering them in the Total row, you can enter a formula to make this calculation for you.

Concept 2: Formulas and Functions

Formulas and functions are used to perform calculations. A **formula** is a expression that contains any combination of numbers, fields resulting in numbers, table references, and operators. Operators are used to specify the type of calculation to perform. The most common operators are + (add), – (subtract), * (multiply), and / (divide).

To use the operators, follow the common arithmetic laws: multiply and divide before adding and subtracting, and calculate whatever is in parentheses first. For example, the formula, 125 + D3 * D5 will multiply the value in cell D3 by the value in cell D5 and then add 125. If you want to add 125 to D3 and then multiply the result by D5, put 125 and D3 in parentheses: (125 + D3) * D5.

A **function** is a prewritten formula. One function you may use frequently is the SUM function. SUM adds the numbers directly above the current cell. Other functions include:

Function	Description
AVERAGE	Calculates the average of a column of numbers.
COUNT	Totals the number of cells in the column.
MAX	Displays the maximum value in the column.
MIN	Displays the minimum value in the column.

To reference cells in formulas and functions, use a comma to separate references to individual cells and a colon to separate the first and last cells in a block. For example C1, C5 references the values in cells C1 and C5, whereas C1:C5 references the values in cells C1, C2, C3, through C5.

Formulas and functions are entered as fields in the table. The calculated result is displayed in the cell containing the formula or function. Because Word inserts the result of the calculation as a field, if you change the data in the referenced cells in the formula or function, you can update the calculation by selecting the field and then pressing F9.

The formulas and functions in Word let you create simple tables and spreadsheets for your documents. For larger, more complex spreadsheets, use Excel and then paste the spreadsheet into your document.

Refer to Concept 4: Fields in Lab 2 for information on this feature.

To enter the formula to sum the values in the 1996 column of data,

■ Move to cell C6.

■ Click 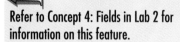 AutoSum.

Your screen should be similar to Figure 4-6.

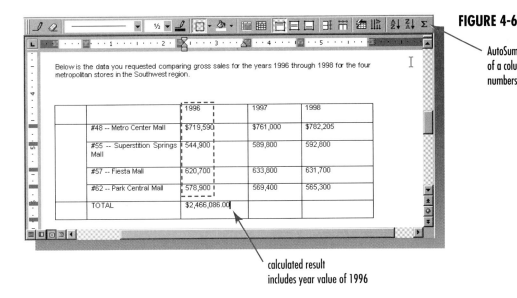

FIGURE 4-6

AutoSum calculates a total of a column or row of numbers

calculated result
includes year value of 1996

The calculated value of $2,466,086.00 is displayed in cell C6. The calculated value for this column is incorrect. It should be $2,464,090. To see the formula used to make the calculation,

- Choose Table/Formula.

In the Formula text box of the Formula dialog box, the function =SUM(ABOVE) is displayed. Using the Σ AutoSum button enters a function that calculates the sum of all the numbers above the current cell. Because it includes the number in cell C1, the year 1996, the calculated total is incorrect. To correct this you need to replace "ABOVE" with the specific table cell references.

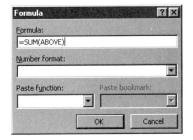

- In place of the word "ABOVE" in the parentheses, enter **C2:C5**

- Click OK.

The formula correctly calculates the result of $2,464,090.00 using the values in the specified cells of the table. Notice that the value is displayed with a dollar sign. This is because Word used the same format as the value in cell C2. It also includes two decimal places by default because most currency entries may include decimals. You decide you do not want the decimal places displayed.

- Select the result and delete the .00 from the entry.

- Enter the functions to calculate the totals for the other two years in cells D6 and E6. Delete the two decimal places from both results.

> If your Total does not display currency symbols, precede the entry in cell C2 with a $, then press F9 in cell C6 to update the display.

> Double-click the word "ABOVE" to quickly select it.

> Because the result is a field, the entire entry is shaded.

The T**a**ble/**I**nsert Columns command is used to add a column to the left of the current column.

The ▦ Insert Cells button on the Standard toolbar can also be used to insert columns and rows.

The menu equivalent is T**a**ble/**M**erge Cells.

Inserting a Row

After looking at the table, you decide to add a row above the years to display a table heading. Because the row will display a table heading centered over all columns of the table, you will also combine the cells in the row to create a single cell.

- ■ Move to cell A1.
- ■ Choose T**a**ble/**I**nsert Rows.
- ■ Click ▦ Merge Cells.
- ■ Click in the cell to clear the highlight.

Your screen should be similar to Figure 4-7.

merges selected cells in table

FIGURE 4-7

inserted row with merged cells

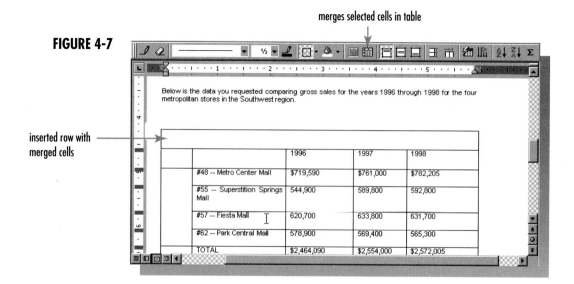

The three column dividers are eliminated, and the top row is one cell. Now you are ready to add the text for the heading and to center it within the cell space. You also want to enter the heading "Store" in cell A3 and align it vertically within the cell space.

- ■ Type **ANNUAL SALES**
- ■ Click ▤ Center.
- ■ Enter **Store** in cell A3.
- ■ Click ▦ Change Text Direction (twice).
- ■ Click ▤ Center.

Your screen should be similar to Figure 4-8.

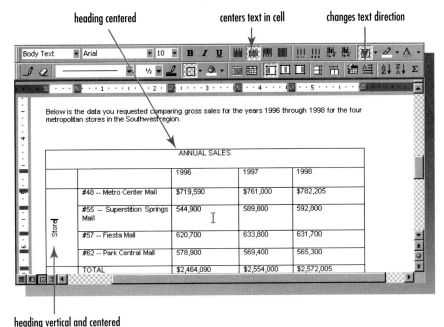

heading centered   centers text in cell   changes text direction

heading vertical and centered

FIGURE 4-8

Changing Column Width

The table is really taking shape. However, it can still be improved by adjusting the size of the columns. You want to increase the width of column B so that the store names are displayed on a single line. To change the width of a column, point to the column divider line and drag it to the right or left to increase or decrease the column width. A temporary dotted line appears to show your new setting.

- Point to the right border of column B. The mouse pointer should be displayed as ⇼.

- Drag to the right to increase the column width to fully display all store names on a single line (approximately 2.5-inch position on the ruler).

You also want to adjust the widths of columns C through E to be equally sized. As you continue to modify the table, many cells can be selected and changed at the same time. The table on page 166 describes how to select different areas of a table.

You can also increase or decrease the height of a row by dragging the row divider line.

The menu equivalent is T**a**ble/Cell Height and **W**idth.

Area to Select	Procedure
Cell	Click the left edge of the cell when the pointer is ⊿.
Row	Click to the left of the row when the pointer is ⊿.
Column	Click the top of the column when the pointer is ↓.
Multiple cells, rows, or columns	Drag through the cells, rows, or columns, or select the first cell, row, or column, and hold down ⇧Shift while clicking on another cell, row, or column.
Contents of next cell	Press Tab⇥.
Contents of previous cell	Press ⇧Shift + Tab⇥.
Entire table	Press Alt + 5 (on the numeric keypad with NumLock off).

> The menu equivalent to select a row is T**a**ble/Select **R**ow, and for a column is T**a**ble/Select **C**olumn.

> The menu equivalent is T**a**ble/Select T**a**ble.

- Select cells C2 through E7.

- Click ⊞ Distribute Columns Evenly.

Your screen should be similar to Figure 4-9.

FIGURE 4-9

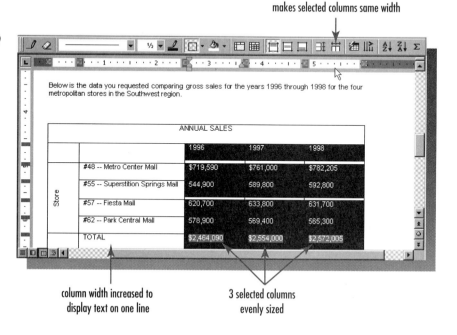

makes selected columns same width

column width increased to display text on one line

3 selected columns evenly sized

Formatting the Table

To enhance the appearance of the table, you can apply many different formats to the cells. This is similar to adding formatting to a document except the formatting affects the selected cells only.

You want the entries in the currently selected range, C2 through E7, to be right-aligned in their cell spaces. You also want the year headings to be centered, 12 pt, and bold, and the table title and the Store heading to be in a different font, larger, and bold. To make these changes,

- Click ▤ Align Right.
- Select cells C2 through E2.
- Change the font to 12 pt and bold.
- Click ▤ Center.
- Change the table title font (cell A1) to Times New Roman, 14 pt, and bold.
- Change the Store heading (cell A3) to Times New Roman, 12 pt, and bold.

Finally, you want to add color shading behind the table title.

- Move to cell A1.
- Open the ▨ ▾ Shading Color drop-down list and select a color of your choice from the color palette.
- Clear the highlight.

Your screen should be similar to Figure 4-10.

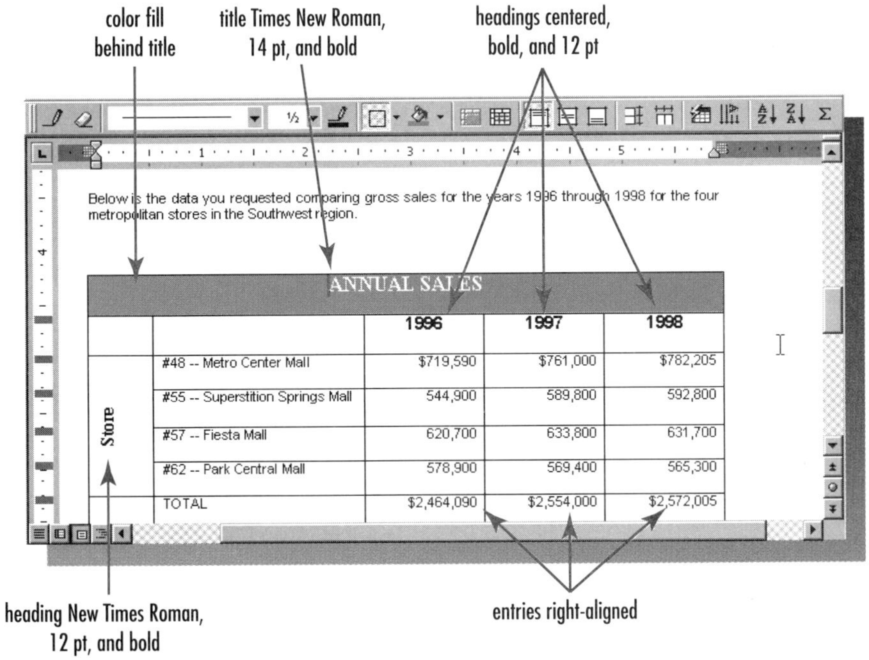

To change the format settings of all text within a cell, simply move to the cell and apply the formats.

You can also use T**a**ble/Table Auto-**F**ormat or ▣ to apply a predesigned table design and layout to an entire table.

color fill behind title / title Times New Roman, 14 pt, and bold / headings centered, bold, and 12 pt

FIGURE 4-10

Below is the data you requested comparing gross sales for the years 1996 through 1998 for the four metropolitan stores in the Southwest region.

ANNUAL SALES			
	1996	**1997**	**1998**
#48 -- Metro Center Mall	$719,590	$761,000	$782,205
#55 -- Superstition Springs Mall	544,900	589,800	592,800
#57 -- Fiesta Mall	620,700	633,800	631,700
#62 -- Park Central Mall	578,900	569,400	565,300
TOTAL	$2,464,090	$2,554,000	$2,572,005

Store

heading New Times Roman, 12 pt, and bold

entries right-aligned

- Apply any additional formatting you wish, such as shadings, different border line weights, text and line colors, and so on, to the table.

- When you are done, close the Tables and Borders toolbar.

The memo is now complete.

- Save the document as Sales Summary Memo.

- Preview, then print the memo (select the appropriate printer).

- Close the file.

Part 2

The Mail Merge Feature

Next you will change the letter sent to new credit card customers to a form letter.

- Open the file Credit Card Letter 4. If necessary, maximize the document window and switch to Normal view.

- If necessary, set the zoom to Page Width so that the entire document width is visible.

This letter is similar to the credit card letter you saved as Revised Credit Card Letter 2 in Lab 2. Notice that the date in the letter on your screen is the same date the file was saved. When this letter is printed, the date will automatically be updated to print the current system date. This is because you entered a date field in the document. To manually update the date displayed on your screen,

- Move to the date field.

- Select Update Field from the Shortcut menu.

To create the personalized form letter to be sent to all new credit card recipients, you will use the Mail Merge feature of Word.

Concept 3: Mail Merge

The **Mail Merge** feature combines a list of data (typically a file of names and addresses) with a document (commonly a form letter) to create a new document. The names and addresses are entered (merged) into the form letter in the blank spaces provided. The result is a personalized form letter.

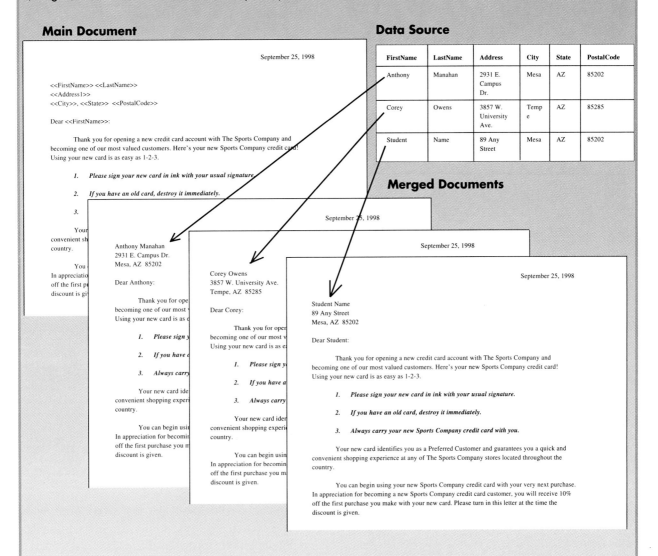

Main Document

Data Source

FirstName	LastName	Address	City	State	PostalCode
Anthony	Manahan	2931 E. Campus Dr.	Mesa	AZ	85202
Corey	Owens	3857 W. University Ave.	Tempe	AZ	85285
Student	Name	89 Any Street	Mesa	AZ	85202

Merged Documents

Mail Merge usually requires the use of two files: a main document and a data source. The **main document** contains the basic form letter. It directs the merge process through the use of merge fields. A **merge field** is a field code that controls what information is used from the data source and where it is entered in the main document. The **data source** contains the information needed to complete the letter in the main document. It can also be called an **address file** because it commonly contains name and address data. Each category of information in the data source is called a **data field**. For example, the customer's first name is a data field, the last name is a data field, the street address is another data field, the city a fourth data field, and so on. All the data fields that are needed to complete the information for one person (or other entity) are called a **record**. Commonly, a database file created using a database application is used as the data source. However, the data source can also be created using Word.

Creating the Main Document

To start the Mail Merge feature,

■   Choose **T**ools/Mail Me**r**ge.

The Mail Merge Helper dialog box on your screen should be similar to Figure 4-11.

FIGURE 4-11

directions ─────

3 steps to create
a merge document

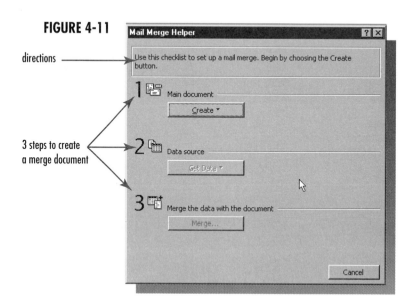

This dialog box is designed to take you step by step through the process of creating a merge. The three steps are:

1.   Create a main document.

2.   Create a data source.

3.   Perform the merge.

The credit card letter will be modified to be the main document. Then you will create the data source of customers' names and addresses using Word. When you perform the merge, Word takes the data field information from the data source and combines or merges it into the main document. The merge fields in the main document control what data fields are used from the data source and where they are entered in the main document.

   To create the main document form letter from the credit letter in the active window,

■   Choose [**C**reate ▾]/Form **L**etters/[**A**ctive Window].

The dialog box now shows the type of merge (Form Letters) and name of the file (Credit Card Letter 4) that will be used as the main document, along with a second button, [Edit ▾], which is used to edit your main document.

Creating the Data Source

The dialog box also now indicates that the next step is to create the data source file. This file will contain the customers' names and addresses, which will be merged with the main document. To create this file,

■ Select [Get Data ▾]/**C**reate Data Source.

The Create Data Source dialog box on your screen should be similar to Figure 4-12.

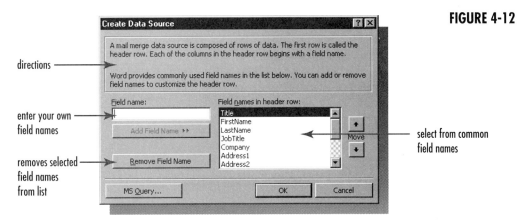

FIGURE 4-12

directions

enter your own field names

removes selected field names from list

select from common field names

In this dialog box you specify the field names for the data that will be entered in the data source file.

Concept 4: Field Names

Field names are used to label each data field in the data source. A field name can contain only letters, numbers, or the underline character. It can be a maximum of 40 characters and cannot contain spaces. The first character of a field name must be a letter. Field names should be descriptive of the contents of the data field.

Commonly used form letter field names are displayed in the Field Names in Header Row list box. You can remove from the list field names that you do not need in your letter, or you can add additional field names to the list by typing them in the Field Name text box. In this case, you will remove field names that you do not want to use in the credit card letter. The first field you do not need is Title. To remove it,

> The Move buttons to the right of the list let you rearrange the order of fields.

■ Click [**R**emove Field Name].

■ In the same manner select and remove the following field names: JobTitle, Company, Address2, Country, HomePhone, and WorkPhone.

The list now reflects only those fields you will include in the data source.

- ■ Click [OK].

- ■ Save the file as Credit Data Source on your data disk.

The informational dialog box displayed on your screen advises you that you need to add the record information to the data source file and edit the main document to include the merge fields. You will add data to the data source file first.

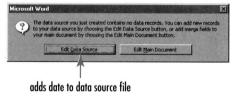

adds date to data source file

- ■ Click [Edit Data Source].

The Data Form dialog box on your screen should be similar to Figure 4-13.

field names

fill in the information for each field to create a record

FIGURE 4-13

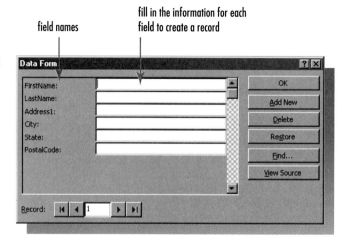

This dialog box displays the field names and a text box to be used to enter the data for each record. The data must be entered exactly as you want it to appear in the letter. If you do not have the information needed to complete a field, you can leave it blank. To enter the data for the first field of the first record, the customer's first name,

- ■ Type **Anthony**

- ■ Press [Tab ⇥] or [←Enter].

- ■ Enter the information for the remaining fields for this record using the following information:

  LastName: **Manahan**

  Address1:   **2931 E. Campus Dr.**

  City: **Mesa**

  State: **AZ**

  PostalCode: **85202**

- ■ If you see any errors in the field data, move back to the entry and edit it.

The dialog box on your screen should be similar to Figure 4-14.

completed information for the first record

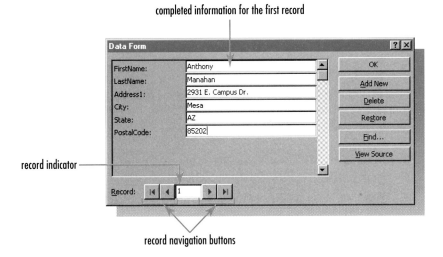

FIGURE 4-14

record indicator

record navigation buttons

To add this record to the data source file and display a new blank data form,

■ Click [Add New].

Notice that the record indicator shows that the current data form will be used to hold the data for the second record.

■ Enter the field data for the second record using the following information:

FirstName: **Corey**

LastName: **Owens**

Address1: **3857 W. University Ave.**

City: **Tempe**

State: **AZ**

PostalCode: **85285**

■ Enter your name and address as the third record in the data source.

■ Move to each of the records and verify the data you entered. If necessary, correct any errors.

You can also view multiple records at once in the window. To see the three records,

■ Choose [View Source].

The record navigation buttons [Record:] can be used to quickly move between records.

The number of records you enter into the data source is limited only by your disk space. At any time, you can add more records using the Data Form as you just did.

Your screen should be similar to Figure 4-15.

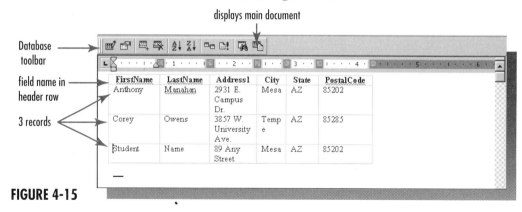

FIGURE 4-15

The data source is displayed in a document window in table form. The field names are displayed as the top row of the table, and each record is displayed as a row. In addition, the Database toolbar shown below is displayed.

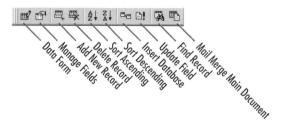

■   If necessary, move the Database toolbar below the Formatting toolbar.

■   Now that the data source contains records, save the file again.

■   Click 🔲 Mail Merge Main Document.

The main document is displayed in the window along with the Mail Merge toolbar shown below.

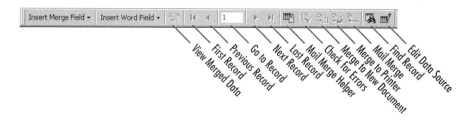

Entering Merge Fields in the Main Document

How will Word know where to enter the customer's name and other source data in the main document? Word uses merge fields to do this. Merge fields direct the program to accept information from the data source at the specified location in the main document. To prepare the credit card letter to accept the fields of information from the data source, you need to add merge fields to the letter.

The credit card letter needs to be modified to allow entry of the name and address information for each preferred customer from the data source. The inside address will hold the following three lines of information:

> FirstName LastName
> Address1
> City, State PostalCode

The first line of the inside address, which will hold the preferred customer's full name, will be entered as line 5 of the credit card letter.

A merge field needs to be entered in the main document for each field of data you want copied from the data source. The location of the merge field indicates where to enter the field data. To position the insertion point on the line where the preferred customer's name will appear as the first line of the inside address, and to enter the fields into the main document,

■ Move to the blank line above the salutation.

■ Click Insert Merge Field ▾ .

A drop-down list of field names from the data source file is displayed. To insert the FirstName merge field at the location of the insertion point,

■ Select FirstName.

Your screen should be similar to Figure 4-16.

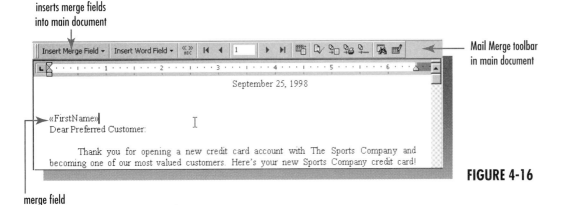

inserts merge fields into main document

Mail Merge toolbar in main document

merge field

FIGURE 4-16

The merge field <<FirstName>> is displayed at the insertion point location in the main document. It is a field code that instructs Word to insert the information from the first name data field (from the data source) at this location in the main document when the merge is performed.

The next merge field that needs to be entered is the preferred customer's last name.

- Press (Spacebar).

- Enter the LastName merge field.

- Press (←Enter).

- Enter the remaining merge fields in the inside address using the punctuation as shown in Figure 4-17.

- Enter a blank line between the inside address and the salutation.

- Then select and replace the words "Preferred Customer" in the salutation with the FirstName merge field.

> The same merge field can be used more than once in the main document.

Your screen should be similar to Figure 4-17.

FIGURE 4-17

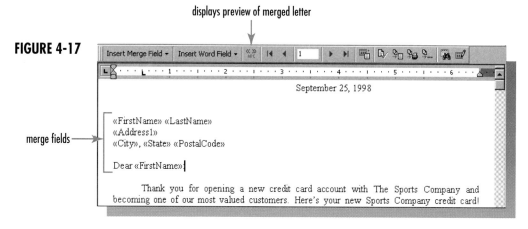

To see how the form letter will appear with the merged data,

- Click [«»] View Merged Data.

Your screen should be similar to Figure 4-18.

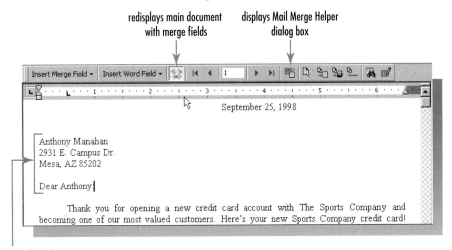

FIGURE 4-18

The data in the first record of the data source is displayed in place of the merge fields. To redisplay the merge fields and check that the entire letter still fits on a single page,

■ Click ⟨⟨⟩⟩ View Merged Data.

■ Preview the letter.

If your letter is longer than one page,

■ Click 🗇 Shrink to Fit.

■ Close the Print Preview window.

■ Save the main document as Credit Main Document.

Performing the Merge

Now that you have created the main document and data source document, you are ready to combine them to create the new personalized credit card letter. During this process a third file is created. The original main document and data source file are not altered or affected in any way. The third file is the result of merging the main document with the data source file.

■ Click 🖼 Mail Merge Helper.

■ Click Merge... .

The Merge dialog box on your screen should be similar to Figure 4-19.

FIGURE 4-19

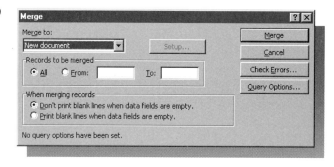

From the Merge dialog box you specify the output you want the merge to create. You can direct the merge to create a new document that contains copies of each form letter generated by the merge, or you can merge directly to the printer to print each form letter. You can also direct the merge to output the form letters to e-mail or a fax if your system is set up to include these features. Finally, if you do not need all records in your data source to receive copies of the form letter, you can specify a range of records to merge or criteria for records to meet. To merge all the records in the data source to a new document,

■ Click .

At the completion of the merge, the file containing the three merge letters is displayed. It has a default file name of Form Letters1.

Your screen should be similar to Figure 4-20.

default merge file name

FIGURE 4-20

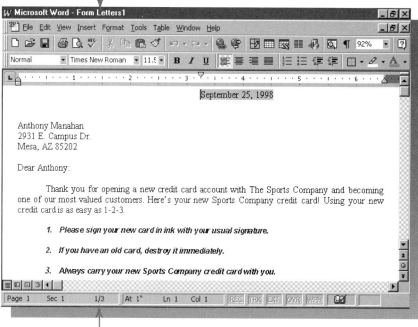

first of three letters created from the merge

Now each time you need to send credit card letters, all you need to do is to edit the preferred customer data source file and issue the Merge command. Because the Date field was used, the date will automatically reflect the date the letter is printed.

- ■ Scroll the document to see the three letters.

- ■ Save the Form Letters1 document to your data disk as Credit Merge Document.

- ■ Print only the letter containing your name and address information.

- ■ Close all document windows, saving the files as necessary.

- ■ Exit Word.

> Each letter is separated by a section break. If a page break line is also displayed, use ▣ Shrink to Fit in the Print Preview window.

LAB REVIEW

■ ■ ■ ■ ■ ■ ■ ■ ▪ ▫

Key Terms

address file   (WP169)
cell   (WP158)
click and type   (WP157)
column   (WP158)
data field   (WP169)
data source   (WP169)
field name   (WP171)
formula   (WP162)
function   (WP162)
Mail Merge   (WP169)
main document   (WP169)
merge field   (WP169)
placeholder   (WP157)
record   (WP169)
row   (WP158)
table   (WP158)
table reference   (WP158)

Command Summary

Command	Button	Action
Table/Draw Table		Creates a table using the Draw Table feature
Table/Insert Table		Inserts a table where you drag in document
Table/Insert Rows		Inserts new rows in a table
Table/Insert Columns		Inserts new columns in a table
Table/Merge Cells		Merges cells in a table
Table/Table AutoFormat		Applies predesigned table layouts to table
Table/Select Row		Selects row in table
Table/Select Column		Selects column in table
Table/Select Table		Selects entire table
Table/Distribute Columns Evenly		Evenly sizes selected columns
Table/Convert Text to Table		Converts existing text separated into columns to a table
Table/Formula		Inserts a formula into a table
Tools/Mail Merge		Starts Mail Merge feature

Matching

1. merge field _____
2. template _____
3. column _____
4. table _____
5. record _____
6. =SUM (ABOVE) _____
7. main document _____

8. row _____

9. data source _____
10. cell _____

a. data that runs vertically in a table

b. function that adds the numbers directly above the current cell

c. intersection of a row and a column in a table

d. data that runs horizontally in a table

e. file that contains the data for a main document

f. display of data that contains rows and columns

g. controls what information is used from the data source and where it is entered in the main document

h. all the fields of data that are needed to complete the information for one entity

i. a predesigned document

j. the basic form letter that directs the merge process

Discussion Questions

1. There are several methods you can use to create a table. Describe each and explain when they would be used.

2. What is the significance of using a column and row format in tables? How are the rows and columns labeled?

3. Describe the use of formulas and functions in tables. How are they an advantage over entering fixed values?

4. Describe how the Mail Merge feature works. What are some advantages of using Mail Merge?

5. What steps are used to create the data source file? How is the data used in a main document?

Fill-In Questions

1. Complete the following statements by filling in the blanks with the correct terms.

   a. To create a merged document you need a _____ file and a(n) _____ file.

   b. The data source consists of _____ made up of _____.

   c. The _____ is used to create a complex table.

   d. The _____ identifies the cells in a table.

   e. _____ and _____ are used to perform calculations in tables.

Hands-On Practice Exercises

Step by Step

	Rating System		
		☆	Easy
		☆☆	Moderate
		☆☆☆	Difficult

1. In this exercise you will create a memo informing employees that a new time sheet form will be used effective next Monday.

   a. Create the memo below using the Professional Memo template.

Note: You will only have to press ⊣Enter once after each paragraph in the body of the memo. If you open the Paragraph dialog box and look at the Indents and Spacing tab, you will notice that this template includes 11 pt spacing after each paragraph. If you set up your document in this manner before typing, you can eliminate the need to press ⊣Enter two times after each paragraph.

To: [Your Name]
From: Mr. J. B. Briggs
CC: Payroll Department
Date: [Current Date]
Re: New Time Sheets

This Friday will mark the last day that you will use the old time sheets. Below is a sample of the new time sheets we will be using effective next Monday.

Please make sure that your time sheet is turned in no later than 9:00 a.m. the Monday after each pay period ends so that Payroll can process your check on time.

Thank you for your cooperation in this matter.

	Date	Time In	Time Out	Regular Hours	Overtime Hours	Total Hours
Monday	1/6/97	8:00	5:00	8	0	8
Tuesday	1/7/97	8:00	5:00	8	0	8
Wednesday	1/8/97	8:00	5:00	8	0	8
Thursday	1/9/97	7:00	6:00	8	3	11
Friday	1/10/97	7:00	6:00	8	3	11
Total Hours						46

b. Select and delete the Company Name Here box in the upper right corner.

c. Create the sample time sheet (as shown above) below the memo using the Draw Table feature.

d. Apply a table autoformat of your choice to the table.

e. Use a formula to calculate the Total Hours column. Make sure all numbers are right-aligned.

f. Enter and format a row to display a table title.

g. Adjust the column widths appropriately and make additional formatting changes to improve the appearance of the table as needed.

h. Document the file and save it as Time Sheet Memo. Print the document.

2. As the owner of Susie's Sundries, you are replenishing your stock of some very popular items: widgets, gadgets, smidgens, and do-dads. In this exercise you will create an order form.

Item	Vendor	Quantity	Unit Cost	Total Cost
Widgets	Wonder Widgets	100	.50	
Gadgets	Gadgets Galore	100	2.00	
Smidgens	Smidgen Sensations	50	12.00	
Do-Dads	Do-Dad Delights	250	10.00	
Grand Total				

a. Use Draw Table to create the table shown above.

b. Enter the formula =c2*d2 to calculate a total for widgets. While you are in the Formula dialog box, use the Number Format drop-down list to apply the second format (#,###.00) to the value. Using this logic, calculate totals and apply the same number format to all values representing total amounts for gadgets, smidgens, and do-dads.

c. Calculate a grand total at the bottom of the Total Cost column. Format the grand total amount to display a dollar sign (third Number Format option). Bold the grand total value. Merge this row to a single cell.

d. Select the entire table and use the AutoFit option located in the Column tab of the Cell Height and Width dialog box to accommodate the widest entry in each column.

e. Insert a row at the top of the table and merge the cells. Enter the title "Order Form" in a different font that is larger than the text in the rest of the table. Center this title.

f. Left-align all entries in the first two columns, and right-align all number entries (and their column headings) in subsequent columns.

g. Insert your name and the current date in a header.

h. Document the file and save it as Order Form Table. Print the form.

3. To complete this exercise, you must have completed Practice Exercise 4 in Lab 1. In this exercise, you will create a form letter to be sent to the friends and relatives who want a copy of Grandma Gertie's cookie recipes.

a. Open the file Cookie Letter from your data disk.

b. Follow the procedures you learned in this lab to define the document in the active window as the main document, and create the data source. Assign the file name Cookie Data Source. Enter the following records and at least three more of your own choice:

Susan
Wagner
463 E. Tioga Ave.
Forty Fort
PA
18704

George
Peterson
832 Colonial Dr.
Wellesley
MA
02181

c. When you are finished entering the records, view the data source file. Save the data source file again.

d. In the Cookie Letter document, create an inside address by inserting data source merge fields above the salutation. In the salutation replace "Friends and Family" with the FirstName merge field.

e. Insert the current date as a field above the inside address and right-align it.

f. Increase the font size for the letter to 12 pt. Justify the letter. Center your return address. When you are finished, document the file and save the letter as Cookie Main Document.

g. Merge the data source and main document files. Document the merge file and save the merged letters as Cookie Merge Document. Print the letters.

4. To complete this exercise, you must have completed Practice Exercise 2 in Lab 2. In this exercise, you will modify the document Acceptance Letter to be a form letter.

a. Open the file Acceptance Letter from your data disk. Define Acceptance Letter as the main document, and create a data source named Student Data Source consisting of the following fields. (Hint: After you have removed all unnecessary fields, enter the field name Major in the Field Name text box. Then click the Add Field Name button.)

Title
FirstName
LastName
Address1
City
State
PostalCode
Major

b. Enter information that pertains to you as record 1 of the data source, and then enter records for three of your friends. When you have finished entering records, view the data source. Document the file and resave it.

c. Modify the Acceptance Letter to contain appropriate merge fields where your name, address, or major appears throughout the letter. Insert the cur-

rent date as a field. You might have to right-align the date again. Increase the font size to 12 pt for the entire letter. Use the Shrink to Fit command if the entire letter does not fit on one page. Document and save the modified main document as Student Main Document.

d. Merge the letters. Document and save the file as Student Merge Document. Print the letters.

5. Murphy's Department Store is holding a private sale for its preferred customers. As CEO, you are sending a "personal" letter to each of these customers inviting them to the sale.

a. Open the file Preferred Customer from your data disk. Cut the first line ("murphy's") to the Clipboard, and paste it (Ctrl + V) into the WordArt Enter Your Text Here dialog box. Create a title using the WordArt features you learned in Lab 3. Center the title, and enter another blank line below it.

b. Go to the line of text below the title. Set a centered tab at the 3-inch position, and a right-aligned tab at 6 inches. Move the street address to the centered tab, and move the city, state, and postal code information to the right tab. Draw a box around this line.

c. Use Find and Replace to locate and replace "preferred customer" with "Special Preferred Customer" in the first and third paragraphs only. Bold and italicize those two occurrences of "Special Preferred Customer." Italicize the text "Any day this month" at the beginning of the second paragraph.

d. Use the Insert Date and Time command to replace [Current Date] at the top of the document.

e. Use the active document to create a form letter. Create a data source named Customer Data Source that contains the following fields:

Title
FirstName
LastName
Address1
City
State
PostalCode

f. Enter the following records:

Mr. Joel Allen
316 River St.
Wilkes-Barre, PA 18702

Ms. Ronnie Lee
452 Valley View Dr.
Shavertown, PA 18706

Mr. Dean Walter
409 Laurel Rd.
Mountain Top, PA 18707

g. When you are finished entering records, view the data source. Document the file and resave it.

h. In the main document, insert fields representing the customers' names and addresses above the salutation line. Remove "Preferred Customer" from the salutation, and replace it with the customer's FirstName merge field. Remove [Customer's First Name] from the third paragraph, and replace it with the appropriate merge field code. Insert your name as the CEO in the closing.

i. Document the file and save the main document as Customer Main Document. Merge the main document and the data source. Document the merged letter file and save it as Customer Merge Document. Print the letters.

On Your Own

6. Use Draw Table to create a schedule of your classes for the semester. The column headings should display the days of the week, and the row headings should display hours. The cells below the column headings should display the classes you have on those days. Include a merged cell to display a table title. Appropriately format the table to improve its appearance. Document and save the file as Schedule. Print the document.

7. In this exercise you will use the Draw Table feature to create a resume.

Create a table with two columns and sixteen rows.

Apply the Grid 1-AutoFormat and clear the Borders check box under Formats to Apply so that no borders will print.

Note: When the table is displayed, dotted grid lines will be displayed for you to use as a guide. These lines will not print, however.

Career Objective		Type your objective(s) here.
Education		
	Date: [Enter Date Here]	Institution City Degree Courses included:
Work Experience (most recent first)		
	Date: [Enter Date Here]	Your Job Title Name of Company Duties Included:
Activities		List Activities
Honors and Awards		List Honors and Awards (Dean's List, Who's Who)
Special Skills		List skills that would enhance your job performance
References		List References or "Available upon request from…"

Enter the resume headings in column A as displayed in the table above.

Enter resume information into column B. Cells follow the same formatting rules as a paragraph. If you right-align a cell, all entries in the cell will be right-aligned. When listing information that exceeds the width of a cell, overflow information will wrap to the next line. You can press ⏎Enter to add multiple lines (for example, the date, job title, company, and duties) to a cell. If you had more than one job or graduated from more than one school, you can enter additional information below the first set of information in the same cell.

When you are finished, increase the font size to 12 pt.

Create a centered return address above the table. The return address should contain your name, address, city, state, postal code, and phone number(s). It can be slightly larger than the resume text, and you can use a different font to attract attention. Just don't get too carried away! Remember . . . keep it conservative.

If the document does not fit on one page, reduce the margins to 1 inch all around. If the document still does not fit, use the Shrink to Fit command.

When you are finished, document and save the file as Resume. Print the resume.

☆☆☆

8. To complete this exercise, you must have completed Practice Exercise 7 in Lab 1. Open the file Cover Letter from your data disk. In this exercise you will create a data source and convert the Cover Letter to a main document file.

Create the data source containing at least three prospective employers, using information of your own choice. Use the fields that are described in the return address of the Lab 1 exercise. Save the file as Cover Data Source.

Insert the data source fields into the appropriate locations of the Cover Letter to create a main document. Increase the font size of the letter to 12 pt and change the font.

Hint: Use a font for the cover letter and resume that is conservative and easy to read. When in doubt, use Times New Roman and/or Arial. Fancy fonts (script, for example) can be difficult to read, and Courier looks as though you just "cranked it out" on a typewriter. You're better than that!

Save the file as Cover Main Document.

Merge the two files. Document the merged letter file and save it as Cover Merge Document. Print the letters.

Concept Summary

Creating a Table and Merging Documents

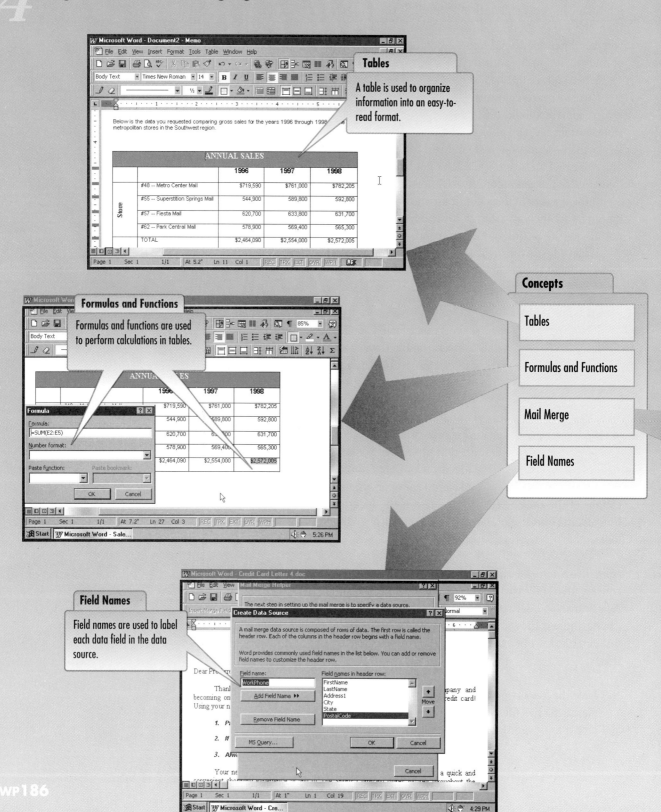

Tables

A table is used to organize information into an easy-to-read format.

Formulas and Functions

Formulas and functions are used to perform calculations in tables.

Field Names

Field names are used to label each data field in the data source.

Concepts

- Tables
- Formulas and Functions
- Mail Merge
- Field Names

Main Document

September 25, 1998

<<FirstName>> <<LastName>>
<<Address1>>
<<City>>, <<State>> <<PostalCode>>

Dear <<FirstName>>:

Thank you for opening a new credit card account with The Sports Company and becoming one of our most valued customers. Here's your new Sports Company credit card! Using your new card is as easy as 1-2-3.

1.   *Please sign your new card in ink with your usual signature.*

2.   *If you have an old card, destroy it immediately.*

3.   *Always carry your new Sports Company credit card with you.*

Your new card identifies you as a Preferred Customer and guarantees you a quick and convenient shopping experience at any of The Sports Company stores located throughout the country.

You can begin using your new Sports Company credit card with your very next purchase. In appreciation for becoming a new Sports Company credit card customer, you will receive 10% off the first purchase you make with your new card. Please turn in this letter at the time the discount is given.

Additionally, each month you will receive The Sports Company Update, a newsletter about new products, sports trends, sports safety tips, and upcoming events. The newsletter will also include announcements of special sale days for our preferred customers only. If you have questions about an event, call 1-800-555-9839 or come in and speak to the Customer Service representative.

We are the leading sports store in the Southwest with a tradition of personal, friendly service. As you use your new Sports Company credit card, you will discover the many conveniences that only our credit customers enjoy.

We are delighted with the opportunity to serve you and we look forward to seeing you soon.

Sincerely,

The Sports Company Manager

Data Source

FirstName	LastName	Address	City	State	PostalCode
Anthony	Manahan	2931 E. Campus Dr.	Mesa	AZ	85202
Corey	Owens	3857 W. University Ave.	Tempe	AZ	85285
Student	Name	89 Any Street	Mesa	AZ	85202

Merged Documents

September 25, 1998

Anthony Manahan
2931 E. Campus Dr.
Mesa, AZ 85202

Dear Anthony:

Thank you for opening a new credit card becoming one of our most valued customers. Here's Using your new card is as easy as 1-2-3.

1.   *Please sign your new card in ink*

2.   *If you have an old card, destroy i*

3.   *Always carry your new Sports C*

Your new card identifies you as a Prefer convenient shopping experience at any of The Sport country.

September 25, 1998

Corey Owens
3857 W. University Ave.
Tempe, AZ 85285

Dear Corey:

Thank you for opening a new becoming one of our most valued custom Using your new card is as easy as 1-2-3.

1.   *Please sign your new card*

2.   *If you have an old card*

3.   *Always carry your new*

Your new card identifies you convenient shopping experience at any of country.

September 25, 1998

Student Name
89 Any Street
Mesa, AZ 85202

Dear Student:

Thank you for opening a new credit card account with The Sports Company and becoming one of our most valued customers. Here's your new Sports Company credit card! Using your new card is as easy as 1-2-3.

1.   *Please sign your new card in ink with your usual signature.*

2.   *If you have an old card, destroy it immediately.*

3.   *Always carry your new Sports Company credit card with you.*

Your new card identifies you as a Preferred Customer and guarantees you a quick and convenient shopping experience at any of The Sports Company stores located throughout the country.

Mail Merge

The Mail Merge feature combines a list of data (typically a file of names and addresses) with a document (commonly a form letter) to create a new document.

Creating a Web Page

COMPETENCIES

After completing this lab, you will know how to:

1. Design a Web page.
2. Create an HTML document.
3. Insert inline images.
4. Create hyperlinks.
5. Make a Web page public.

CASE STUDY

The Sports Company has decided to join the Internet by creating a World Wide Web site for the company. They hope to be able to promote their products through the Web site and broaden the audience of customers. In addition to the obvious marketing and sales potential, they want to provide an avenue for interaction between themselves and the customer to improve their customer service. They also want the Web site to provide articles of interest to the customers. The articles would include topics such as nutrition and fitness and would change on a monthly basis as an added incentive for readers to return to the site.

You have been asked to develop an overall design and layout for the Web site. Your completed Web page will look like that shown below.

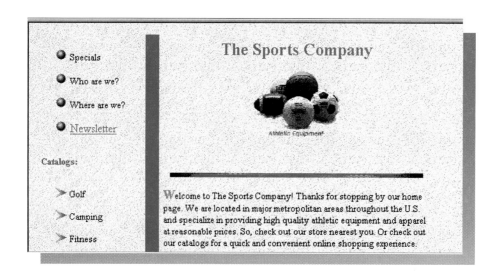

Concept Overview

The following concepts will be introduced in this lab:

1. Web Sites and Home Pages — The World Wide Web is a massive collection of Web sites. The top-level or opening page of a Web site is called the home page.

2. Web Page Design — You can add many elements to a Web page, such as graphic objects, images, art, and color, to make it attractive and easy to use.

3. Hypertext Markup Language — All pages on the WWW are written using a programming language called HTML (Hypertext Markup Language).

4. Inline Images — Word inserts graphics in Web pages as inline images, which are positioned directly in the text at the insertion point.

5. Hyperlinks — Hyperlinks provide a way to quickly jump to other documents, objects, or Web pages.

Designing Your Web Page

The Sports Company's plans for the Web site include a home page that will link to additional Web pages such as a catalog, order form, newsletter, and customer service. You have been asked to develop an overall plan for the Web site and to design the home page for the site.

Concept 1: Web Sites and Home Pages

The **World Wide Web** (WWW or Web for short) is a massive collection of Web sites. Web **sites** are locations on computers called **servers** that store the documents contained at the site. The basic document of the WWW is a **page**. Each site usually consists of many pages. Some large servers support multiple sites.

The top-level or opening page of a site is called the **home page.** It is displayed by default when a user visits your Web site. A site may even have many home pages if it is very large. The home page usually contains an introduction to the site along with connections that allow you to jump to another location on the same page, to another page in the same site, or to another page on a different site altogether. These connections may also be to a multimedia file such as a video or audio clip or even to a program.

When creating or **authoring** a Web page, you want to make the page both attractive and informative. You also want it to be easy to use and you want it to work right. It is important therefore to plan the design of the Web site and the pages it will include.

Concept 2: Web Page Design

You can add many elements to a Web page to make it attractive and easy to use. Graphic objects, images, art, and color are perhaps the most important features of Web pages. They entice the user to continue to explore the Web site.

You can also use forms to make your Web page interactive. **Forms** are collections of fields that you can use to get information or feedback from users. When the user submits a completed form, it is sent to a form handler where it is processed.

Other elements, such as animations, scrolling banners, blinking text, audio, and video can be added to a Web page to make it even more dynamic. With all these elements available, it is easy to add too many to a page and end up with a cluttered and distracting mess. Keep the following design tips in mind when authoring your own Web pages.

- Text should be readable against the background. Check for proper spelling and grammar.

- Background colors and patterns add interest and pizazz to a page, but be careful that they do not make the page hard to read. Additionally, keep in mind that more complex patterns take longer to download. Since many users have 256-color monitors, higher-resolution colors will be lost and may not look good on their monitors.

- Adding graphics and animations to a page make it more interesting, but keep them simple to speed up downloading, and avoid busy animations and blinking text. A good suggestion is to keep images less than 100K in file size. Smaller is even better.

- At the bottom of each page, include navigation links back to the home page and other major site pages so users will not get lost. Also include text links for users who have turned off graphics loading in their browsers to improve their speed.

- Page dimensions should be the same as the browser window size. Because many users have their screen resolution set to 640 x 480 pixels, designing a page for 600 x 800 pixels will be too large for their screens.

- Get permission before using text, sounds, and images that are copyrighted. Copyright laws and infringement fines apply to pages posted on the Internet.

You and the marketing manager have discussed the features that The Sports Company wants to include in their Web site pages. For example, the manager suggested that the site use the company colors of blue and green, and wanted to include a graphic image on the home page to make the site more interesting to view. After considering these features, you drew a sample page layout that you feel may be both interesting and easy to use.

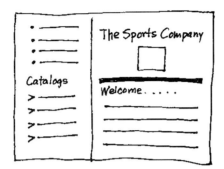

You have already entered in a Word document the text that will be displayed on the home page.

- ■ If necessary, turn on your computer and load Word.
- ■ Open the file Home Page Text from your data disk.

Your screen should be similar to Figure 5-1.

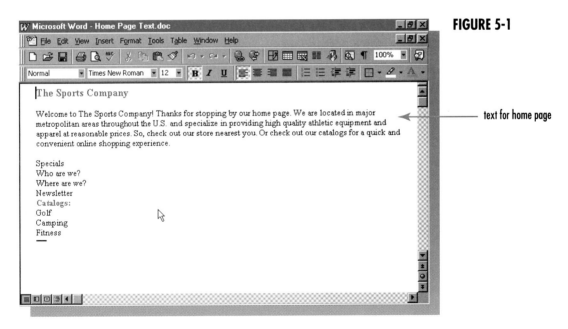

FIGURE 5-1

As you can see, this is a simple text document. The only enhancements you have made to this document are a few text formats.

Creating an HTML Document

Your next step is to change this document into an HTML (Hypertext Markup Language) document that can be used on the WWW, and to add the design elements to the page.

> ### Concept 3: Hypertext Markup Language
>
> All pages on the WWW are written using a programming language called **HTML (Hypertext Markup Language)**. HTML commands control how the information on a page is displayed, such as font colors and size, and how an item, such as a form, will be processed. HTML also allows users to click on highlighted text or images and jump to other locations on the same page, other pages in the same site, or to other sites and locations on the WWW altogether.
>
> HTML commands are interpreted by the browser software program you are using to access the WWW. The **browser** is a program that connects you to the remote computers and displays the pages you request. The server stores the pages and sends them to a browser when requested.
>
> Every item on a Web page has properties associated with it that are encoded in HTML **tags**, which are embedded codes that supply information about the page's structure, appearance, and contents. They tell your browser where the title, heading, paragraphs, images, and other information are to appear on the page. In addition, they designate links to other Web pages. Examples of some simple tags and their effects are shown below.
>
> | Tagged text | Effect |
> | --- | --- |
> | <B> Hello </B> | **Hello** (makes it bold) |
> | <P> text </P> | Marks the beginning and end of paragraph |
> | <TITLE>The Sports Company</TITLE> | Displays text as a title for the page |
>
> All Web pages commonly include a title, different levels of headings, and text design elements such as horizontal rules. Each of these elements has its own tag.

Tags do not show when you load the HTML page on your browser.

This document needs to be changed to HTML format. Word includes an authoring tool that lets you create a Web page without needing to know the HTML codes. It generates the HTML tags automatically while you are using many of the same features that you would use to create a text document, such as spelling and grammar checking, AutoText, and tables. You can apply bold, italic, underline, strikethrough, superscript, and subscript formats to selected text. Some features, such as graphical bullets and lines, are customized for use in pages to make Web authoring easier.

Features that are not supported by HTML or other Web browsers are not available when you author Web pages. This includes the emboss, shadow, and engrave character formatting effects, line spacing, margins, and spacing before and after paragraphs. Tabs are not available because they are displayed as spaces by many Web browsers. Instead, to shift the first line of text to the right, you can use an indent.

Word offers three ways to create Web pages. You can use the Web Page Wizard to help you quickly create a Web page. The Web Wizard provides dialog boxes from which you select a layout and graphical designs. The Web Wizard creates a sample Web page based on your selections, which you then can modify to your own needs. The second method is to convert an existing Word document to HTML. Finally, you can start with a blank Web page.

You will convert the simple text document to an HTML document. Word converts the file by adding the HTML tags to the document and then by saving it to a new file with an .html file extension.

- Choose File/Save as HTML.

- Save the file as Sports Company Home Page on your data disk.

- Click [Save].

Your screen should be similar to Figure 5-2.

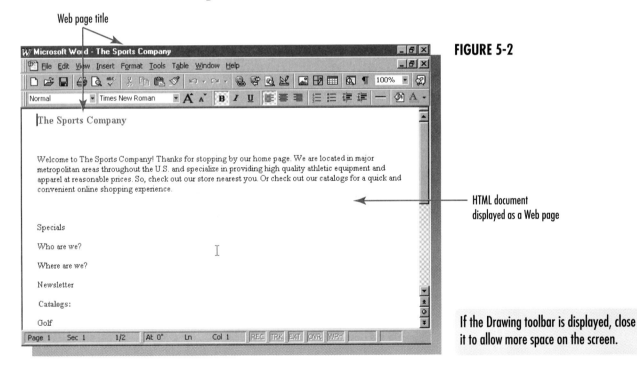

FIGURE 5-2

If the Drawing toolbar is displayed, close it to allow more space on the screen.

Word displays the HTML document as a Web page in a format that is similar to how it will appear in a Web browser. The formatting and features that are supported by HTML, in this case the text size and color attributes, have been converted to HTML format. To see the HTML code,

- Choose View/HTML Source.

The Web page title, rather than the file name, is displayed in the title bar.

Your screen should be similar to Figure 5-3.

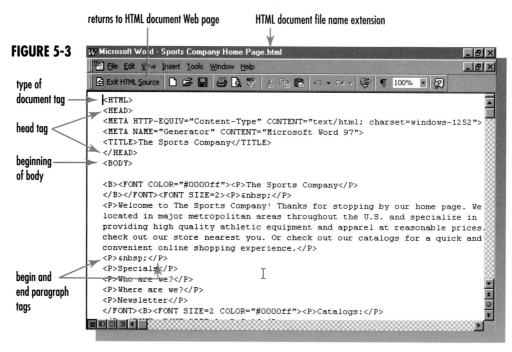

returns to HTML document Web page   HTML document file name extension

FIGURE 5-3

type of document tag

head tag

beginning of body

begin and end paragraph tags

All HTML document files begin with the <HTML> tag, which tells the browser that the document it is reading is an HTML document. They also contain a <HEAD> tag, which includes basic information needed by the browser, and a <TITLE> tag identifying the text to be used as the title of the page, which is usually displayed in the browser window title bar. The <BODY> tag indicates the area where the body of the page will appear. Each paragraph begins and ends with a paragraph tag (<P> </P>). Converting this document to HTML format using Word was a lot easier than learning to enter the code yourself. To return to the Web page,

■ Click  .

Inserting Inline Images

Below the company name on the Web page, you want to display a picture. Pictures and other types of graphic objects are one of the most important features of Web pages. Authors use images to provide information or decoration, or to communicate their personal or organizational style. They are also commonly used to display graphic artwork or pictures of products for sale. Graphic objects that appear when a Web page is loaded are called inline images.

Concept 4: Inline Images

Graphics cannot be embedded in Web pages as they can in Word documents. Therefore Word inserts graphics as inline images. **Inline images** are inserted directly in the text at the insertion point, as opposed to graphics, which are inserted in layers that stack. Thus you can position inline images precisely on the page or in front of or behind text or other objects.

Each graphic you insert in an HTML file is stored in a separate file that is accessed and loaded by the browser when the page is loaded. Word creates a link, which includes the location and file name, to the object's file in the HTML file. When graphic files are added to a page, they are copied to the same folder location as the page. They must always reside in the same location as the HTML document file in which they are used.

Graphic objects are commonly inserted into HTML documents in GIF and JPEG file formats. If you insert an image that is not in either of these formats, the image will be saved in the GIF format when the file is saved.

You can also add drawing objects, such as shapes created using the Drawing toolbar and WordArt, to a Web page. When the HTML file is closed, however, and they have been converted to GIF file format, they can no longer be edited in Word when you reopen the HTML file. In these cases, it is a good idea to also save the Word file as a regular document in case you want to edit these objects at a later date. Then you can insert the edited object in place of the original object in the HTML page.

JPEG files use the file name extension .jpg.

You want to add to the Web page a picture that is representative of some of the items The Sports Company sells, along with a colored and textured background.

- Move to the blank space below the company name.

- Click [⊞] Insert Picture.

- Change the location to your data disk and select the picture file Balls.gif.

- Click [Insert].

- Select the picture and reduce the size to be similar to that in Figure 5-4. Deselect the picture.

Drag the corner handle to maintain picture proportions.

- Click [⬧] Background.

- Select **F**ill Effects.

- From the Texture palette, select Blue Tissue Paper.

the menu equivalent is F**o**rmat/ Bac**k**ground.

- Click [OK].

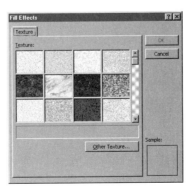

Your screen should be similar to Figure 5-4.

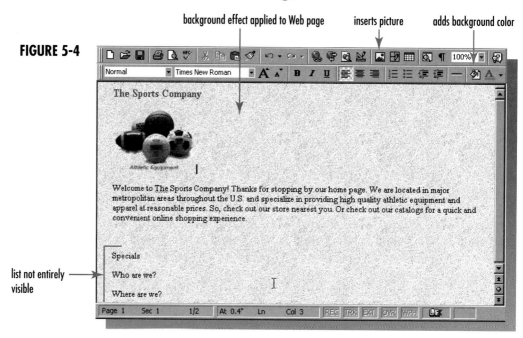

FIGURE 5-4

background effect applied to Web page   inserts picture   adds background color

list not entirely visible

So far your page is very plain and contains a lot of blank space. In addition you want the entire list to be visible without scrolling the page. You will continue to make several changes to improve the appearance of the page. First you will change the layout of the page so that the list of items will appear to the left of the company name and welcome text, making it unnecessary to scroll the page. Unlike a regular document where you could use columns to display text side by side, in a Web page you need to use a table to control the page layout. The table allows you to place items in different locations on the Web page. You want to create a table the full width of the text on the page (6 inches) and approximately 2 inches deep with three vertical cells.

The mouse pointer changes to a pen so you can draw a table.

Display the ruler by pointing to the top boundary of the window. The ruler will temporarily display so you can check the table size and line locations.

- ■ Click [⊞] Tables and Borders.

- ■ Drag to create the outside boundary of the table (approximately 6 inches wide by 2 inches high) starting at the very top of the page above the company name.

- ■ Draw a vertical column line at the 2-inch position and another about 0.25 inch to the right of the first (refer to Figure 5-5).

- ■ Click [⊞] Tables and Borders.

Your screen should be similar to Figure 5-5.

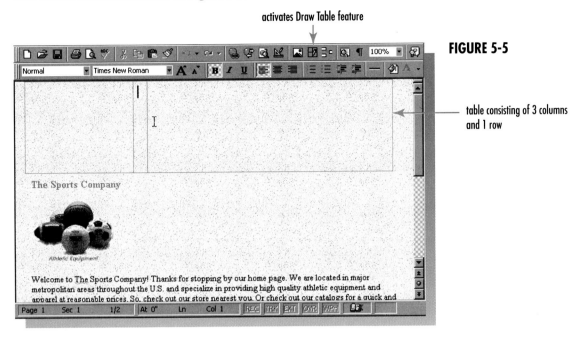

activates Draw Table feature

FIGURE 5-5

table consisting of 3 columns and 1 row

Next you need to move the text and picture into the appropriate cells of table.

- Select the title, picture, and welcome paragraph. Cut and paste (or drag) this selection into the rightmost cell of table. Clear the highlight.

- Select the list of items. Cut and paste (or drag) this selection into the leftmost cell of the table. Clear the highlight.

Your screen should be similar to Figure 5-6.

text and graphics moved into table cells

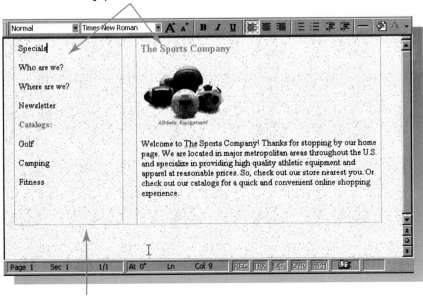

FIGURE 5-6

table boundary increases to accommodate cell contents

As you moved the selections into the table cells, the table boundary increased to accommodate the cell contents. It expands the table to the maximum size that can be displayed in the window. If additional space were needed, a new cell would be created to hold the overflow.

To see how your page will look when displayed by your browser, you can preview it.

> The menu equivalent is **File/Web Page Preview**.

- Click  Web Page Preview.

You are prompted to save the changes you have made to the HTML file before previewing the page. This is necessary so that the links to the inline image graphic files are correctly saved, and so the browser can load and display the most up-to-date version of your page.

- Click [OK].

Your screen should be similar to Figure 5-7.

FIGURE 5-7

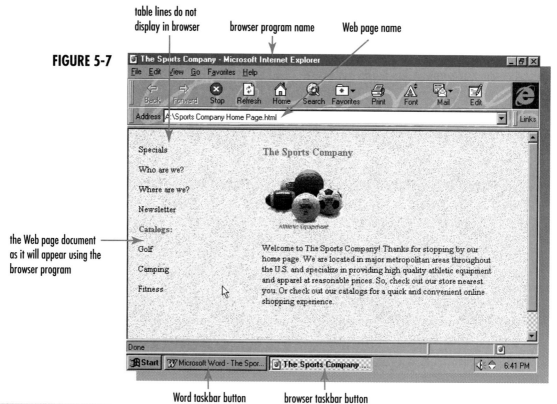

table lines do not display in browser   browser program name   Web page name

the Web page document as it will appear using the browser program

Word taskbar button   browser taskbar button

> Your screen will display the Web page in the browser that is on your computer system.

The browser on your system is loaded offline, and the page you are working on is displayed in the browser window.

> Offline means the browser program is not connected to the Internet.

All the information you want is visible in the browser window, but it is still not very visually appealing. You want to add formatting, lines, bullets, and other enhancements to improve its appearance. To return to the Word document,

■ Click [📝 Microsoft Word - The Spor...] in the taskbar.

First you will increase the size of the title and center it. In HTML documents, font sizes are not measured in points, but in a range from 1 to 7. When a file is converted to HTML, point sizes are converted to the closest HTML size.

■ Select the company name.

■ Click [A] Increase Font Size (2 times).

■ Click [≡] Center.

■ Select and center the picture.

Your screen should be similar to Figure 5-8.

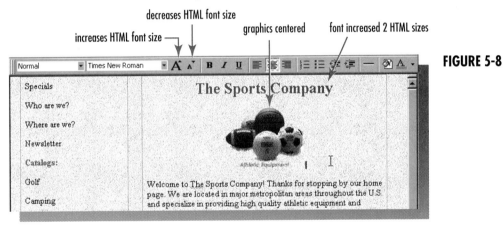

increases HTML font size —
decreases HTML font size
graphics centered
font increased 2 HTML sizes

FIGURE 5-8

Next you want to separate the headline area from the welcome paragraph with a horizontal line. Word includes special graphic horizontal lines that can only be used in Web pages.

■ Move to the beginning of the paragraph.

■ Select Insert/Horizontal line.

■ Select the fifth line style (rainbow).

■ Click [OK].

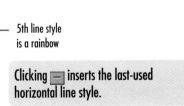

5th line style
is a rainbow

Clicking [━] inserts the last-used horizontal line style.

With the addition of the horizontal line, the text in the paragraph may have overlapped below the cell space.

■ If this happened, reduce the size of the picture to allow the entire paragraph to display in the cell space.

You also want to add emphasis to the paragraph by increasing the font size of the first letter of the word Welcome and adding color to it.

- ■ Select W.

- ■ Click **A̅** Increase Font Size (2 times).

- ■ Change the format to bold and the text color to green.

- ■ Clear the highlight.

Your screen should be similar to Figure 5-9.

FIGURE 5-9

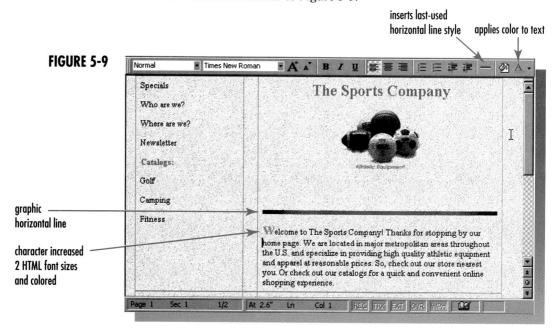

graphic
horizontal line

character increased
2 HTML font sizes
and colored

inserts last-used
horizontal line style   applies color to text

Next you want to add bullets to the items in the list. Like the special graphic horizontal lines, Word includes special graphic bullets that can be used on Web pages.

- ■ Select the top four items in the list.

- ■ Choose F**o**rmat/Bullets and **N**umbering/ Bulleted/ More... /Green Ball.gif/ Insert .

- ■ Select the bottom three items and add the

  > bullet style.

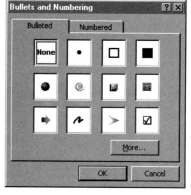

> Like regular bullets, these bulleted items are also automatically indented.

You would like again to see how your changes look. Each time you want to preview how your changes will look in the browser, you need to save the Web page file. In addition, because the browser is already open, you can simply switch to the window.

■ Click 💾 Save.

■ Switch to the browser window.

The browser still displays the original page. To see the changes you have made,

■ Click Refresh.

Your screen should be similar to Figure 5-10.

> Click the browser's taskbar button.

> On some browsers, the button is 🔄 Reload.

graphic bullets   reloads file and updates image display

FIGURE 5-10

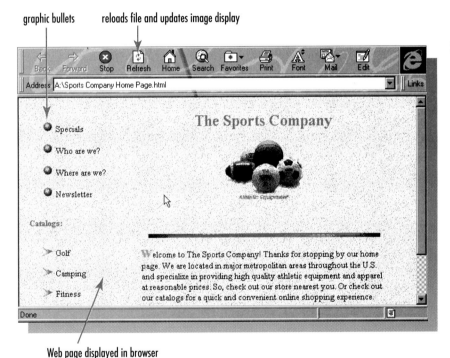

Web page displayed in browser

The Web page is almost done. The last improvements you want to make are to add a vertical color bar to visually separate the list of items from the welcome text, and to add a hyperlink to the newsletter page. First you will add color to the narrow vertical cell separating the two areas of the table.

■ Switch back to Word.

■ Move to the narrow vertical cell to the right of the bulleted list.

■ Choose Table/Cell Properties/Background/Blue/ OK .

Your screen should be similar to Figure 5-11.

table cell with color

FIGURE 5-11

Creating Hyperlinks

Next you want to create a hyperlink to the newsletter.

Concept 5: Hyperlinks

As you have learned, **hyperlinks** provide a quick way to jump to other documents, objects, or Web pages. Hyperlinks are the real power of the WWW. You can jump to sites on your own system and network as well as to sites on the Internet and WWW. A hyperlink can also be to an object within a Word document, such as a cross-reference.

When you create a hyperlink in a document, you can make the path to the destination of the hyperlink an absolute link or a relative link. An **absolute link**, also called a **fixed link**, identifies the file location of the destination by its full address, such as c:\Word Data File\Sales.doc. Fixed links are usually only used if you are sure the location of the object will not change. A **relative link** identifies the destination location in relation to the location of the HTML file. A relative link is based on a path you specify in which the first part of the path is shared by both the file that contains the hyperlink and the destination file.

Hyperlinks to other Web sites should typically use a fixed file location that includes the full path to the location or address of the page called the Uniform Resource Locator (URL). All URL's have at least two basic parts. The first part presents the protocol used to connect to the resource. The **protocol** is the set of rules that control how software and hardware on a network communicate. The protocol http (Hypertext Transfer Protocol), shown in the example below, is by far the most common. The protocol is always followed by a colon (:). The second part presents the name of the server where the resource is located (www.eatright.org). This is always preceded by two forward slashes (//) and each part of the path is separated by a single forward slash (/).

http://www.eatright.org

- Select the word "Newsletter."

- Click 🖰 Insert Hyperlink.

- Click Browse... .

- Select the file Fall 1998 Newsletter from your data disk.

- Click OK .

Your screen should be similar to Figure 5-12.

The menu equivalent is **I**nsert/ Hyper**l**ink, and the keyboard shortcut is Ctrl + k.

inserts a hyperlink into a document

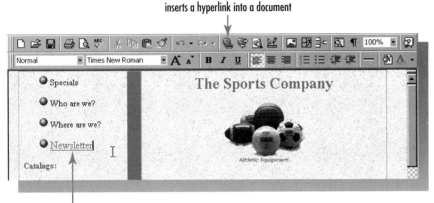

FIGURE 5-12

hyperlink to newsletter document

Typically a text hyperlink appears in a document underlined and in blue.

- Save the page and then preview your changes in the browser.

Clicking on a hyperlink to a page directs the browser to get the page from the server and display it. Clicking on a hyperlink to a file directs the browser to get the file from the server and to open it using the appropriate program, such as an audio program to play an audio file.

To see if your link works correctly,

- Click Newsletter.

The hyperlink color may vary from one browser to another.

Images that are hyperlinked are not identified in any particular way.

The pointer changes to 🖑 over a hyperlink, and the URL appears in the status bar.

The browser locates the file, loads it, and displays it in the browser window. Your screen should be similar to Figure 5-13.

newsletter document loaded and displayed in browser

FIGURE 5-13

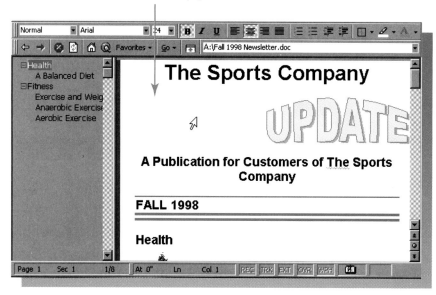

The newsletter file is displayed in Online Layout view.

■ Change to Page Layout view.

■ Scroll the window to see the entire newsletter document.

Next you will try out the link to the American Dietetic Association on the first page of the newsletter. If your system is not connected to the Internet, skip the next three steps.

■ Click www.eatright.org.

■ If your computer displays the screen to access your Internet provider, enter the requested user identification.

Users who do not have Word can use the Word Viewer to display Word documents. Word Viewer is a separate application this is available for free by downloading it from the WWW.

If this file had already been converted to an HTML document, the browser would display it as an HTML document.

If you are using Netscape as your Web browser, your computer may launch another browser window.

Your screen should be similar to Figure 5-14.

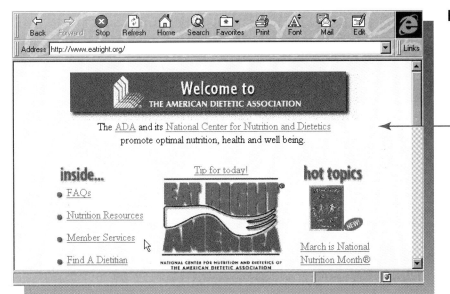

FIGURE 5-14

clicking link in newsletter connects to the Internet and displays associated Web page

To return to The Sports Company home page,

- Click [Back] (2 times).

- Click [X] to exit the browser program.

- If necessary, follow the procedure to disconnect from the Internet.

- Exit Word.

> When you return to a Web page after following a hyperlink, the hyperlink text color changes to purple.

Making a Web Page Public

Before making your Web page available for others to see, you should test that all links work correctly. In addition, because all browsers do not display the HTML tags the same way, it is a good idea to preview your page using different browsers. Many of the differences in how browsers display a page are appearance differences, not structural.

The steps that you take to make your pages public depend on how you want to share them. There are two main avenues: on your local network or intranet for limited access by people within an organization, or on the Internet for access by anyone using the WWW. To make pages available to other people on your network, save your Web pages and related files, such as pictures, to a network location. To make your Web pages available on the WWW, you need to either install Web server software on your computer or locate an Internet service provider that allocates space for Web pages.

LAB REVIEW

■ ■ ■ ■ ■ ■ ■ ■ ■ ■ ■

Key Terms

absolute link   (WP202)
authoring   (WP190)
browser   (WP192)
fixed link   (WP202)
form   (WP190)
home page   (WP189)
hyperlink   (WP202)
Hypertext Markup Language (HTML)   (WP192)
inline image   (WP195)
page   (WP189)
protocol   (WP202)
relative link   (WP202)
server   (WP189)
site   (WP189)
tag   (WP192)
World Wide Web   (WP189)

Command Summary

Command	Shortcut Key	Button	Action
File/Save as HTML			Converts file to HTML format
File/Web Page Preview			Previews Web page in browser
View/HTML Source			Displays HTML codes
Insert/Horizontal Line			Adds graphic horizontal line to Web page
Insert/Hyperlink	Ctrl + K		Inserts a hyperlink in Web page
Format/Background			Applies background color to selection
Table/Cell Properties/Background			Changes background of selected cell

Matching

1. home page   _____   **a.** link that allows user to jump to other documents

2. URL   _____   **b.** creates a hyperlink in Web page

3. hyperlink   _____   **c.** identifies the location of a hyperlink by its full address

4.   _____   **d.** address of the page

5. tags   _____   **e.** basic document of the World Wide Web

6. browser   _____   **f.** embedded codes that supply information about a page

7.   _____   **g.** software program used to access WWW

8. absolute link   _____   **h.** creating a Web page

9. authoring   _____   **i.** previews Web page in browser

10. page   _____   **j.** top-level page

Fill-In Questions

1. Complete the following statements by filling in the blanks with the correct terms.

   a. Web sites are locations on computers called _____ that store the documents contained at the site.

   b. HTML _____ are embedded codes in a Web page.

   c. The top-level or opening page of a site is called the _____.

   d. HTML commands are interpreted by the _____ software program used to access the WWW.

   e. _____ and _____ are the two graphic file formats commonly used in HTML documents.

   f. Web sites use a fixed file location that includes the full path to the location or address of the page called the _____ .

   g. _____ give the ability to quickly jump from one location to another with a simple click.

Discussion Questions

1. Discuss three attributes of a well-designed Web page.

2. Discuss how inline images are saved in an HTML document.

3. Discuss how hyperlinks work.

4. Discuss how to get your Web page on the Internet.

Hands-On Practice Exercises

Step by Step   **Rating System**

1. In this problem you will create a personal home page.

   a. Plan the design of your home page. You may want to visit other personal home pages on the Web to get an idea of what you like and do not like for your page.

   b. Develop a Word document that contains the text of your home page.

   c. Convert the Word document into an HTML document.

   d. Create columns and rows as necessary to align your text.

   e. Add a background.

   f. Add clip art, pictures, and animation to your home page.

   g. Create a list of links to other pages that are of interest to you.

   h. If possible, load your home page to a server so others can enjoy your work.

   i. Print your home page.

2. Andrew Beinbrink has just accepted a job with the Call Animation Studio. He has been asked to create a new Web page to promote the company.

   a. Use the Web Page Wizard to create a two-column layout. Apply the visual style Festive.

   b. Replace the headline with the name of the company.

   c. Replace the paragraph text with the following information about the Call Animation Studio.

   Call Animation Studio specializes in a variety of media services for your corporate, broadcast, and film projects. Check out:

   d. Change the sample text in the list to:

   3D Graphics Animation

   3D Computer Animation

   3D Modeling

   e. Create three new pages for 3D Graphics Animation, 3D Computer Animation, and 3D Modeling. Link the three pages to the list on the home page.

   f. Add clip art pictures of animation characters to the pages to add interest.

   g. Print the four pages.

3. Sarah Harvey has accepted a position with one of her university professors. Her professor has already created a class Web page but would like to include a calendar for the upcoming month. The calendar should include all classroom hours, the professor's office hours, and assignments due.

   a. Use the Web Page Wizard to create a calendar for next month.

   b. Choose the visual style of your choice.

   c. Insert a course title as the main heading and the month and year as the subheading.

   d. Write a short introduction above the calendar to explain its contents.

   e. Add text to the days of the week to represent the information the professor requested.

f. Enhance the calendar by using lines, borders, and pictures as appropriate. Print the Web page.

g. If possible at your school, follow the procedure to load the page to a server so others can enjoy your work.

On Your Own

4. To complete this problem, you must have completed Practice Exercise 1 on page 208. After designing your home page, you would like to know how others feel about what you added to your page. A good way of asking for input is to use a feedback form. With this form you can ask visitors to respond to questions. Use the Web Page Wizard to create a feedback form in the same visual style as your home page. Enhance the page using lines, borders, and pictures as appropriate. Link the feedback form to your home page. Print the page. If possible at your school, follow the procedure to load your new page to a server.

5. To complete this problem, you must have completed the Web page from this lab. You would like to add an order form page linked to The Sports Company home page. Refer to the help topic on Web forms for information on forms. Create an order form for The Sports Company that will allow the user to order information about products available from The Sports Company. Enhance the page using the features discussed in the lab. Link the order form to The Sports Company home page.

Creating a Web Page

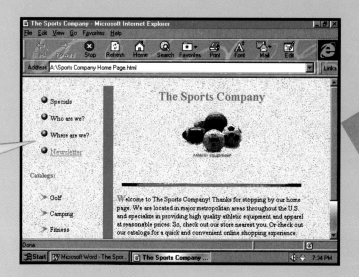

Web Sites and Home Pages

The World Wide Web is a massive collection of Web sites. The top-level or opening page of a Web site is called the home page.

Hyperlinks

Hyperlinks provide a way to quickly jump to other documents, objects, or Web pages.

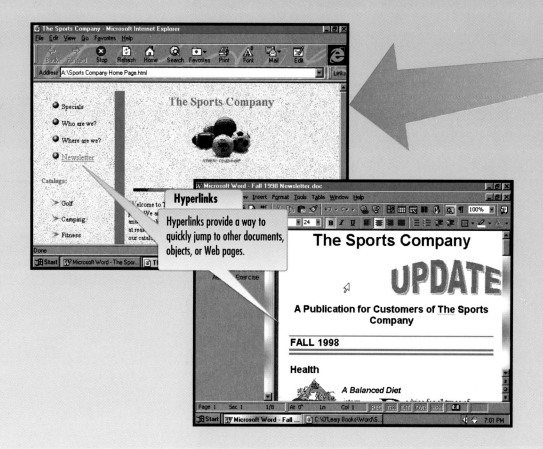

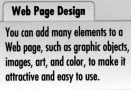

Web Page Design

You can add many elements to a Web page, such as graphic objects, images, art, and color, to make it attractive and easy to use.

Concepts

Web Sites and
Home Pages

Web Page Design
Inline Images

Hypertext Markup
Language

Hyperlinks

Inline Images

Word inserts graphics in Web pages as inline images, which are positioned directly in the text at the insertion point.

Hypertext Markup Language

All pages on the WWW are written using a programming language called HTML (Hypertext Markup Language).

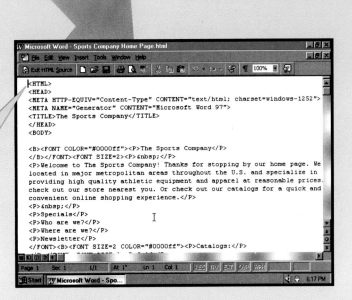

Case Project

Introduction

This project is designed to reinforce your knowledge of the word processing features used in the five Microsoft Word 97 labs. You will also be expected to use the Office Assistant to learn more about advanced features available in Word 97.

Case

Marianne Virgili is the Director of the Glenwood Springs Chamber Resort Association. Semiannually the chamber produces a newsletter called *Trends,* which reviews the latest economic indicators for Garfield county. It is sent to all chamber members. Marianne has compiled much of the data to be included in the next issue and has asked you to work on several of the articles.

Part I

a. Open the file Trends from your data disk. This file contains some of the text that will be used in the newsletter.

b. The first paragraph contains many errors. Use the editing techniques you learned in the labs to correct the paragraph.

c. Spell-check the document. Check that the document has a single space between words and following a period at the end of a sentence.

d. Search for the word "TRENDS" throughout the document and change it to be displayed in italics. Locate all occurrences of incorrect capitalization for Glenwood Springs and replace them with the correct capitalization.

e. Delete the paragraph about school attendance in the Population, Housing, and Construction section. In the same section, use the Document Map to move the paragraph about commercial construction below the paragraph on residential construction.

f. Bold the section headings throughout the document. Change the font type, bold, and enlarge the main heading "Trend Indicators."

g. Save and replace your document. Print the document.

Part II

This issue of *Trends* will contain two tables. The first table will provide employment information for 1996 to 1997 for Garfield county. The second table will provide information on gross sales.

a. The employment information is shown below. Use the Draw Table feature to create a table from this data in a new document. Use the List 8 table AutoFormat.

Job Category	1996	1997	% Change
Agr., For., Fish.	141	174	23.4
Mining	705	813	15.3
Construction	856	1,171	36.8
Manufacturing	284	327	15.1
Trans., Comm., Util.	443	504	13.8
Wholesale Trade	338	410	21.3
Retail Trade	2,580	2,859	10.9
Fin., Ins., Real Est.	522	601	15.1
Services	2,679	2,767	3.3
Government	2,234	2,328	4.2
TOTAL			

b. Right-align the entries in the three data columns, including the column heads. Left-align the row heads. Bold and underline the column heads.

c. Enter functions to sum the 1996 and 1997 columns of data, and average the % Change column. (Hint: You will need to exclude the cells containing the date column headings from being included in the calculated total.) Bold the Total row.

d. Insert a new row above the table. Remove the column dividers. Add the title "JOBS IN GARFIELD COUNTY." Center and bold the title.

e. Enhance the appearance of the table by appropriately sizing the columns and making the gridlines thicker.

f. Save the table. Print the table.

The second table will display the percent of gross sales for the first half of 1998 for the five major cities in the county.

g. Open a new document file. Use the Draw Table feature to create a table from the following data. Select a table AutoFormat of your choice.

City	Sales	% of Total
Glenwood Springs	165.7	61.0
Parachute	2.3	0.8
Silt	3.4	1.3
Carbondale	19.3	7.1
Rifle	34.7	12.8
Remainder of County	46.1	17.0
TOTAL 1st Half		

h. Enter formulas to total the two columns of data.

i. Insert a new row above the table. Clear the column dividers. Enter the title "TOTAL GROSS SALES" on the first line, "JANUARY-JUNE 1998" on the second line, and "(In millions of dollars)" on the third line. Center the title lines.

j. Right-align the data columns. Left-align the City column.

k. Enhance the appearance of the table by adding bold and making other format changes as you like. Appropriately size the table columns.

l. Save the table. Print the table.

Part III

You need to create the newsletter headline next.

a. The headline should display the following information:

Newsletter name:	TRENDS
Subheadings:	A Semiannual Review of Economic Indicators
	Glenwood Springs Chamber Resort Association
[Your Name]	
[Current Date]	

b. Use the following features when designing the headline:

- centered text
- font and type sizes of your choice
- italics
- bold
- borders with different line weights
- WordArt

c. Save the headline as a separate document file.

Part IV

Now you are ready to create the newsletter.

a. Copy the headline to the top of the text file, Trends. Change the newsletter text to display two columns. Make the page margins 0.5 inch. Make the space between columns 0.25 inch.

b. Copy each table into the newsletter near the reference to the table in the text. Add a caption below the tables in the document. Size the tables to fit within the column widths.

c. Hyphenate the newsletter.

d. Display the last paragraph of text in a shaded text box.

e. Save the newsletter. If necessary, select another printer and adjust the newsletter layout (you may need to change font and type sizes, adjust columns, or change the placement of the tables). Print the newsletter.

Part V

The final document you need to create is a cover memo to the Director to accompany a sample copy of the newsletter.

a. Open a memo template of your choice.

b. Enter the information that is needed to complete the template. (Use your name following "FROM:".)

c. Enter the body of the memo. The memo should introduce the newsletter and indicate that you can revise the newsletter as needed.

d. Save the memo. Print the memo.

Glossary of Key Terms

Absolute link: A link that identifies the file location of the destination by its full address. Also called a fixed link.

Active window: The window you can work in. It is identified by a highlighted title bar, the insertion point, and scroll bars.

Address file: The data source file used in a merge; it typically contains name and address data to be combined with the main document.

Alignment: Positioning of text on a line, such as flush left, centered, flush right, or justified.

Anchor: To attach a graphic object to a paragraph.

Authoring: Creating a Web page.

AutoCorrect: A Word feature that makes basic assumptions about the text you are typing and automatically corrects the entry.

AutoText: Commonly used words or phrases that are recognized by the program and can be automatically completed for you.

Browser: Software program used to access the World Wide Web.

Caption: A title or explanation for a table, picture, or graph.

Case sensitive: Capable of distinguishing between uppercase and lowercase characters.

Cell: The space created by the intersection of a vertical column and a horizontal row.

Character style: A combination of any character formats that affect selected text.

Click and type: A feature found in many templates that lets you click on the placeholder and replace it with the text you type.

Clip art: A collection of graphics that is usually bundled with a software application.

Column: A vertical block of cells one cell wide in a table.

Cross-reference: A reference in one part of a document to related information in another part.

Cursor: The blinking vertical bar that shows you where the next character you type will appear. Also called the insertion point.

Custom dictionary: A dictionary of terms you have entered that are not in the main dictionary of the Spelling Checker.

Data field: Each category of information in the data source.

Data source: The file that supplies the data in a mail merge.

Default: Initial Word settings that can be changed to customize documents.

Destination: The location to which text is moved or copied.

Docked: Menus and toolbars that are fixed to the edge of the window.

Document pane: When footnotes are created, the upper portion of the window that displays the document; in Online Layout view, the pane that displays the document text.

Drag and drop: A mouse procedure that moves or copies a selection to a new location.

Drawing object: A simple object consisting of shapes such as lines and boxes.

Drop cap: A large, uppercase character with the top part of the letter even with the line and the rest of the letter extending into the paragraph below it.

Edit: The process of changing and correcting existing text in a document.

Endnote: A reference note displayed at the end of the document.

End-of-file marker: The horizontal line that marks the end of a file.

Field: A placeholder code that instructs Word to insert information in a document.

Field code: The code containing the instructions about the type of information to insert in the document.

Field name: A name used to label each data field in the data source.

Field result: The results displayed in a field according to the instructions in the field code.

Fixed link: A link that identifies the file location of the destination by its full address. Also called an absolute link.

Floating: Menus and toolbars that appear in separate windows.

Font: A set of characters with a specific design. Also called a typeface.

Footer: The line or several lines of text at the bottom of every page just above the bottom margin.

Footnote: A reference note displayed at the bottom of the page where the reference occurs.

Form: Collection of fields on a Web page that you can use to get information or feedback from users.

Formatting: Features that enhance the appearance of the document to make it more readable or attractive.

Formatting toolbar: The toolbar, displayed below the Standard toolbar, that contains buttons representing the most frequently used text-editing and text-layout features.

Formula: Table entry that does arithmetic calculations.

Frame: An invisible box containing text, a table, a graphic, or another object that you can move freely on a page.

Function: A prewritten formula that performs a calculation automatically.

Graphic: Non-text element in a document.

Group: A set of objects that can be minipulated as a single unit.

Handles: Small boxes surrounding a selected object that allow you to manipulate its size and placement.

Header: The line or several lines of text at the top of each page just below the top margin.

Heading style: A style that is designed to identify different levels of headings in a document.

Home page: The top-level or opening page to a site.

Hyperlink: Special type of link that provides a quick way to jump to other documents, objects, or Web pages.

Hypertext Markup Language (HTML): Programming language used to create Web pages.

Hyphenation: Feature that inserts a hyphen in long words that fall at the end of a line to split the word between lines.

Hyphenation zone: An unmarked space along the right margin that controls the amount of white space in addition to the margin that Word will allow at the end of a line.

Inline image: A graphic object that appears on a Web page when the page is loaded.

Insert mode: Method of text entry in which new characters are inserted into existing text, which moves to the right to make space for the new characters; the text on the line is reformatted as necessary.

Insertion point: The blinking vertical bar that shows you where the next character you type will appear on the line. Also called the cursor.

Lock: To keep a graphic and a paragraph together on a page.

Mail Merge: A feature that combines a text document with a data document or file containing names and addresses to produce a merged document or form letter.

Main dictionary: The dictionary of terms that comes with Word 97.

Main document: Document that contains the basic form letter in a merge operation.

Manual page break: Begins a new page regardless of the amount of text on the previous page.

Margin: The distance from the text to the edge of the paper.

Merge field: A field code that controls what information is used from the data source and where it is entered in the main document.

Newpaper columns: Display text so that it flows from the bottom of one column to the top of the next column.

Note pane: Lower portion of the window that displays footnotes.

Note reference mark: A superscript number or character appearing in the document at the end of the material being referenced.

Note separator: The horizontal line separating footnote text from main document text.

Note text: The text in a footnote.

Object: An item that can be sized, moved, and manipulated.

Office Assistant: A feature that automatically suggests help topics as you work.

Optional hyphen: Hyphen inserted by Word when a word is broken between two lines because the full word did not fit.

Overtype mode: Method of text entry in which new text types over the existing characters.

Page: The basic document of a World Wide Web site.

Pane: A division of the workspace.

Paragraph mark: Special hidden character that indicates the end of a paragraph.

Paragraph style: A combination of any character formats and paragraph formats that affects all text in a paragraph.

Picture: An illustration such as a scanned photograph.

Placeholder: Text in a template that marks the space and provides instructions for the text that should be entered at that location.

Point: Measure used for height of type; one point equals 1/72 inch.

Protocol: The rules that control how hardware and software on a network communicate.

Record: All the fields of data that are needed to complete the main document for one entity in a merge operation.

Relative link: Identifies the destination location in relation to the location of the HTML file.

Row: A horizontal block of cells in a table.

Ruler: The ruler located below the Formatting toolbar that shows the line length in inches.

Sans serif font: A font, such as Arial or Helvetica, that does not have a flair at the base of each letter.

Select: To highlight text.

Selection bar: The unmarked area to the left of the document area where the mouse can be used to highlight text lines.

Serif font: A font, such as Times New Roman, that has a flair at the base of each letter.

Server: A computer that stores the documents contained in a Web site.

Site: Web location on a computer.

Soft space: A space automatically entered by Word to align the text properly on a single line.

Standard toolbar: The toolbar, displayed below the menu bar, that gives quick access to editing features.

Status bar: The line of information at the bottom of the screen.

Style: A set of formats that is assigned a name.

Tab alignment selection box: A box on the left end of the ruler from which you select tab alignment types.

Tab leaders: Series of dots between a heading and the page number in the table of contents.

Tab stop: A stopping point along the ruler that marks the locations of a tab.

Table: A grid of horizontal rows and vertical columns; the intersection of rows and columns creates cells in which you can enter data.

Table reference: The column letter and row number that identifies a cell in a table.

Tag: An embedded code that supplies information about a Web page's structure, appearance, and contents.

Template: A prewritten blank worksheet that is used repeatedly to enter text.

Text box: A mini-document that acts as a graphic object in that it is surrounded by a frame.

Thesaurus: The file of synonyms and antonyms provided with Word.

Typeface: A set of characters with a specific design. Also called a font.

Uniform Resource Locator (URL): The address that indicates the location of a document on the World Wide Web.

WordArt: A supplementary application included with the Word program that is used to enhance a document by changing the shape of text, adding 3-D effects, and changing the alignment of text on a line.

Word wrap: Feature that automatically determines where to begin the next line of text; the user does not press ⌐Enter at the end of a line unless it is the end of a paragraph or to insert a blank line.

World Wide Web: A massive collection of sites.

Command Summary

Command	Shortcut Key	Button	Action
File/**N**ew	Ctrl + N		Opens new file
File/**O**pen	Ctrl + O		Opens selected file
File/**C**lose			Closes file
File/**S**ave	Ctrl + S		Saves file using same file name
File/Save **A**s			Saves file using a new file name
File/Save as **H**TML			Converts file to HTML format
File/**W**eb Page Preview			Previews Web page in browser
File/Page Set**u**p			Changes layout of page including margins, paper size, and paper source
File/Page Set**u**p/**L**ayout/Vertical Alignment			Aligns text vertically on a page
File/Print Pre**v**iew			Displays document as it will appear when printed
File/**P**rint	Ctrl + P		Prints file using selected print settings
File/Proper**ti**es			Shows properties of active document
File/E**x**it	Alt + F4		Exits Word program
Edit/**U**ndo	Ctrl + Z		Restores last editing change
Edit/**R**edo or **R**epeat	Ctrl + Y		Restores last Undo or repeats last command or action
Edit/Cu**t**	Ctrl + X		Cuts selected text and copies it to Clipboard
Edit/**C**opy	Ctrl + C		Copies selected text to Clipboard
Edit/**P**aste	Ctrl + V		Pastes text from Clipboard
Edit/**F**ind	Ctrl + F		Locates specified text

Command	Shortcut Key	Button	Action
Edit/**Re**place	Ctrl + H		Locates and replaces specified text
Edit/**G**o To	Ctrl + G		Moves insertion point to specified location in document
View/**N**ormal		▤	Displays document in Normal view
View/Onlin**e** Layout		▣	Displays document best for onscreen reading
View/**P**age Layout		▣	Displays document as it will appear when printed
View/**O**utline		▤	Displays structure of document as an outline
View/**M**aster Document			Shows several documents organized into a master document
View/**T**oolbars			Displays or hides selected toolbars
View/**D**ocument Map		▣	Shows document headings along left side of document
View/**H**eader and Footer			Displays header and footer areas
View/**F**ootnotes			Hides or displays note pane
View/F**u**ll Screen		▣	Shows document without Word's toolbars, menus, scroll bars, and other screen elements
View/**Z**oom		100% ▾	Changes onscreen character size
View/**Z**oom/**W**hole Page			Displays entire page onscreen
View/HTML **S**ource			Displays HTML codes
Insert/**B**reak/**P**age Break	Ctrl + ↵Enter		Inserts manual page break
Insert/**B**reak/Con**t**inuous			Starts next section on same page as current section
Insert/Page Nu**m**bers			Specifies page number location
Insert/Date and **T**ime			Inserts current date or time, maintained by computer system, in selected format
Insert /Foot**n**ote	Alt + Ctrl + F		Inserts a footnote reference at insertion point
Insert/**C**aption			Inserts a caption at insertion point
Insert/Cross-**r**eference			Inserts a cross-reference at insertion point
Insert/In**d**ex and Tables			Inserts an index or table, such as a table of contents
Insert/**P**icture/**F**rom File			Inserts a picture from a file
Insert/Te**x**t Box		▣	Inserts text box
Insert/**H**orizontal Line		▬	Adds graphic horizontal line to Web page
Insert/Hyper**l**ink	Ctrl + K	▣	Inserts a hyperlink in Web page

Command	Shortcut Key	Button	Action
Format/Font			Changes appearance of characters
Format/Font/Size		A	Increases HTML character size
Format/Font/Font Style/Italic	Ctrl + I	I	Makes selected text italic
Format/Font/Font Style/Bold	Ctrl + B	B	Makes selected text bold
Format/Font/Underline/Single	Ctrl + U	U	Underlines selected text
Format/Paragraph/Indents and Spacing/Special/First Line			Indents first line of paragraph from right margin
Format/Paragraph/Indents and Spacing/Alignment/Left	Ctrl + L	≣	Aligns text to left margin
Format/Paragraph/Indents and Spacing/Alignment/Centered	Ctrl + E	≣	Centers text between left and right margins
Format/Paragraph/Indents and Spacing/Alignment/Right	Ctrl + R	≣	Aligns text to right margin
Format/Paragraph/Indents and Spacing/Alignment/Justified	Ctrl + J	≣	Aligns text equally between left and right margins
Format/Bullets and Numbering		⊞ ⊞	Creates a bulleted or numbered list
Format/Borders and Shading			Adds borders and shadings to selection
		⊞	Adds top border
		⊞	Adds bottom border
Format/Columns		⊞	Specifies number, spacing, and size of columns
Format/Tabs			Inserts tab stops
Format/Drop Cap/Dropped			Changes character to a drop cap
Format/Style			Applies, creates, or modifies styles
Format/Background			Applies background color to selection
Format/Picture			Changes picture scaling, size, wrapping, position, and cropping information
Tools/Spelling and Grammar	F7	ABC✓	Starts Spelling and Grammar tool
Tools/Language/Thesaurus	⇧ Shift + F7		Starts Thesaurus tool
Tools/Language/Hyphenation			Specifies hyphenation settings
Tools/Mail Merge			Starts Mail Merge feature
Tools/Customize/Options			Changes display options

Command	Shortcut Key	Button	Action
Tools/**O**ptions/View/**S**paces/ Paragraph **M**arks		¶	Displays or hides special characters
T**a**ble/Draw Ta**b**le			Creates a table using the Draw Table feature
T**a**ble/**I**nsert Table			Inserts a table where you drag in document
T**a**ble/**I**nsert Columns			Inserts new columns in a table
T**a**ble/**I**nsert Rows			Inserts new rows in a table
T**a**ble/**M**erge Cells			Merges cells in a table
T**a**ble/Ce**ll** Properties/Background			Changes background of selected cell
T**a**ble/F**o**rmula			Inserts a formula into a table
T**a**ble/Table Auto**F**ormat			Applies predesigned table layouts to table
T**a**ble/Distribute Columns Evenl**y**			Evenly sizes selected columns
T**a**ble/Con**v**ert Text to Table			Converts existing text separated into columns to a table
Help/Microsoft Word **H**elp	F1	?	Displays Office Assistant

Index

Notes

Appendix A

Additional Microsoft Word 97 User Specialist Certification Topics

- ■ Create and Modify an Outline
- ■ Create a Folder
- ■ Use Alternate Headers and Footers
- ■ Use Tabs with Leaders
- ■ Adjust Line Spacing
- ■ Use Underline Styles
- ■ Edit Styles
- ■ Key and Edit Text in Columns
- ■ Create and Modify 3-D Shapes
- ■ Create and Modify Lines
- ■ Prepare and Print Envelopes and Labels

Create and Modify an Outline

When creating a new document, one of the hardest parts is getting started. Often the best way to start is by creating an outline of the main topics using Outline view. Outline view shows the hierarchy of topics in a document by displaying the different heading levels of a document indented to represent their level in the document's structure. Headings that are level 1 appear as the top level of the outline, level two headings appear indented below level 1 headings and so forth. The

Heading 1
Heading 2
Heading 3
Heading 3
Heading 2
Heading 3
Heading 3
Heading 3

arrangement of headings in a hierarchy of importance quickly shows the relationship between topics.

You can use Outline view to help you create a new document or to view and reorganize the topics in an existing document. In a new document, Word automatically applies the built-in heading styles as you enter and rearrange the topic headings and subheadings. In an existing document, you need to apply the heading style levels before viewing the document in Outline view.

First you will create a new document using Outline view. As you enter each heading, it is initially formatted with a Heading 1 style. Then as you construct the outline, different heading levels are applied based upon the position of the topic within the outline hierarchy.

■   Start Word and switch to Outline view.

■   Close the Document Map.

■   Type the following headings pressing Enter after each.

Health and Fitness
Health
A Balanced Diet
Controlling Fat in Your Diet
Improving Your Eating Habits
Attaining a Healthy Weight

Your screen should be similar to Figure A-1.

Use **View/Outline** or click 🗐 to switch to Outline View.

The Outline toolbar contains buttons that make it easy to modify the outline.

FIGURE A-1

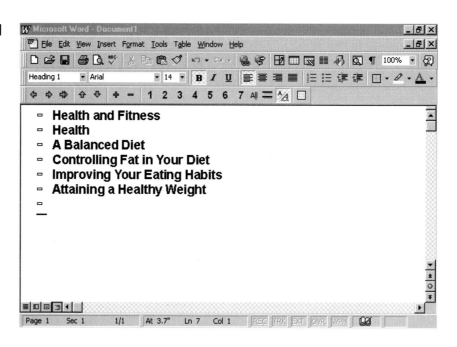

Next, you need to arrange the headings by outline levels. The outline symbols (▭ and ✛) to the left of the headings are used to select and move the heading to a new location or level within the document. To demote a heading to a lower level, drag the symbol to the right and to promote a heading to a higher level, drag the symbol to the left. You need to demote the Health heading so that is is a subtopic below the main heading.

■ Drag the ▭ of the Health heading to the right one level.

■ Demote the heading A Balanced Diet two levels.

Your screen should be similar to Figure A-2.

You can also click ⬅ to promote levels and ➡ to demote levels.

The mouse pointer changes to ⟷ indicating dragging it will move the heading.

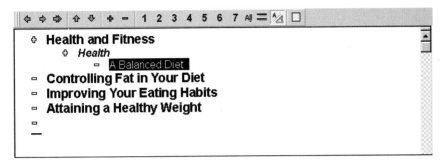

FIGURE A-2

The Health heading has changed to a Heading 2 style and the heading is indented one level to show it is subordinate to the heading above it. The A Balanced Diet heading is a Heading 3 style and is indented two levels in the outline. The ✛ outline symbol indicates the topic heading includes subtopics.

■ Demote the 3 remaining topics to the heading levels shown below.

Controlling Fat in Your Diet	Level 3
Improving Your Eating Habits	Level 2
Attaining a Healthy Weight	Level 2

Next you want to change the order of topics. To move a heading to a different location, drag the outline symbol up or down. A horizontal line shows where the heading will be placed when you release the mouse button.

You can also click ⬆ and ⬇ to move a topic.

■ Drag the Attaining a Healthy Weight heading up above the Improving Your Eating Habits heading.

Your screen should be similar to Figure A-3.

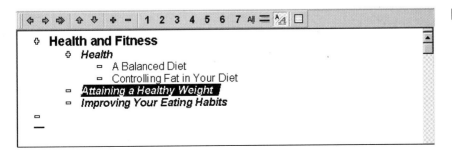

FIGURE A-3

When you are satisfied with the organization of your outline you can switch to normal view or page layout view to add detailed body text and graphics.

- ■ Switch to Normal view.
- ■ Add your name and date as a header.

Create a New Folder

Next you will save the outline you have created in a folder on your data disk that you will use to hold files related to the newsletter. You can create a new folder at the same time you save a file.

- ■ Choose File/Save As.
- ■ Change the Save In location to the drive containing your data disk.
- ■ Click [⬛] Create New Folder.

The New Folder dialog box displays the path of the active directory. The new folder will be created as a subfolder in the active directory.

- ■ Enter the folder name **Newsletter** in the Name text box.
- ■ Click [OK].
- ■ Change the active directory to the new folder, Newsletter.
- ■ Enter the file name **Outline.**
- ■ Click [Save].
- ■ Print the document.
- ■ Close the file.

Checking an Existing Document in Outline View

Next you will open an existing document that is already formatted with heading styles and check its organization using Outline view.

- ■ Open the file Newsletter Topics from your data disk.
- ■ Switch to Outline view and close the Document Map.
- ■ Scroll the window to view the entire document outline. Return to the top of the second section.

This file was saved at the end of Part 1 in Lab 3.

Your screen should be similar to Figure A-4.

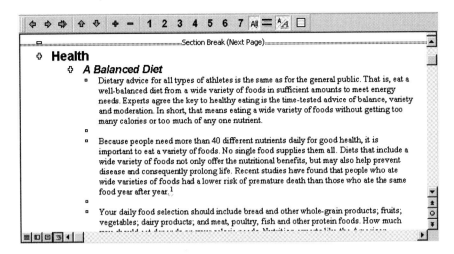

The document is displayed as an outline with the topic headings indented appropriately. In Outline view you can display as much or little of the document text as you want. To make it easier to view and reorganize the document's structure, you can collapse the document to show just the headings you want. Alternatively, you can display part of the body text below each heading or the entire body text. The body text is any part of the document that is not formatted with a heading style. You can then easily move the headings around until the order is logical. The body text will follow the heading. The following tables show how you can expand and collapse the amount of text displayed in Outline view.

To expand	Do this
All headings and body text	Click **All**
All collapsed subheadings and body text under a heading	Double-click ✤ next to the heading.
Collapsed text under a heading, one level at a time	Click the heading text, then Click ✚ Expand

To collapse	Do this
Text below a specific heading level	Click the numbered button for the lowest heading you want to display.
All subheadings and body text under a heading	Double-click ✚ next to the heading.
Text under a heading, one level at a time	Click the heading text, and then click ▭
Text below all headings to show only the first line of body text	Click ▭ Show First Line Only
All body text	Click All

■ Double-click ✚ of the A Balanced Diet heading.

Your screen should be similar to Figure A-5.

FIGURE A-5

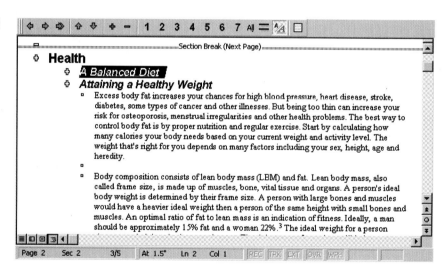

All the body text below this heading is hidden. You would like to see only the 4 heading levels of the document, not the body text so you can quickly check its organization.

■ Click **4** Show Heading 4.

Your screen should be similar to Figure A-6.

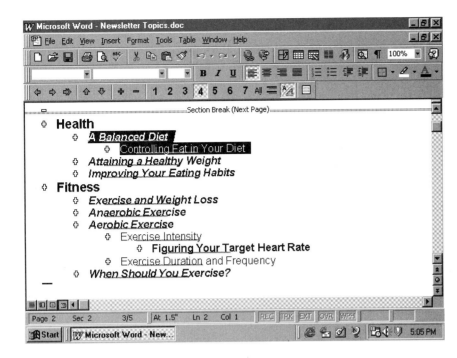

Now you decide the discussion of controlling fat in your diet should appear as a subtopic in the Attaining a Healthy Weight topic.

■ Move the heading Controlling Fat in Your Diet as a subtopic below Attaining a Healthy Weight.

Your screen should be similar to Figure A-7.

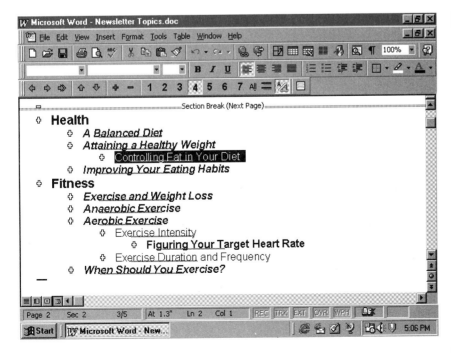

When you move or change the level of a heading that includes collapsed sub-ordinate text, the collapsed text is also selected and any changes you make to the heading such as moving, copying, or deleting it also affect the collapsed text. To verify this, you will display all body text again.

■   Click   [All]   Show All Headings.

The body text appears below the heading you moved.

Use Alternate Headers and Footers

You can also design the headers and footers in a document to have different content displayed on odd and even numbered pages.

■   Change to Page Layout view.

■   Move to the top of page 2.

You will change the headers and footers in section 2 of this document to display different information on odd and even-numbered pages.

■   Choose View/Header and Footer.

■   Click   [📖]   Page Setup.

■   If necessary, open the Layout tab.

■   Select Different odd and even.

■   Click   [OK]   .

You will leave the header on the odd page the same as it is and will change the footer to display the date.

■   Switch to the odd page footer.

■   Clear the existing footer information.

■   Click   [Insert AutoText ▾]   .

■   Choose -PAGE-.

Odd Page Footer -Section 2-
-1-

You will make the even page footer the same as the odd page footer.

■   Click   [🖼▶]   Next.

■   Click   [Insert AutoText ▾]   .

■   Choose -PAGE-.

Next you will change the even page header to display your name and the date.

- ■ Click 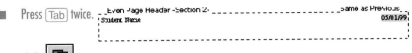 Switch.

- ■ Type your name in the header text box.

- ■ Press `Tab` twice.

- ■ Click [ ].

- ■ Click Close.

- ■ Change the zoom to Two Pages and scroll the document to check the header and footer text on the odd and even pages of section 2.

Your screen should be similar to Figure A-8.

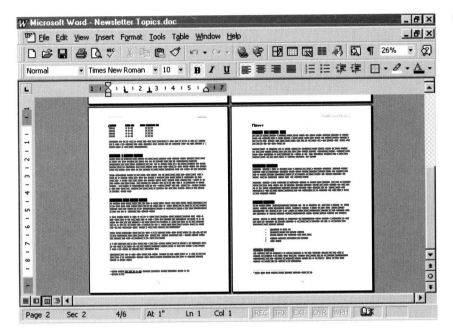

FIGURE A-8

- ■ Return the zoom to Page Width.

Use Tabs with Leaders

To make the fat grams table of data even easier to read you will add tab leaders to the two tab stops you specified for the table.

- • Select the fat gram table on page 2 of Section 2, excluding the heading line.

■ Choose Format/Tabs

The current tab leader setting is set to none for the 1 inch tab stop position. There are three styles of tab leaders you can select. You will use the style three tab leader for both tab stop settings.

■ Select 3 ------ .

■ Click [Set] .

■ Select the 2.25 inch tab stop setting from the Tab Stop Position list box.

■ Select 3 ------ .

■ Click [Set] .

■ Click [OK] .

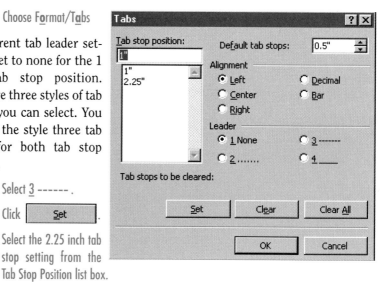

Calories	Total Fat	Total Saturated Fat
1,600	53 or less	18 or less
2,000	65 or less	20 or less
2,200	73 or less	24 or less
2,500	80 or less	25 or less

Adjust Line Spacing

You will also change the line spacing for the table. Line spacing is the vertical space between lines of text. The default setting of single line spacing accommodates the largest font in that line, plus a small amount of extra space. The other line spacing options are described below.

Spacing	Effect
1.5 Lines	Spacing is one-and-one-half times that of single line spacing.
Double	Spacing is twice that of single line spacing.
At Least	Uses the point value in the At text box as the minimum line spacing amount that can be used to accommodate larger font sizes or graphics that would not otherwise fit within the specified spacing.
Exactly	Uses the point value in the At text box as a fixed line spacing amount that is not changed making all lines evenly spaced.
Multiple	Uses the percentage value in the At text box as the amount to increase or decrease line spacing. For example, a 1.3 multiple line spacing setting will increase the space by 33 percent.

Line spacing is a paragraph format setting, therefore it effects the selected paragraph or selection.

- Select the fat grams table including the heading line.

- Choose Format/Paragraph.

- If necessary, open the Indents and Spacing tab.

- Choose 1.5 lines from the Line Spacing drop-down list.

- Click OK.

Calories	Total Fat	Total Saturated Fat
1,600	53 or less	18 or less
2,000	65 or less	20 or less
2,200	73 or less	24 or less
2,500	80 or less	25 or less

Use Underline Styles

Finally, you will add underlines to the fat gram table heading. In addition to the default single underline style, there are eight other types of underlines.

- Select the heading line of the table.

- Choose Format/Font.

- Open the Underline drop-down list box and select each underline type and look at how it appears in the Preview box.

- Select a type of your choice.

- Click OK.

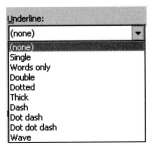

Calories	Total Fat	Total Saturated Fat
1,600	53 or less	18 or less
2,000	65 or less	20 or less
2,200	73 or less	24 or less
2,500	80 or less	25 or less

Edit Styles

You would also like to improve the appearance of the title page by applying a style to the title. Currently, the title has been formatted individually, however, you want to see if there is a predefined style that you can use to quickly improve the title.

- Move to the title line on the title page.

- Choose Format/Style.

- Select Title from the Styles list box.

The Title style settings are very similar to the settings that were applied individually to the title; Arial, 16 pt, bold and centered. Using this style will not change the appearance of the title, so you decide to create your own special style. You can do this by modifying an existing style or by creating a new style that you name. You will create a new style that you will name Fancy Title.

> If the Fancy Title style is listed in the Styles text box, select it and press [Delete].

- Click [New...].
- Type **Fancy Title** in the Name text box.
- Click [Format ▾].
- Choose Font.
- Select a font of Times New Roman, size of 20 and the Shadow effect.
- Click [OK] twice.
- Click [Apply].

Your screen should be similar to Figure A-9.

FIGURE A-9

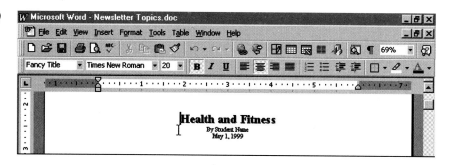

The style you designed is applied to the title. The name also appears in the Style button. You can also create styles by selecting text that contains the formatting you want included in the style and then naming the style in the Style button.

- Save the file as Newsletter Topics2 in the Newsletter folder.
- Print pages 2-3 of the report.
- Close the file.

The style you created is saved with the document. If you want to use the style in other documents you can copy it to the Normal.dot template or another document using the Organizer option in the Style dialog box.

Enter and Edit Text in Columns

You still have a few changes you want to make to the text of the newsletter. Although it is easier to enter and edit text when a document is in single column format, it is sometimes necessary to make changes when the document is formatted with multiple columns. As in a single column document, the text is automatically reformatted on a line when insertions and deletions are made. Using the [→] and [←] keys moves the insertion right or left along a line in a column. When it reaches the margin of the column it moves up or down to the next line in the column. Using the [↑] and [↓] keys moves the insertion point up or down line by line in a column. When it reaches the beginning or end of the column it moves to the bottom or top of the next column in the direction you are moving. Similarly, if you are dragging to select text, it highlights down then across columns. You want to add a paragraph to the end of the second article.

- Open the file Fall 1998 Newsletter on your data disk.

- If necessary, change to Page Layout view.

- Move to the end of the third column on page 2.

- Move the Special of the Month box to the bottom of the column.

- Type the following paragraph below the list of bulleted items.

  Two important factors of an aerobic workout are intensity and duration. Intensity is measured by checking your heart rate. A heart rate between 65 and 80 percent of its maximum is needed for the greatest cardiovascular improvement and most efficient fat burning. The duration recommended ranges from 12 to 60 minutes. Generally, 30 minutes of moderate-intensity physical activity on most days of the week is needed to maintain and improve weight.

- Delete the words "maintain and" from the last sentence of the paragraph.

This file was saved at the end of Lab 3.

Your screen should be similar to Figure A-10.

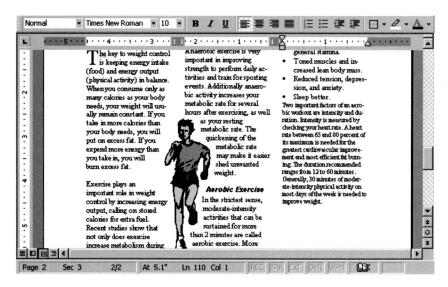

After reading over the section on aerobic exercise, you decide to move the paragraph above the preceding paragraph.

- ■ Select the paragraph.

- ■ Drag it to the beginning of the paragraph above it.

- ■ Insert a blank line between the paragraphs.

Create and Modify 3-D Shapes and Lines

Since this is the first issue of the company newsletter, you want to add a special graphic to the headline to catch the reader's attention.

- ■ Move to the top of the newsletter.

- ■ Display the Drawing toolbar.

- ■ Click AutoShapes ▾.

- ■ Click Stars and Banners ▸.

- ■ Click Explosion 1.

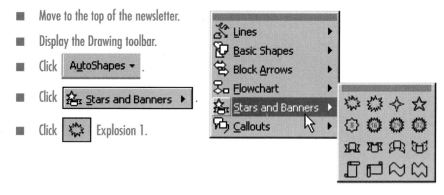

- In the upper left-hand corner of the headline, click and drag to draw a shape similar to that shown in Figure A-11.

- Fill the drawing with the Light Green color.

The AutoShape object should be similar to Figure A-11.

Click ✏️ ▾ Fill Color and then select Light Green.

FIGURE A-11

Next you will add text to the drawing.

- Right-click on the shape to open the Shortcut menu.

- Click Add Te**x**t.

- Change the font to Arial, size 12, bold, italic and center.

- Type **Premiere**

- Press (Enter).

- Type **Issue!**

Next you will add depth to the object.

- Click 📦 .

- Select any shape from the 3-D pop-up menu.

Your screen should be similar to Figure A-12.

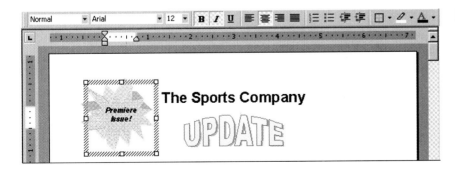

FIGURE A-12

■ Select several other 3-D shapes to see how they look when applied to the object.

In addition, you can modify the 3-D settings using the 3-D Settings toolbar. To open this toolbar,

■ Click [■] and choose 3-D Settings.

The buttons in this toolbar are used to modify the depth (the extrusion) of the object and its color, rotation, angle, direction of lighting, and surface texture.

■ Use each of the 3-D settings to modify your shape.

■ Select a 3-D design that you think looks good.

■ Click anywhere outside the graphic.

■ Close the 3-D Settings toolbar.

The object should be similar to Figure A-13.

FIGURE A-13

Finally, you want to add a line after the Health and Fitness heads to further distinguish the sections of the newsletter. You will create a straight graphic line consisting of a series of colored boxes.

> The other Lines options can be used to quickly create many common line types as well as create non-straight lines.

■ Move to the end of the word Health.

■ Click AutoShapes ▾ .

■ Select Lines.

■ Click [\] .

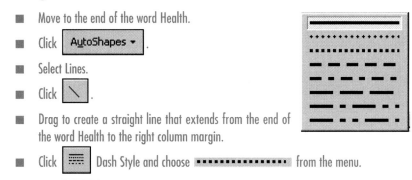

> Clicking [\] on the Drawing toolbar is the same as choosing it from the Autoshapes menu.

■ Drag to create a straight line that extends from the end of the word Health to the right column margin.

■ Click [▤] Dash Style and choose ▪▪▪▪▪▪▪▪▪▪▪▪▪ from the menu.

■ Click [✎ ▾] Line Color and choose the Sea Green color.

Your screen should be similar to Figure A-14.

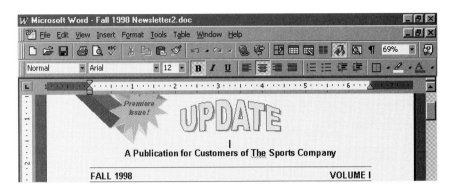

■ Copy the line object and paste it to the right of the Fitness heading on page 2.

■ Size the line appropriately.

■ Save the revised newsletter as Fall 1998 Newsletter2 in the Newsletter folder.

■ Close the file.

Fitness ················

Exercise and Weight | Loss

The key to weight control

Prepare and Print Envelopes

Word 97 helps you easily create and print address information directly on an envelope on mailing labels that are applied to envelopes. You will address an envelope for the credit card letter.

■ Open the file Credit Card Letter 4 from your data disk.

■ Add your name and address above the salutation as the inside address.

■ Choose Tools/Envelopes and Labels.

■ If necessary, open the Envelopes tab.

The Labels tab is used to create labels rather than to print the address directly on the envelope.

The dialog box on your screen should be similar to Figure A-15.

FIGURE A-15

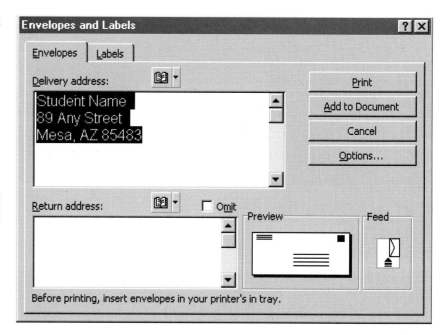

You can also type an address directly in the Delivery Address text box.

Word automatically copies the inside address from the letter into the Delivery Address text box. To complete the information for the envelope, you need to add the return address. Then you will check the options for printing and formatting the envelope.

■   Enter your school's address in the Return Address text box.

■   Click   Options... .

■   If necessary open the Envelope Options tab.

The dialog box on your screen should be similar to Figure A-16.

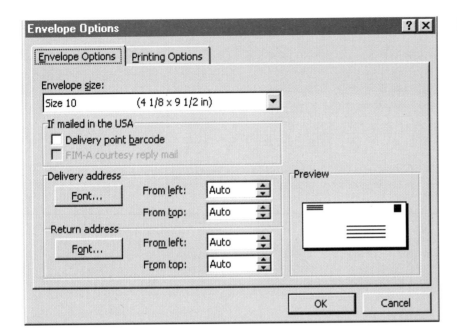

Using this dialog box you can change the envelope size and the font and placement of the delivery and return addresses. The Preview area shows how the envelope will appear when printed using the current settings. To see the envelope size options,

■ Open the Envelope Size drop-down list.

The default envelope size of 10 is for a standard 8 1/2 x 11 inch letter paper size. This is the appropriate size for the letter. Next you will check the print options.

■ Open the Printing Options tab.

Envelope size:	
Size 10	(4 1/8 x 9 1/2 in)
Size 10	(4 1/8 x 9 1/2 in)
Size 6 3/4	(3 5/8 x 6 1/2 in)
Monarch	(3 7/8 x 7 1/2 in)
Size 9	(3 7/8 x 8 7/8 in)
Size 11	(4 1/2 x 10 3/8 in)
Size 12	(4 3/4 x 11 in)
DL	(110 x 220 mm)
C4	(229 x 324 mm)
C5	(162 x 229 mm)
C6	(114 x 162 mm)
C65	(114 x 229 mm)
Custom size...	

The dialog box on your screen should be similar to Figure A-17.

FIGURE A-17

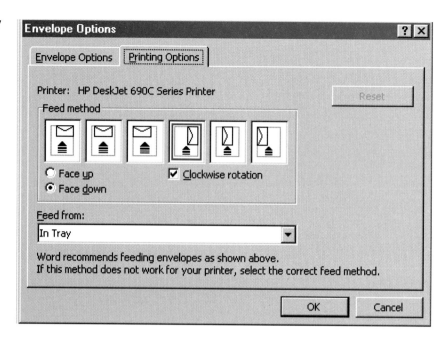

The options in this dialog box are used to specify how the envelope is fed into the printer. Word automatically selects the best option for the selected printer. You do not need to change any of the envelope options.

■ Close the dialog box.

Next, you will print the envelope. Before printing you would need to insert the correct size envelope in the printer. However, you will simply print it on a sheet of paper.

■ Click | Print |.

■ Click | No | in response to the prompt to save the return address as the default.

■ Close the letter without saving it.

Use the [Add to Document] button to add the envelope to the beginning of the active document so that you can print the envelope at the same time you print the document.

Responding yes displays that address automatically whenever envelopes are printed.

Prepare and Print Labels

You can also create mailing labels using Word 97 from address information that is stored in a data source file. You want to print mailing labels for recipients of the merge credit card letter. A sample of a mailing label appears below:

> Anthony Manahan
> 2931 E. Campus Dr.
> Mesa, AZ 85202

The Mail Merge feature includes a Mailing Labels option that will create mailing labels.

- ▣ Open a new document window.

- ▣ Choose Tools/Mail Merge

- ▣ Click [Create ▾] .

- ▣ Choose Mailing Labels

- ▣ Click [Active Window] .

- ▣ Click [Get Data ▾] to specify the data source

- ▣ Choose [Open Data Source...] .

- ▣ Change the location to the drive containing your data disk and select the Credit Data Source file.

  This file was created in Part 2 of Lab 4.

- ▣ Click [Open] .

- ▣ Click [Set Up Main Document] .

The dialog box on your screen should be similar to Figure A-18.

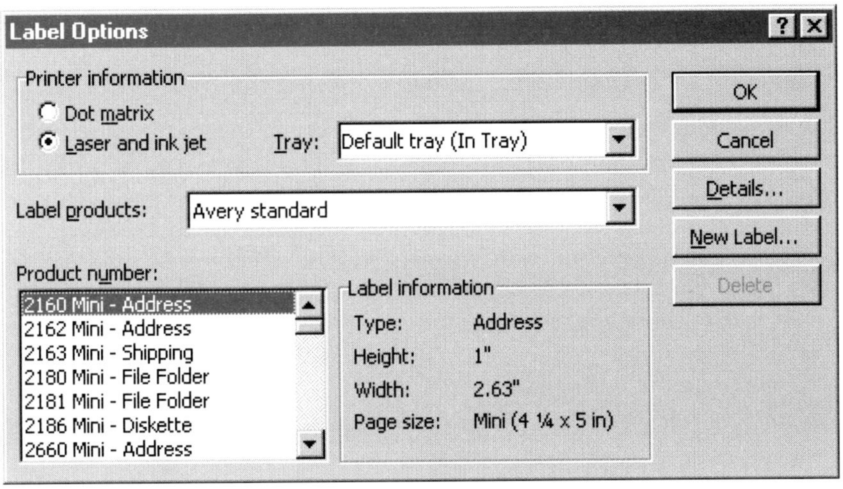

FIGURE A-18

In this dialog box you specify the printer and label product information. You can either use a predefined label or create a custom label. You will use a standard mailing label made by Avery. These labels appear three across the width of the paper.

- ▣ If necessary, select Avery standard from the Label Products drop-down list.

  Word remembers and displays the last selected label type.

- ▣ Select 5160 - Address from the Product number list.

- ▣ Click [OK] .

The dialog box on your screen should be similar to Figure A-19.

FIGURE A-19

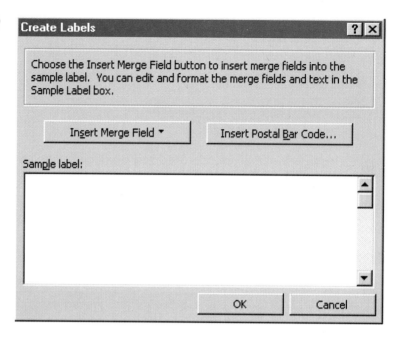

Just as you did when you entered the merge fields into the letter, you select the merge fields from the data source to include in the labels. As you select the fields you also design the label layout in the Sample Label text box. You may type any additional text, such as punctuation or a holiday message, directly into the text box.

- Click **Insert Merge Field ▾**.

- Choose the FirstName field.

- Press ⎵Spacebar.

- Add the LastName field to the sample label.

- Press ⏎Enter.

- To complete the rest of the label, add the Address, City, State, and PostalCode fields to the sample label box using the punctuation and spacing shown here.

- Click **OK**.

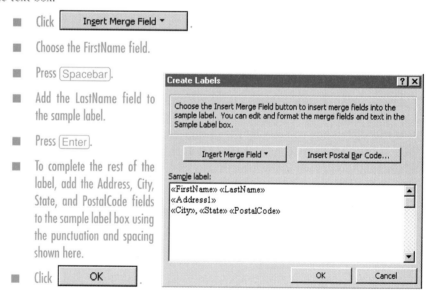

Your merge label settings are complete and the Merge Helper dialog box is displayed. The open document behind the dialog box shows how the active document has been formatted with the merge codes and labels. You are now ready to perform the merge.

■ Click  .

The dialog box on your screen should be similar to Figure A-20.

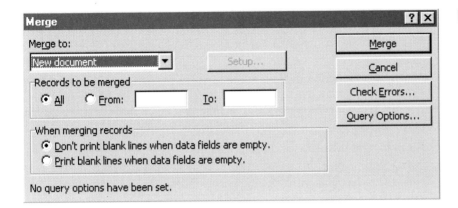

FIGURE A-20

You can merge to a new document or directly to the printer. It is safest to merge to a document so that you can check your output before printing the labels. This is the default setting.

■ Click [Merge] .

Your screen should be similar to Figure A-21.

FIGURE A-21

Three mailing labels appear across the width of the page. The placement of the labels on the page corresponds to the 5160 Avery labels you selected. Before printing the actual labels, you would need to insert the correct label paper in the printer. However, you will simply print it on a sheet of paper.

■ Print the document.

■ Close all open documents without saving.

Practice Exercises

1. Open the Cookie Merge Document you created in problem 3 of Lab 4. Follow the procedures you learned in this appendix to add envelopes to the file in front of the letters. Add your address as the return address. Print the first two letters with envelopes (you can print the envelopes on regular paper). Save the document to your data disk.

2. Open the Scenic Drives Newsletter you created in problem 6 of lab 3. Delete the WordArt on the title page and replace it with an AutoShapes banner that contains the same words. Add 3-D effects to the banner. Print the title page. Save the document as Scenic Drives Newsletter Revised on your data disk.

3. Open the Camera Ready B&B Ad you created in problem 4 of Lab 3. Insert a [Tab] after each item in the bulleted list. Add tab leaders to the table. Delete the WordArt and replace it with an AutoShape of your choice that contains the same words. Add 3-D effects to the shape. Print the document. Save the document at B&B revised on your data disk.

4. Open the Customer Main Document you created in problem 5 of lab 4. Format the paragraphs with 1.5 line spacing. Merge the document again. Create envelopes that contain your address as the return address adds the envelopes to the file. Print the first two letters and envelopes. Save the document as Revised Customer Merge.

5. Open the file How to Create a Resume. Create and apply a style of your own to the title and another style to the name and date lines below the title. Add Heading 1 styles to all topic heads then view the document in Outline view. Adjust the heading levels appropriately. In the Overview of Resumes section, arrange the paragraphs in the following order: Name, Address, and Phone Number, Career Objectives, Education, Work Experience, Activities, Honors and Awards, Special Skills, and References. Change to Page Layout view and indent the five items to include in a resume and precede each item in the list with dot leaders of your choice. Set the line spacing for the list to 1.5. Bullet the list of basic principles of resume construction. Add a different underline style to each of the eight paragraph topic headings in the Organizing Your Resume section. Add a header and alternate footer of your own choosing. Save the document with a new file name to a new folder named Resume on your data disk. Print the document.